ASTOR PIAZZOLLA

Astor Piazzolla at the Montreux Jazz Festival, Switzerland, 1986.
Photo by Dany Gignoux

Astor Piazzolla
A Memoir

by
Natalio Gorin

Translated, annotated, and expanded
by
Fernando Gonzalez

AMADEUS PRESS
Portland, Oregon

Jacket/cover illustration by Alberto De Piero for Manzi Publishing, *Aerolíneas Argentinas Magazine*

Unless otherwise indicated, photographs are from the collection of Natalio Gorin.

The author also gratefully acknowledges:
Dedé Wolff for family photographs
Daniel Piazzolla for photographs
Víctor Oliveros for documents and photographs
Atilio Talín for photographs
Aldo Pagani for photographs
César Luongo for photographs
Roberto Fernández for bandoneon drawings
Fernando Gonzalez for the translation and additions to the English-language edition
Mariana Grugni for the translation of the Italian edition
Academia Nacional del Tango
Sociedad Argentina de Autores y Compositores (Argentine Society of Authors and Composers)
Asociación Argentina de Interpretes (Argentine Association of Interpreters)

Published in 2001 by
AMADEUS PRESS
(an imprint of Timber Press, Inc.)
The Haseltine Building
133 S.W. Second Avenue, Suite 450
Portland, Oregon 97204 U.S.A.

Printed in Singapore

Library of Congress Cataloging-in-Publication Data

Piazzolla, Astor.
  [Astor Piazzolla. English]
  Astor Piazzolla : a memoir / by Natalio Gorin ; translated, annotated, and expanded by Fernando Gonzalez.
    p. cm.
  Translation of: Astor Piazzolla ; a manera de memorias.
  Includes discography (p.), bibliographical references (p.), and index.
  ISBN 1-57467-066-2—ISBN 1-57467-067-0 (pbk.)
    1. Composers—Argentina—Biography. 2. Bandoneon players—Argentina—Biography. I. Gorin, Natalio. II. Gonzalez, Fernando, 1954–

ML410.P579 A3 2001
'80'.92—dc21
3]
                                                              2001022151

To Carola, my wife
To Pablo and Verónica, my children
To Raquel Gorin
To Mario Schapchuk
To Jack Roitman
To Eduardo and David Kurman

Contents

Preface *9*
Introduction *13*
Prologue *23*

1. Alevare *25*
2. New York, New York (First Movement) *29*
3. Maestro, Why Don't You Play a Tango? *39*
4. Suite Troileana *59*
5. Nadia of Paris, Alberto of Barracas *69*
6. New York, New York (Second Movement) *75*
7. For Fans Only *79*
8. Aria for Chorus *93*
9. Love Theme *117*
10. Love Theme (Encore) *123*
11. Self Portrait *125*
12. Bandoneon *141*
13. 500 Motivations *147*
14. Triunfal *151*

Postscript *157*
  The Penultimate Goodbye *159*
  Milonga for Four *191*
  My Crazy Bandoneon *207*

Piazzolla's Musicians and Singers *213*
Discography of Recordings by Astor Piazzolla *220*
Chronology *249*
Bibliography *252*
Index *255*

Preface

After the hug, the anxious question: "Did you bring the tape recorder?" He was true Piazzolla from the first minute, careful with all the details of this meeting, which he had agreed to and encouraged and for which he had set the date and place: "The first days of March 1990, in my house in Punta del Este."

The answer made him smile. It calmed him down. The precautions were mutual: "You go on tour with two bandoneons, right? Well, I also brought two tape recorders." Perhaps the mood for our work was set.

His music had moved me for more than thirty years; we were not unknown to each other. This idea was not new. Astor had been aware of it for some time. It had been maturing; some homework had to be done.

My modest and at the same time enormous ambition was to leave a testimony for the future. Who was Astor Piazzolla? What did he do? What did he think about? How did he travel the arc of his life?

He was jokingly alarmed to see the old clippings from my archives. "Who gave you all this, the secret service?" Some of them we eventually discarded. Some we kept as valid.

Because I always suspected his tendency, in the style of Jorge Luis Borges, to say certain things for the fun of it, to provoke, I showed him an old letter of his with a very personal line, very much his, in his own hand: "Never believe what I tell journalists." The reminder was a way of making a commitment: we had to tell his true story. He accepted the rules. The proof is in his prologue: it is devastating.

After that, we turned the tape recorder on. The chapters to be developed had been agreed upon in Buenos Aires. So was the technique we would use: first a dialogue between us and afterward my work. I'd organize his tales, give them book form, and choose the pictures and documents to illustrate them.

Three consecutive days of work in Punta del Este cemented the structure. On 16 April 1990 we met at his apartment on Avenida Libertador in Buenos Aires to go over some details that I had questions about. Then we left an open parenthesis. Astor was going on tour to Europe. We agreed to meet in September to polish a chapter that needed his special attention. It was "Bandoneon."

But on the fourth of August, in his beloved Paris, a major stroke trapped him. Now I was alone with the work. I completed the book by myself, moved by this blow of fate and by a huge sense of responsibility.

Astor Piazzolla and author Natalio Gorin in Punta del Este, Uruguay, in 1990, when the interviews that make up the core of this book took place.

The first version of *Astor Piazzolla: A Manera de Memorias* (literally, Astor Piazzolla: By way of a memoir) arrived in bookstores in March 1991. I am proud of the book because people who read it have let me know their opinion in a thousand ways. They recognized Astor's thinking in these pages. Many went even further: "I felt I could hear him," they said.

Piazzolla died in Buenos Aires on 4 July 1992. From that date on, as was to be expected, every return to the original text suggested a revision, first, to complete the portrayal of his life, and secondly, because it was possible to enrich the memoir with testimonies that are key to the story.

There is also a rigorously updated discography. It is dedicated to all the fans—and to those who are not—who are in search of more information.

Finally, I felt the need to write a penultimate goodbye, bringing forth personal memories, experiences, and ideas explored over hundreds (can it be thousands?) of hours of conversations with his friends, his acquaintances, his enemies, and most of his musicians. Of such treasures I held back nothing.

This is the definitive version.

NATALIO GORIN
Buenos Aires, Argentina

Introduction

FERNANDO GONZALEZ

Tango is a music of paradoxes.

For *porteños*, as the inhabitants of the port city Buenos Aires are called, it is the deepest expression of their identity. But this music, born at the turn of the century in the muddy outskirts of the city, is a porridge of African, European, and indigenous cultures. Its quintessential instrument is the bandoneon, a button squeezebox invented in Germany as a poor man's organ. It was created to play sacred music, but it flourished in the whorehouses of Buenos Aires. Moreover, the dance might be understood as a macho ritual, but in the first step, the man backs down.

It is only fitting, then, that the man who revitalized tango, the man who heard in the music possibilities others couldn't, or wouldn't, imagine, was the same man once accused of killing it. It is only fitting that he wasn't even a *porteño*.

Astor Piazzolla was born in 1921 in Mar del Plata, a seaside city four hundred kilometers (approximately 248 miles) south of Buenos Aires. Two years later his father, Vicente, a barber, and his mother, Asunta, a hairdresser, took him to New York. There was a short-lived return to Mar del Plata, but in all, Piazzolla spent fourteen years in New York. He grew up in Greenwich Village, in a world of hard-working immigrants and gangsters, Catholic school and street gangs, his father's tango records, and Cab Calloway at a Harlem club.

In an interview in his New York apartment in 1987, he told me that back then he didn't even speak Spanish that well. "*Cocoliche*," he called it, pidgin Spanish. Over the years he gave both eight and nine as the age at which he received his first bandoneon as a gift from his father. And then, he once recalled, "I started to look for the notes by myself." In time he learned not only tango but also Bach, Schumann, Gershwin, and Ellington.

When he finally arrived in Buenos Aires, Piazzolla was sixteen, but his destiny as an outsider was set. He had been an outsider in New York, not just for being Argentine (everybody was a foreigner) but because of his physical limitations. Piazzolla was born lame, and because he limped he felt he had to prove his endurance and toughness over and over again. This might have been the perfect training for what was to come.

Tangueros, as both fans and players of the music are known, can seem to be a cult, such is their intense, ritualized devotion to certain artists and traditions. There is no room for heretics.

"The *tanguero* is a very strange animal," Piazzolla told me when we spoke in 1987. Evoking the tango stars of the 1930s and '40s, he said, "They live on Corsini and Magaldi and Gardel and Troilo, and you can't take them out of that because of sentimental reasons. It's one of the plagues of Argentina." In fact, *tanguero* is sometimes used as an adjective, implying melancholy, as in "He (or it) is very *tanguero*." Deeply emotional responses to tango suggest that there is more than just musical taste at play. After all, this is the music of a city, indeed, a country, of immigrants searching for an identity and yearning for unifying myths.

In the 1880s as tango emerged around the edges of Buenos Aires in the fabled *arrabal*, the tough, lowly suburbs, Argentina was a country in the making. Born of the mostly immigrant working class and the disenfranchised, early tango carried echoes of *zarzuelas* and *habaneras*, *candombes* and polkas, waltzes and *milongas*. Originally it was played by a trio comprising violin, flute, and guitar.

And because some places where this music was played did not accept women, some early tangos were danced between men. The music became part of the entertainment in the whorehouses, and the more expensive bordellos even made room for a piano. The bandoneon arrived decades later.

Tango inched closer to the prosperous downtown and entered the *conventillos*, the poor, working-class tenements of Buenos Aires. There was resistance. Tango was "indecent" music, favored by people best known for their talent with a knife and their penchant for violence.

Yet this reputation also attracted the sons of the upper class who went slumming and eventually brought the music into their palaces, like a forbidden fruit, to be savored behind closed doors. In fact, the "good families" in Argentine society, historically tone deaf regarding anything Creole, embraced tango only after they heard of the approval of Paris and Hollywood. (Similarly the tango revival in Argentina in the 1980s was largely credited to the success of the show *Tango Argentino* on Broadway.)

Tango had arrived in France in the late 1890s, some say in an Argentine navy training ship while others talk about a Frenchman who fell in love with tango and brought sheet music back; yet others suggest traveling musicians who found a receptive audience and stayed. Whatever the true story, by the early 1910s tango—*le tango* for Parisians—was a hit. This, and the success of tango in Hollywood where Rudolph Valentino danced it in *The Four Horsemen of the Apocalypse* (1921), started a chain reaction that reached Italy, England, and even Germany.

Back home the music found a defining voice in its greatest icon, Carlos Gardel, a singer and songwriter who conveyed a mix of street toughness, sensitivity, and sophistication. He not only performed the definitive versions of some classic tangos but also starred in five Hollywood films and headlined shows in New York, Madrid, and Paris. His work also marked the peak of the *tango canción*, the tango song. The lyrics, once typically obscene in their preoccupation with life in the brothel, grew thematically. By the 1930s during the Depression, tango was not only lamenting lost love but was also telling the stories of the working poor and those who were falling by the wayside.

A decade later, riding a wave of prosperity, tango became a staple of radio and the ballrooms. It was a time of great orchestras, bandleaders, singers, and songwriters, many of whom Piazzolla—a stu-

dent of the music—recalls in this memoir as if invoking magical spir-
its, names such as Aníbal Troilo, Alfredo Gobbi, Osvaldo Pugliese,
and Miguel Caló.

It was the golden era of tango. But by the mid 1950s, political,
economic, and social changes in Argentina brought a sharp decline
in tango's fortunes, and then Elvis Presley and the Beatles hit. The
combination was disastrous. For the next two decades, tango in
Buenos Aires became the music of old folks and tourists. It became
an industry of nostalgia and the picturesque. But Piazzolla was in-
tent on pushing the music forward.

In the 1940s he had already served notice by reworking tango's
traditional form and sound even for standard orchestras and within
the unwritten but clear demands of the dance floor. By the mid '50s,
after his stay in Paris, his studies with Nadia Boulanger, and his
epiphany the night he heard saxophonist and composer Gerry Mulligan leading an octet, Piazzolla was ready to do away with the rules
and make his move.

He retained tango's poignancy and lyricism while rejecting its
tendencies toward sentimentality and bouts of morbid self-pity. He
revised its harmonic language by incorporating the influences of
Maurice Ravel, Claude Debussy, Giacomo Puccini, and Olivier Messiaen, as well as the occasional nod to the cool jazz of Mulligan and
Lennie Tristano. He moved away from the dance floor but infused
the music with a new vitality by using three-part fugues, a walking
bass, jazz-style improvisation, and urgent, brutish accents in echoes
of Béla Bartók.

In a word, he enraged the tango traditionalists. To make matters
worse in his detractors' eyes, Piazzolla was not just an iconoclast
but an iconoclast who happened to be a brilliant musician with impeccable *tanguero* credentials. While still a kid in New York he had
appeared with Gardel occasionally on stage and even in film—a
cameo in *El día que me quieras* (The day you love me) for which Piazzolla received twenty-five dollars. Back in Argentina he did his
apprenticeship as a player and arranger in Aníbal Troilo's tango
orchestra. Moreover, his early writing shows the influences of such
classic figures as Pugliese, Gobbi, and Orlando Goñi.

Yet he was also an outsider, an oddball who could play Mozart and Gershwin on his bandoneon and who wrote *orquesta típica* arrangements featuring cello solos in tangos for club dancers. This was highly unorthodox: the *orquesta típica*, a sort of tango big-band, was expected to feature strings, a front line of bandoneons, and piano. *"Terminá con esa fantasía; marcáme un tango"* (Cut it out with those fantasies; just give me a tango), he was told by bandleader Francisco "El Tano" Lauro in his audition. He was seen by traditionalists as the tango Antichrist and was nearly treated as such.

But as is clear from this memoir, Piazzolla fought back with relish, with the pride of the kid from the Village who never backed down and with the shrewdness of a PR man who knows the benefits of scandal. He told the truth as he saw it and had the courage and wherewithal as a musician to back it up. And he also knew how to get the publicity he couldn't buy. Piazzolla never sold many records in Argentina—not while alive, not since his passing—but he got many column inches of copy in magazines and newspapers.

And then there was the other Piazzolla, the one who "wanted to be Stravinsky," as he once put it. In this world he was also an outsider, an unusual popular musician, educated, curious not only about his craft but also about the visual arts, film, and literature. Furthermore, he was a bandoneon player who wrote competent, although hardly groundbreaking, neoclassical pieces. (Piazzolla was less charitable in his own assessment. "Symphonic trash," he called it in our 1987 interview.)

Only toward the end of his life and even more so after his death did Piazzolla reach the place in classical music he had once set out to find as a budding composer. Groups such as the Kronos Quartet and musicians such as Daniel Barenboim, Gidon Kremer, the Assad Brothers, Emanuel Ax, and Yo-Yo Ma have embraced his music. Ironically, he reached his place in contemporary classical music with tango, his tango.

It all adds up to a brilliant, funny, complicated man, author Natalio Gorin told me in a conversation in 1999. A longtime fan and personal friend of Piazzolla's, Gorin said, "Astor had a great sense of humor. He was a great raconteur. He was great fun to be with. But he was also very difficult."

Gorin discovered Piazzolla on a television show in the early 1960s soon after Piazzolla's return to Argentina from the United States (it was called "Welcome, Mr. Piazzolla," in English, he recalls) and heard him live for the first time in 1962 at Jamaica, "a dive in downtown Buenos Aires, for thirty or forty people."

Gorin was a journalist by profession and a *tanguero* by birthright, having been born in Almagro, a hardcore tango neighborhood of Buenos Aires. Far from rejecting Piazzolla's music, he saw it as "a natural evolution" from that of the more progressive figures in traditional tango.

"I'm one of those who believe that the most authentic fans of Astor Piazzolla come either from tango or from jazz. I don't think they come from anywhere else," he said. Referring to the conservative tango bandleader Juan D'Arienzo, Gorin explained, "I was a Pugliese fan. I never met a guy who'd say, 'I'm a fan of D'Arienzo and Piazzolla.' But Pugliese and Piazzolla have historic continuity. For all the talk of Piazzolla's being a revolutionary, he is actually an 'evolutionary'—he is part of a chain."

Gorin became part of a small group of fans who devotedly followed Piazzolla's career, and their friendship began in 1971 in Paris. He was vacationing in Europe with his wife when he remembered reading about Piazzolla's living in Paris. "So I got it in my mind to meet him. Through the information in the paper I figured out the address, looked for the place, and rang the bell, and Piazzolla opened the door. I said 'Hi. I'm Argentine and I'm a big fan of yours,' and he invited me in."

It was the beginning of a friendship that continued until Piazzolla's death, although there was a small matter of an eight-year interruption. Angered by what he perceived as Gorin's slight of his wife, Laura, after a concert in 1978, Piazzolla banished him from his life. They reconciled in 1986.

"I was wrong, but it was an ugly reaction," Gorin said with a shrug. "But I was not the only one who suffered from his temper.

That's why for me, for many of us in that group that followed him, it was never '*La vida por Piazzolla!*' (My life for Piazzolla) but '*La vida por la* musica *de Piazzolla!*' (My life for Piazzolla's *music*), which is a very different thing. I'm a fan. I owe Piazzolla what many people owe him: he opened my mind, sharpened my musical taste. After Piazzolla, I could get into jazz, into classical music."

But while the personal relationship suffered an interruption, Gorin's admiration for Piazzolla's music only grew: "I loved the music more and more."

He approached Piazzolla with his idea for a memoir in 1989. It was a proposal "very similar to what this book is but with a lot more questions and answers. He said, 'There is only one place to do this.' It was to be in Punta del Este in March of the following year. Gorin and Piazzolla talked for three days in Punta del Este and for two more days in Buenos Aires some weeks later. Gorin was to go over the material and in September follow up with any questions. It never happened: Piazzolla suffered a cerebral hemorrhage and stroke on 4 August 1990.

"Now Astor was ill and we knew he would not come back to life. Someone, in heaven or hell, said, 'You are going to be the guy who will do Piazzolla's book.' So I thought of doing it by way of a memoir. Many important issues were still pending. Astor had left me alone with them, to fend for myself.

"I listened to the tapes again, and it struck me that at the time I hadn't realized all the references to death he made in our conversations," said Gorin. " Now I am sure he *knew*. Something must happen in our life that we know something is coming."

Perhaps. After all, looking back, Astor Piazzolla seems to have created a musical life that unfolded like one of his extended pieces. His life as a musician is one of themes and variations, counterlines and echoes, calculation and passion unfolding with implacable logic.

In Piazzolla nothing was ever lost, neither his father's tango records nor the Bach he heard through a door as a child; neither the exact rules of counterpoint and fugue he learned with Nadia Boulanger nor the cool swing of Gerry Mulligan or the style of Pedro Laurenz. He even alchemized the jagged, insistent rhythms of Eastern European Jewish music overheard at parties in the Village into the relentless, driving pulse of his New Tango.

Every lesson, every experience, every encounter seemed to lead inevitably to the next lesson and the next experience. Even his recording with Mulligan (*Summit,* 1974) suggests the paying of an old debt to a musician who, without knowing it, had opened a universe to him back in Paris in 1955. And his recording with vibraphonist Gary Burton seems a search for redemption of his unhappy experiments with jazz tango in New York nearly thirty years earlier.

It is also ironic, but not surprising, that Piazzolla reached the kind of recognition he looked for and deserved not in his most creative years but in a long recapitulation that began after his heart attack in 1973. With his last, superb Quintet, with which he found fame and fortune not only in Europe but also in the United States, Piazzolla was no longer breaking ground as a composer. Rather, he was the master craftsman, revisiting his work and painstakingly polishing it for a definitive version.

It is a process that reaches its pinnacle in *La camorra* (1989), his last recording with his last Quintet. In it Piazzolla both offers an extraordinary summation of the history of tango and sets a challenge. It is his masterpiece—a nod to his teachers, a thank-you note to his bandoneon idols, a peace offering to his critics, a coming to terms with his life, a testament, and a dare to those coming behind, all wrapped into one.

By then, even his critics in Argentina had been silenced, although the grudging acceptance he enjoyed in his later years was probably more the result of his international success than of any sudden enlightenment.

"The famous Quintet, his last one, the one with which he travels around the world, played in Shams for fifty people," recalled Gorin, referring to the small jazz club in Buenos Aires. "That's where he premiered 'La camorra,' before fifty people. I was there. And the group went from that show to the studio. He might have been filling theaters everywhere else, but here . . ." he says, his voice trailing off. But even that couldn't obscure his triumph.

What does not fit in his story is that slow, painful, unfair coda from the stroke in Paris in August 1990 to his clinical death nearly two years later in Buenos Aires. "Nothing came easy to Astor, not even death," writes Natalio Gorin in this remarkable oral history. Then again, who knows if such a spirit would have wanted it any other way?

Translating Natalio Gorin's *Astor Piazzolla: A manera de memorias* was a challenge I did not relish. Being true to the spirit of the word is difficult enough in any translation, but Gorin's book often suggested a conversation between two educated, streetwise, and passionate *tangueros*. Good luck. But that, of course, is one of the very elements that make this book special.

If I took on the challenge it was because, as a *porteño* and Piazzolla fan, I felt that providing an accessible social and musical context for English-speaking readers was crucial to an appreciation of Piazzolla, his music, his struggle, and Natalio Gorin's work.

I did not wish to create a tango encyclopedia in the footnotes and drown the book's voices in numbing detail. The appendix entitled "Piazzolla's Musicians and Singers" provides basic information about the artists called upon by Piazzolla over the years. Other figures, such as singer and songwriter Carlos Gardel and bandoneonist and bandleader Aníbal Troilo, have been dealt with in greater detail in the text because of their historical importance or their role in Piazzolla's life. Some notes provide Natalio Gorin's comments from our conversations. My hope, in all cases, has been to remain unobtrusive while helping the reader along and to provide enough information to pique his or her interest in a more personal search. An advantage of globalization is that nowadays many recordings by the tango artists mentioned in this book are widely available, and I trust that when you find them, you will not be disappointed.

Thanks to Natalio Gorin for his trust and for his generosity with his knowledge and his time, Eve Goodman for her patience and persistence, and the musicians, as always, for their willingness to share their insights into the music, especially Horacio Malvicino Sr., Pablo Ziegler, Kip Hanrahan, Gary Burton, Yo-Yo Ma, and, of course, *el maestro*, Astor Piazzolla himself. In memory of Piazzolla's (and later Burton's) sometime tour manager, the late Fernando Basabru, journalist, producer, and dear friend. His stories of the road and his love of life opened a window into the heart of Astor's music.

PROLOGUE

I have to tell the most absolute truth.
I could make it a story of angels,
but that would not be the true story.
Mine is one of devils mixed with angels,
and some miserliness.
One must have a bit of everything
to move forward in life.

ASTOR PIAZZOLLA
Punta del Este, Uruguay
March 1990

Marking the beginning of the music with the four beats of the *alevare*, Piazzolla in a gesture still vivid in the memories of all who watched him lead his groups.

1

Alevare

I have a hope: that my music will be heard in the year 2020—and in 3000, too.* Sometimes I am sure of it because the music I make is different, because in 1955 one kind of tango began to die so another one was born, and in its birth certificate is my Buenos Aires Octet.

I am going to have a place in the story, like Carlos Gardel. But this does not mean we are going to be archived. Gardel endures, and the same is going to happen with me because I am not a mediocrity.

I am a tango man, but my music makes people think, people who love tango and people who love good music. All ballet companies in the world are dancing my works. The jazz people love and enjoy what I do. Chamber groups that play classical repertoire are asking me to write for them.

I had two great teachers: Nadia Boulanger and Alberto Ginastera. The third I found in a cold room in a boarding house, in the cabarets in the 1940s, in the cafés with balconies and orchestras, in the people of yesterday and today, in the sound of the streets. That third teacher is called Buenos Aires: it taught me the secrets of tango.

I am not a charlatan. People might like my music or not, but no one is going to deny its craftsmanship: it is well orchestrated, it's

---

Alevare: The first gesture in the performance of a tango. In addition to its symbolic meaning, *alevare* also alludes to the opening piece in Piazzolla's tango opera, *María de Buenos Aires*.

* Piazzolla alludes to the lyrics of Enrique Santos Discépolo's tango "Cambalache," which laments that the world has been and is a mess, that it was that way in 506 and will be in the year 2000.

new, it is of this century, and it smells of tango. That's why it is so attractive to the world.

It cost me a lot to arrive at this position. I am neither a millionaire nor anything resembling one. I only know that I will live the last years of my life comfortably, which is also a reward for so many years of struggle. Many times I haven't had a dime. When I was over fifty years old I had to leave for Europe to start over again from scratch.

Far from my country, they didn't ask me if I played tango. My music could be well liked or not, but it was always respected. In Argentina I believe I've achieved that in recent years, although there is always a joker still out there who yells, "Play a tango, maestro." He

Carlos Gardel (1890?–1935)

Singer, composer, movie star, and man about town, Carlos Gardel captured the imagination of his audiences as few other popular twentieth-century artists anywhere have been able to do. Even decades after his death—Gardel died in a fiery collision as his plane was taxiing on the runway at the Olaya Herrera Airport in Medellín, Colombia, on 24 June 1935—tango fans still declare that *"Cada día canta mejor"* (He sings better every day). In fact, Gardel not only defined great tango singing in his unerring intonation, nuanced phrasing, and astute reading of the lyrics, but he also wrote such classics of the genre as "Mi Buenos Aires querido," "Volver," "Soledad," and "El día que me quieras." He performed and recorded in Europe as well as throughout Latin America. Between 1934 and 1935 he starred in five Hollywood films. Some consider him the first international pop star from the Southern Hemisphere.

The fact that he was a handsome man with a mysterious smile and an impeccable dresser of a certain roguish elegance didn't hurt. He also was a figure shrouded by intrigue. His family roots and national origin, as well as his place and date of birth, remain in dispute. Some say he was born in Toulouse, France, others in Montevideo, Uruguay, and still others insist he was Argentine.

must be one of the few left of those listeners who criticized me for decades. I had to defend myself, fight, argue, but I also must confess, I had fun. Without realizing it, they helped to create Astor Piazzolla's reputation.

Soon I will celebrate my sixty-ninth birthday. It is a good excuse to tell this story, my story.

The Piazzollas in New York: Vicente Piazzolla (Nonino), Asunta Manetti de Piazzolla (Nonina), and Astor. Graduation day 1934, the end of Piazzolla's formal schooling.

2

New York, New York
(First Movement)

My dad, Nonino, traveled the road I myself would follow years later. He picked up his family and emigrated. He traveled by himself at first, found work, and came back to take us with him. I was four years old—I'm talking about 1925—and leaving Mar del Plata, my grandparents, my uncles, and my cousins was the first great pain I felt in life. Perhaps it was the second, because by then I had undergone four operations on my right leg. I was born with a defect caused by infantile paralysis during my mother's pregnancy, at least that was what the doctors said.

In those days people traveled by boat so the first image I had of New York City was the same as so many other immigrants have had: the Statue of Liberty. I can't say it moved me. I was a kid. I remember those moments as if in a fog.

My dad had made contact with a Sicilian family, that of Vicenzo Baudo, very good people who helped him and lent him a room in their house until he found a job. These were hard times in the United States, but in Mar del Plata things had become even worse. That's why we were in New York.

After a fashion, helped by another Italian guy from Trani,* the same village where my grandfather Pantaleón was born, my dad found work as a barber. He had learned a bit and started working at

---

* Trani: A port town in the Italian province of Bari, in the Puglia region of southern Italy.

a mafioso's barbershop. The mafioso's name was Nicola Scabutiello. This was a genial guy and he adored me, but he was who he was. Everything people saw in *The Godfather* or *The Untouchables*, I lived up close. That was my daily life.

I remember one time when a guy named Jimmy wanted to open a barbershop on the same street where Scabutiello's was. It was closed down before it opened. Someone put a "watermelon" to it and it blew up.

We lived on Eighth Street, which at that time was not the best place in Manhattan. Today it's a bohemian neighborhood where many painters, musicians, and artists live. In those days Greenwich Village was a cursed place. Next door to our house was a synagogue where one Saturday, in the middle of a wedding party, fourteen or fifteen Jews were murdered. They killed the whole family.

In that neighborhood the clash was between gangster gangs, and they came from every kind: Italians, Jews, Irish. I grew up in that violent climate. That's why I became a fighter. Perhaps that also marked my music. That kind of stuff gets under your skin. My rhythmic accents—three plus three plus two—are similar to those of the popular Jewish music I heard at their weddings.

To help, because my dad's salary was barely enough, my mother started to work at home, assembling overcoats of synthetic hair. It was a madman's job because you had to glue thousands of synthetic hairs one by one. She finished the day with her eyes irritated and whopping allergies, because the fuzz would get in her nose. That's why she had to change jobs.

Dad didn't like the idea of her working away from the house because she had to leave me alone. Mom found a solution: she enrolled me in school. There something happened that hurt her for a long time. In my clothes she would put a religious stamp of the Sacred Heart, and every time they found it at school, they would take it and throw it away. Because I would come back home crying, my mother went there to complain with all her Italian pep—and then she found out. "Madam," the school's director told her, "this is a Protestant school. We don't believe in those things."

In her new job, at a hairdresser shop called Mary and Susan, things started to go well for my mother. Many years later, back in Mar del Plata—I was an adult then—she showed me the old notebook where she kept a log of everything she had earned. She made nearly two hundred dollars a week. She also went to a cosmetics school and learned to make an almond beauty cream that she sold on the side to her clients. When we went back to Mar del Plata she continued making it until she died. Her formula was not lost. She left it to a niece as inheritance. It's a skin purifier. Here in Argentina one of her clients was Zita Troilo,* and she would always tell me: "Astor, your old lady's cream leaves my skin like an orchid's."

The beauty shop where my mother worked in New York also had to adapt to the neighborhood. Half the clients were Jews, the other half, Italians. They had to accommodate them at different times so that they, and their husbands, didn't kill each other.

By the time I was six, I had been kicked out of two schools because of my fighting. The kids in my gang called me Lefty because my punch had become famous. I was violent. Truly bad. I was part of a very strong gang, all sons of Italians, and we fought the Jews. It was the junior version of what was happening among adults. Our thing never went beyond fistfights, but you had to have guts to take sometimes terrible beatings. Escaping when things got bad was cowardly.

I was very short, and perhaps because of it and the problem with my leg, which forced me to use special shoes, I wanted to excel. It was me against the world. If my dad forbade me to go out on the street, I would run away. If the doctors said it was not good for me to play sports, I jumped into the baseball games and ran like everyone else. I also won several 100- and 200-meter events in swimming meets. I liked the challenge. What others didn't dare do, I tried. With a right leg two centimeters shorter, I took tap-dancing lessons and even danced in public.

Mom and dad worked on Sundays and I wandered alone in the streets of New York. Actually that's in a manner of speaking because

---

* Zita Troilo: Wife of tango bandoneonist, composer, and bandleader Aníbal Troilo.

I was part of a large gang. My best friends were Willy and Nicky. I also had as pals Jake La Motta, who later became middleweight world champion, John Pomponio, who was to manage great boxers, and Joseph Campanella, who in time became a famous baseball player. I saw them all later when I went back to play in the United States. The rest of the gang, people have told me, ended up in jail.

That could have been my fate because I was very rowdy and was always forward. My friends couldn't understand how I could play baseball with the problem I had with my right leg.

Many years later, back in Argentina, someone invited me to play for a club in Buenos Aires, but I didn't have time. I was playing in Aníbal Troilo's orchestra and at the same time I was studying with Alberto Ginastera. I remember once in Montevideo [Uruguay] at Carrasco Beach, a lot of people stood around watching two crazy guys having fun taking swings. The crazy guys were El Negro Esteban, a great saxophone player who had his heyday in the 1940s, and me. El Negro was Cuban and knew a lot about baseball. That's why one day he asked me, "But *chico* [man], you are a good player. Who taught you to throw the ball this way?" Actually no one had taught me. I had learned by watching, copying what others did. I always had a lot of determination in everything I did. If I had put my mind to it, perhaps I could have been the best gangster in New York.

In one of those schools music entered my life. It was funny. One time, a teacher had us listening to a Brahms symphony. A few days later she brought a Mozart symphony. Then she would test us and I would recognize the composer of the passage before anyone else. I had found music but had not discovered it yet. I took it for a game. In the choir I was a disaster. The only thing I wanted was to laugh and make others laugh, another way to stand out.

My dad had already bought me a bandoneon, but as the tango says, I left it in the closet.* I felt a sort of repulsion for that music he listened to almost every night, mostly tangos recorded by Julio De

---

* "Bandoneon . . . in the closet" is a reference to "the guitar in the closet," a line from the classic tango "Mi noche triste."

Caro's orchestra. By that time, my first music lessons with an Italian professor who lived around the block—I studied solfège [sightreading], violin, and mandolin—were already a failure.

On the other hand, I learned to make pasta sauce for a lifetime. While I did my solfège, this Italian guy put on an apron and prepared his spaghetti sauce. The room filled with the smell of basil and sautéed garlic. It got me hungry. Forget about music. Forget about solfège. At one time I asked him and he gave me the recipe. It is the same one I still use today when I cook for my friends. They tell me I make it well.

I always remember the Italian professor's original recipe: "Heat up the oil, drop in the garlic, and when it is golden, not burnt, add tomato, a pinch of pepper, basil, salt, and oregano. Do not let it boil, ever, because if it does, it turns sour and then it gives you an acid stomach."

When I was nine years old, my parents decided to return to Argentina. I think both missed it a lot. I, on the other hand, was very much adapted. At that age everything is easier. Many neighbors went to the port to see us off, as did Nicola Scabutiello and my friends Willy and Nicky. For me it was very sad. But it turned out to be a round-trip, a brief experience.

Shortly afterward, my father decided to return to New York. This time I think it was his decision. I believe my mother did not agree, although both shared the same feeling. Argentina was not the same. The Depression was hitting hard, and the barbershop my father opened in Mar del Plata was a failure.

Of that brief return to Argentina I remember the bandoneon lessons I took with Homero Pauloni* and how hard it was to adapt to school. I was Argentine, but the language I knew best was English, so I took longer to answer the teacher's questions and sometimes I used the wrong words. Because of that and the clothes my mother had bought me in New York, people made fun of me. But that was also brief. Once Lefty started to punch, the laughing stopped.

---

* Homero Pauloni: Argentine musician, friend of Piazzolla's father.

We returned to New York a little more than a year later, and we settled in an apartment as modest as the one we had had before. This one was on Ninth Street. We had different neighbors. Willy and Nicky had moved. The area where we lived was known as Little Italy. Nearby we had the Poles, the Russians, and the Romanians. At

Bandoneon

The bandoneon, a button squeezebox, may have been invented as early as 1835 by Heinrich Band, who was born in Hamburg in 1805 and died in 1888. The term *bandoneon*, or bandonion originally, was known in the region of Krefeld, Mainz, and Cologne by the 1850s. While Heinrich Band is generally credited as the creator of the instrument, musicologist Michal Shapiro has suggested in the notes for her accordion music compilation *Planet Squeezebox: Accordion Music from Around the World* (Ellipsis Arts, 1995) that there was evidence that a C. Zimmerman of Saxony may have invented the bandoneon and presented it at the Industrial Exposition in Paris in 1849.

The bandoneon is from the concertina family, but it is square, not polygonal. It actually is a portable wind instrument in which sound is produced, singly or many notes at a time, by two systems of metal tongues (one called *canto* or melody, the other *bajo* or bass) which vibrate in two acoustic wooden boxes that also hold two sets of buttons.

The instrument is similar to the accordion in that both are free reed instruments—the reeds vibrate freely in their openings, unlike those of beating reed instruments such as the pipe organ and clarinet, in which the reeds vibrate against the edges of air openings. But while the keys in the accordion, usually set up as on the piano, play chords (hence the name, accordion), the buttons on the bandoneon play single notes, some while the instrument is closing in and others while it is opening up. Initially diatonic, bandoneons later became chromatic.

The definitive design has thirty-eight buttons in the *canto* box,

Second Avenue began the Jewish neighborhood. New York, that part of Manhattan, seemed partitioned off.

I completed my schooling at the Maria Aussiliatrice school, run by the Salessian fathers. That was also the school where the gangsters' sons went, which was evident on Sundays. It was mandatory

---

played with the right hand, and thirty-three in the *bajo* box, played with the left hand. A cardboard bellows creates the air pressure that makes the metal tongues vibrate. The earlier, primitive models, before 1900, had no more than forty-four voices between both keyboards.

The bandoneon was originally used as a portable organ in religious events and burials and also to play old popular German songs. Alfred Arnold initiated industrial production of bandoneons in 1864, stamping his instruments with a brand that would become the mark of quality: A-A.

The intellectual development of the bandoneon took place in Argentina. The first professional bandoneon players (1910–1920) asked the instrument makers to add new voices. They were placed in the same design as the original keys, like a fan.

This instrument produces good sound volume, but it also offers considerable freedom to create chords because the keyboard sits comfortably in the space of one hand. The range is generous: almost five octaves. The left hand is written on the bass clef in F major, with some exceptions. The right hand is in G major. Playing with all five fingers is not advised because the instrument becomes destabilized. The right thumb must be held over the air valve. The left thumb should be on the box.

The bandoneon, closed, measures thirty-five centimeters (fourteen inches) wide, twenty-three centimeters (nine inches) high, and twenty-five centimeters (ten inches) deep. When open it is almost a meter or just under forty inches long.

For this information the author acknowledges the collaboration of bandoneonists Daniel Binelli, Marcelo Nisinman, and Antonio Ibars, with additional background from Fernando Gonzalez.

to go to church, parents and students, and here came the godfathers looking circumspect. As they say in literary circles, fiction is never better than reality.

I made friends with a kid my age, a son of Polish parents, Stanley Sommerkovsky. Today, because of the ease with which you can change your name in the United States, his name is Stanley Sommers. I know this because he lives in Houston, and I saw him again in 1987 when I was there with the Quintet. It was a great thrill for both of us. That Stanley who was a swimming champion now weighs 120 kilos [approximately 264 pounds] and has a hip problem. It was

The Piazzolla family lived in this building (center) in the East Village at 313 E. Ninth Street, between First and Second Avenues. Courtesy César Luongo

hard for me to see him that way, aged, just waiting for a pension. He was not only my friend but also my great pal in New York.

By then we were not children but teenagers. Stanley remembered our late night escapades, without our parents' knowledge, to play dice under the lights of 42d Street. It was a heavy game in which people cheated, and sometimes it was better to just run away and save the bucks.

In those days you could go to Harlem. Today it has become a ghetto. With Stanley we would go to hear Cab Calloway, who was not an unknown to me because my father liked him. The difference was that he listened to him on the radio.

One time we decided to run away from our homes forever. But the adventure, on bicycle, got as far as Long Island, which is right next to New York. The one who backed down, as Stanley reminded me in Houston, was me. So he called me "Fairy!" again, this time in jest just as he had in anger back then.

The greatest adventure with Stanley was stealing a harmonica at Macy's, a place I knew well because I had gone there many times with Carlos Gardel. That harmonica, a chromatic Hohner, was the dream I had asked my father for so many times. Instead, he had given me a bandoneon.

Stealing didn't seem like a big deal to me, perhaps because the neighborhood and the school had this mafia air. I must admit that I was attracted to the stories that I heard and could see every day.

I told Stanley my plan and he agreed to go along. In the summertime, I had observed, the saleswomen of the section would snooze a bit while waiting for customers, especially by midday. "We approach together," I told him. "You ask something, and I make the grab for the harmonica." Everything went as planned until a woman guard stopped us close to the door. It was a mess. She took away the harmonica, took us out into the street, and started out for the police station. At one point Stanley and I looked at each other and decided to make a run for it. We took off and she couldn't catch up. We jumped on a delivery truck passing by and got away.

I don't know if for something like that they would have sent us to reform school, something done even today in the United States. Perhaps because of the possibility, or the scare, I never thought of doing anything like that again.

My parents decided to return to Argentina for good when I was sixteen. At that age it is very unlikely that the children would be involved in the parents' discussion, and I was no exception.

In New York I left Stanley, jazz, two or three girlfriends, because I already knew the troubles of the heart, and a world in which I wandered about feeling safe. The prospect of traveling by ship, arriving in Buenos Aires, and then getting to Mar del Plata was not exciting.

At that moment I might have thought a thousand things except one: that years later I would travel the same route with my wife and kids. It would be part adventure and part out of need, just as it had been for Vicente Piazzolla.

3

Maestro, Why Don't You Play a Tango?

One time I went with the Quintet to San Pedro in the province of Buenos Aires. In that city we had a great following. We sold out the theater.

It was fashionable at the time to play a concert and then have a discussion with the audience. In those days, the early 1960s, the musicians did not look at their watches so much. They were looser. After we played, the coordinator of the event introduced me, I talked about what I thought about tango at the time, and I then asked for questions. In truth, I was unlucky right from the start because I gave the microphone to this guy who looked like a weasel and kept staring at me.

The guy stood up and put it to me without blinking: "Maestro, now that the concert is over, why don't you play a tango?" And all hell broke loose. I believe I threw a notebook at him. It was not the last time that happened. "Maestro, play a tango" followed me like a curse. I even heard it from some who thought of themselves as experts, which bothered me doubly.

I made a revolution in tango. I broke the old molds: that's why they attacked me and why I had to defend myself, saying at times a word too many. That curse made me feel bad because if there is something no one could deny, it is my roots: I have tango stamped around my edges. And my career, another source of pride for me, started out from way down.

Not long ago here in my home in Punta del Este, a young guy with many aspirations was already playing bandoneon in Horacio Salgán's orchestra. His name is Marcelo Nisinman. He told me he wanted to do modern stuff. I put my arm around him, took him for a walk, and told him: "Listen to me. For now there is nothing modern. If you continue with Salgán, great; if not, go play with a group in the Old Guard style and put your time in, like I did with El Tano Lauro doing the *chan-chan* night after night. Go spend a few years in that hell of music and you'll see how you discover what's truly modern."*

That's why I went crazy every time someone asked me to play a tango. So what did I just play, a *lambada*?**

Now, if my music is more elaborate, if it is harder to listen to, they can blame it on one thing: I killed myself studying. I am who I am today because I knocked myself out against a wall a hundred times and a hundred times I got up.

My relationship with tango started in New York, having to listen, to my chagrin, to those records that my dad had. I was also moved one time when I went to see a movie featuring "La Negra" Bozán and Pedro Maffia playing bandoneon.‡ And certainly something changed in my life after I crossed paths with Carlos Gardel, something that at the time, because of my age, I didn't appreciate in all its significance. All that must have been like a love pill for tango.

---

* Marcelo Nisinman: Years later, ironically, Nisinman played Piazzolla's part in *Astor Piazzolla Reunion* (Concord Records, 1998), a CD tribute to Astor Piazzolla by vibes player Gary Burton featuring the members of Piazzolla's last Quintet.

Francisco "El Tano" Lauro (?–1960): Piazzolla played in bandoneonist and bandleader Francisco Lauro's orchestra in 1938. *Tano* is *porteño* slang for Italian or Italiano.

Chan-chan: An onomatopoeic allusion to the typical V–I (dominant–tonic) closing tango cadence and traditional tango beat, and hence shorthand for something conventional.

** *Lambada*: A Brazilian dance style that became wildly popular worldwide in the early 1990s, a novelty like the Macarena.

‡ Sofia "La Negra" Bozán (1894–1977): Popular actress and singer in Argentine vaudeville and, later, film.

Pedro Maffia (1900–1967): A crucial player in the history of tango, Maffia set the stylistic canon for the bandoneon in the music.

But the definitive arrow-through-the-heart experience was still missing. I got that back in Mar del Plata when I was already a teenager. I heard the Elvino Vardaro Sextet. I went crazy and said, "I want to do that." I sent a note to the maestro and he was kind enough to reply with an autographed photo. Many years later Elvino would be a soloist in my own groups.

I was on. I formed Cuarteto Azul and imitated his sound. I had it in my head that some day I would play "Arrabal," a tango by José Pascual, with the same mastery as that of the Elvino Vardaro Sextet. Nothing happens by chance in life. When I got back from Paris in 1955, the first piece I arranged for the Buenos Aires Octet was just that, "Arrabal."

I became a fan of other orchestras, those of Pedro Laurenz, Pedro Maffia, Aníbal Troilo. One day Miguel Caló dropped by Mar del Plata. He came to play at Confitería Porta, at the old fishermen's wharf, near what is now known as the Bristol beach. Of course, I didn't miss his debut.*

My dad, Nonino, stopped me at the door. He was curious that I was going out so dressed up. When I told him what I was doing, his smile showed how happy he was. He even needled me, "Don't tell me now that tango got into you." He knew that was the case and felt happy.

Hearing Caló had a big impact on me, so much so that the next day I stopped by the boarding house where the musicians were staying. There I met up close [bandoneonists] Chupita Stamponi, Argentino Galván, and Julio Ahumada. I drove them crazy with questions. I wanted to know everything. I even took my bandoneon and played Gershwin's "Rhapsody in Blue" for them and a tango I had written, dedicated to Caló, called "Mi ensueño." Many years later Chupita Stamponi, one of the great friends life gave me, said I had impressed them. "You seemed possessed," he said.

It was Miguel Caló who advised me to go to Buenos Aires, and I

---

* Pedro Laurenz (b. Pedro Blanco Acosta, 1902–1972): Superb bandoneonist as well as a bandleader and premier tango composer.

Miguel Caló (1922–1972): Bandoneonist, composer, and bandleader.

did. I installed myself at the Alegría, a boarding house at 1492 Sarmiento, where Líbero Pauloni was waiting for me. Líbero was the brother of Homero Pauloni, who had given me bandoneon lessons, and that was the arrangement my dad had made with them.

The beginnings were very hard. I had left my parents' house, where I was pampered, to go live alone in a cold boarding house, although I shared the room with a good guy like Pauloni. Buenos Aires is not an easy place for someone who comes from the outside. I was not some country bumpkin—I had grown up in one of the worst neighborhoods of New York—but it wasn't the same. Besides I was not a kid but a grown man looking for a job as a musician.

The first thing I did was brief, with the orchestra of Gabriel Clausi, until I got a call from Francisco Lauro, El Tano Lauro. He was not top-of-the-line, but he worked a lot. I got my bandoneon and got ready. I wanted to shock him. I rehearsed a little Mozart, a little Gershwin. When I met Lauro he impressed me. He was as big as a house. He asked me to play something and I took off with some Mozart. El Tano looked on without so much as blinking. I think he didn't know what to make of it.

I finished and followed up with Gershwin. That did it. He got up, hands on his waist, bent over, and said, "Cut it out with those fantasies; just give me a tango in four, *chan-chan, chan-chan*." I did that and two minutes later he stopped me: "Done. Tomorrow you start with the orchestra."

Lauro played at the Novelty cabaret, which was low class but it was at a good spot, just meters away from Corrientes y Esmeralda.* I had a thousand fantasies go through my head: the night, the babes. The reality was very different. There were fights almost every night. The women were exploited. They had to drink and dance until the last customer was gone. It saddened me. This was a feeling about the cabaret life that never left me. And I was not a saint. I started to know about life after dark in New York. I knew how drugs flowed.

---

* Corrientes y Esmeralda, a classic Buenos Aires address, is the corner of Corrientes Avenue, an important place rich in tango history, and Esmeralda Street.

One day I also tried cocaine. They told me it was a stimulant, that it helped you play better, besides other things. I didn't think it would take me to paradise. It was a good vaccine—I didn't become a fanatic. I was saved. That Lauro orchestra was truly bad. Alfredo De Angelis* was the pianist. I played worse every day. This rejection of an environment I didn't like and a music I didn't feel made me do many wicked things. I had great fun.

I played a practical joke on El Tano that drove him crazy. He almost killed me. Without his realizing it, I loosened the screws in his bandoneon and told him, before going onstage, that a customer had requested "Loca," a tango in E minor in which he had to open the instrument. He started playing, and in the middle of the tune the screws went flying and the bandoneon came unhinged. He gave me a look and knew, immediately, who was the guilty party. The owners of the cabaret took the opportunity to tell him about other messes I had been involved in.

I was with Lauro three months. I left because I could not stand that setting and because El Tano couldn't stand me. Something like that would happen later with Troilo: three times he wanted to fire me because of things I had done in the cabaret.

Since my arrival in Buenos Aires I had become a regular at Café Germinal, where the Aníbal Troilo orchestra played. I looked up to him as if he were a god. I did the same with his musicians. I would go crazy when I heard pianist Orlando Goñi doing "Comme il faut," the Eduardo Arolas tango. I dreamed of playing like them, with them.

The 1940s, which to my mind extended artistically until 1955, were the high-water mark of the great tango orchestras. I was lucky enough to suck all that in: Aníbal Troilo, Alfredo Gobbi, Osvaldo Pugliese, Francini-Pontier, Miguel Caló, and Horacio Salgán. I even had the pleasure of meeting and hearing Pedro Maffia, who was on the Julio De Caro records that my dad played, entranced, in New York.

Tango also has its heroes, composers of fundamental pieces. These are men such as Agustín Bardi, Eduardo Arolas, Vicente Greco,

---

* Alfredo De Angelis (1912–1992): Pianist, composer, and bandleader.

Joaquín Mora, the brothers Francisco and Julio De Caro, Juan Carlos Cobián, Pedro Maffia, Pedro Laurenz. Then the famous '40s generation would arrive. The people of Buenos Aires loved that music. I underscore Buenos Aires because the tango scent exists right up to General Paz Avenue,* perhaps a little beyond, but that's where it ends.

Ariel Ramírez can play an irreproachable version of "Comme il faut." Mercedes Sosa can sing "Los mareados" very well.** But they don't have the same experiences that a *porteño* has. That's why I've always said that although tango and folk music† are two very authentic Argentine expressions, they cannot be played at the same time. You have to pick one or the other. The man from Buenos Aires is different from the one from Salta, Tucumán, or Mendoza. I don't say better or worse. I say different.

If I were twenty years old today, I don't believe I would go in the direction of tango. I would buy an electric guitar and take off in the direction of rock.

Where can you hear tangos in Buenos Aires? There are just five or six places in San Telmo [the old, colonial part of the city]. How have we come to this? Many things happened that marked its decline. The great tango creators disappeared. There was a rock invasion.

I still can't believe that some pseudocritics continue to accuse me of having murdered tango. They have it backward. They should look at me as the savior of tango. I performed plastic surgery on it. Without Piazzolla there would not have been the Rodolfo Mederos, the Dino Saluzzis, the Daniel Binellis, and all the people who came out

---

* General Paz Avenue encircles Buenos Aires and serves as a natural border of the city proper.

** Ariel Ramírez (b. 1921): A classically trained folk pianist and composer.

Mercedes Sosa: A folk-pop singer.

† Folk music: For North American and even European audiences, "folk" may evoke images of coffeehouses and singers accompanying themselves on steel-string acoustic guitars. Here, though, in the context of Argentine popular music, "folk" refers to the rural music of the Argentine countryside. Tango, in contrast, is not only urban music but a distinctly *porteño* music.

to take a chance for something new in tango, including Eduardo Rovira, who, sadly, died young.*

I also opened new roads in Europe. Now it's fashionable everywhere. But twenty-five years ago when I started traveling around the world with the Quintet, tango was nowhere, missing.

The attacks were so many, the lack of understanding so great, that I was left nearly flat on my back. It's a long story. When I directed the Fiorentino** orchestra—by then I was already out of Troilo's orchestra—I did an arrangement of Mariano Mores's tango "Copas, amigos, y besos." I wrote an introduction featuring a solo cello, and something grotesque happened. The women who worked at the Marabú cabaret took the dance floor and did a parody of a ballet. They were making fun of me. The piece did not work, and I had to change the arrangement. I think that was the first step toward leaving Fiorentino. He also didn't like that kind of audacity.

It was time to form my own orchestra. The year was 1946. That orchestra was very modern for its time and because of this, it had little work. That I wouldn't get calls from clubs to do dance dates was understandable. I put counterpoint, fugues, and new harmonic forms into the music. Those who followed me preferred to have a coffee and listen. For them dancing was secondary. I had proof of it at Tango Bar, at the Marzoto, places where people would go to listen to music. But because I didn't get offers from the radio I realized that things were not working out. Three years later I put the bandoneon away and dissolved the orchestra.

---

* Rodolfo Mederos (b. 1940): Bandoneonist, composer, bandleader, and pioneer in the fusion of rock and tango in the 1970s.

Dino Saluzzi (b. 1935): Bandoneonist, composer, and bandleader, Saluzzi earned a reputation as a brilliant interpreter of both tango and folk music in Argentina before developing an international career with his own highy idiosyncratic jazz-classical-tango fusion recording for the German label ECM.

For Daniel Binelli, see "Piazzolla's Musicians and Singers."

Eduardo Rovira (1925–1980): An innovative bandoneonist, pianist, composer, arranger, and bandleader.

** Francisco Fiorentino (1905–1971): Tango singer.

Today, from a distance, listening to the records I see the intention to change, but at the time it was not clear what I actually wanted. I found the true seam, the one that brings me to where I am today, in 1951 when I wrote "Para lucirse."

I had dissolved the 1946 Orchestra and was writing arrangements for the Aníbal Troilo, Osvaldo Fresedo, José Basso, and Francini-Pontier orchestras and others. That was barely enough to live on so the contract to write music for film was a godsend. The first film I had to work with was *Con los mismos colores*, directed by Leopoldo Torre Ríos, the father of Leopoldo Torre Nilson, with a book by Borocotó and a soccer theme. The music I wrote had nothing to do with the images. In truth, until the emergence of Maradona, of whom I became a furious fan, I didn't understand a thing about soccer. But

Piazzolla (first on the left in the row of bandoneonists) with his 1946 Orchestra. To his left is Roberto Di Filippo, whom Piazzolla called a master bandoneonist. At the piano is Atilio Stampone. The photo, signed "Astor, Sept., 46," is dedicated to his mother and father.

they gave me a seventy-piece orchestra and complete freedom. So here we had Mario Boyé kicking the ball with a symphonic background. They gave me freedom, and I used it to fly.*

They must have liked the final product because the following year the same producers called me to write music for a film about car racing, *Bólidos de acero.* For each film they paid me seven thousand pesos [approximately $2000], which at that time was a lot of money, at least for me.

Writing arrangements for other orchestras I discovered that the melodic elements also had a rhythmic foundation. I began to enjoy the swing in tango. In those days I had started to enjoy jazz again, like I did as a young man in New York. But instead of Cab Calloway I'd buy records by Stan Kenton, Art Tatum, and Oscar Peterson. For *tangueros* in the 1940s, jazz was always a four-letter word. That was something I saw as a mistake because there are many points of contact. Juan Carlos Cobián** also realized this. He was one of the few *tangueros* who said publicly that he loved jazz.

I enjoyed how the Stan Kenton orchestra sounded, the rhythm it had. That was what I wanted to do, work similar harmonies but with a difference: in place of brass I had strings and bandoneons. When I used trumpets, trombones, and saxes, it was horrendous. When I directed Radio Splendid's orchestra in 1952, I wrote atrocious arrangements. At the time I thought they were good, but they sound horrible to me now, tasteless.

That rhythmic idea I had found for "Para lucirse" was the push for "Prepárense," "Lo que vendrá," and "Triunfal." But I still was not a true creator. I arranged music for others and barely wrote a piece of music a year. The composer would emerge when Nadia Boulanger helped me see where the true Piazzolla was.

I think I would have saved myself many fights if I had kept my

---

* Piazzolla refers to sportswriter Ricardo Lorenzo "Borocotó," Argentine soccer star Diego Armando Maradona (b. 1960 in Buenos Aires), and Mario Boyé, Argentine soccer star of the 1940s.

**Juan Carlos Cobián (1896–1953): Pianist, composer, and bandleader.

mouth shut. But the tango world wanted to isolate me and I fought back as well as I could. Even Pedro Laurenz, a musician I greatly appreciated, eventually had to admit he had been wrong. He also had said that what I did was not tango. But when I recorded his "Berretín," one of his most beautiful works, he admitted, "How nice. He even respected my melodic line." Others didn't have such magnanimity, and I defended myself by swinging wildly at everything—and everybody got it, both the guilty and the innocent.

I was once in Montevideo, where I always had a great following, and someone asked me about Donato Racciatti, a local idol, and I answered that I didn't know him. Someone asked me about "La cumparsita," and I said it was the worst tango I'd ever heard in my life. They asked me about Mariano Mores, and I said his orchestra was like that of Francisco Canaro* but with a few more violins.

In my answers there was a bit of fun, a bit of provocation, and my truth. A musician can speak ill of a colleague but only if his opinions have a foundation. If I don't like how so and so plays, I say it. That's why I always had groups that sounded good. When I chose my musicians I didn't pick friends or someone who someone recommended. I chose the best.

All this clashed with certain codes the tango world has. It was the same thing when I said we had to get to the books, that we couldn't keep playing *a la parrilla*.** At first many jumped on me, but later everybody saw it as natural. Osvaldo Pugliese said a line no one challenged: "Piazzolla forced us to study, all of us."

That kind of message is one I want to pass along to the kids who play rock. Long hair and a guitar bought in the best shop in New York are not enough. It's not by chance that Sting called on Gil Evans for arrangements. Sting had the courage to admit that his music lacked preparation.

---

* Francisco Canaro (1988–1964): Violinist, composer and bandleader. His very popular bands played a highly rhythmic style, perfect for dancing but harmonically elementary, hence Piazzolla's disparaging allusion.

** *A la parrilla*: Playing by ear without the music, although not quite improvising.

I have been, I am, and I will be a fan of many tango orchestras. To hear "Negracha" or "La beba" by Osvaldo Pugliese is to be before two jewels. Same thing with "Jueves" by Alfredo Gobbi or "Comme il faut" and "Amurado" by Aníbal Troilo, tangos I did not arrange.

Now if pressed against a wall, just as I say that Polaco Goyeneche is the greatest singing "La Uruguayita Lucía," if I have to pick a song I'd pick "Arrabal" by the Elvino Vardaro Sextet. These are things I hold dear in my *tanguero* heart. That's why Ernesto Sábato* did an almost perfect X-ray of my music: "Piazzolla's tango has the eyes, the nose, and the mouth of its grandfather, the tango. The rest is Piazzolla."

The tango that fills my life is expressed most fundamentally in two groups: the Quintet—first, last, and always—and the Nonet.** The latter, I'm sorry to say, lasted only two years. Around that time was the most creative time in Astor Piazzolla's life. It starts with *María de Buenos Aires* in 1968, continues with the Nonet in 1971–72, and climaxes in the second Quintet, the one that starts in 1978. As in everything, there is a progression.

In "Aria de los analistas" from *María de Buenos Aires* is the germ of the idea for "Balada para un loco." The success of "Balada," which lost the Festival of Buenos Aires in 1969 but won in the people's hearts, is the core of a repertoire Horacio Ferrer and I wrote which includes some nice things: "Chiquilín de Bachín," "Balada para mi muerte," "El Gordo triste," "La bicicleta blanca," and "La última grela." Horacio Ferrer is the best poet I ever had with me.

"Balada," sung by Amelita Baltar, could not lose the first prize because, to begin with, it was a well-written song and, second, because the tango it was competing against, "El último tren," was truly ugly. But the rules changed as the festival went on. The jury was set aside and the popular reaction became most important—

---

* Ernesto Sábato (b. 1911): Important Argentine novelist, recipient of the Cervantes prize for literature, also known for his civic and cultural work. Piazzolla quotes a comment made on television. In 1963 they collaborated on the album *Tango contemporáneo*, on which Sábato recites text from his most famous novel, *Sobre héroes y tumbas*.

** Although Piazzolla decided to call this nine-piece group Conjunto 9 (Ensemble 9), in conversation he always referred to it as the Nonet.

and the lefties gave me a bill for my old anticommunist stance. They filled up Luna Park* with their own people and got a win for a sad-sack of a song that no one remembers and that was never sung again.

But justice always comes. The next day Hugo Guerrero Mar-thineitz** ("the Peruvian") started to play "Balada" on his show, even doing some needling: "*Hasta el último tren esta cargado de bal-adas*" [Even the last train is full of ballads], an allusion to the title of the winning song.

"Ballada" was a hit. It was a great success and went around the world. The true popular verdict, the one not manipulated by anyone, did it justice. A member of the festival's jury was Laura Escalada. In her vote "Balada" had won. She told me so herself many years ago, when we met. Today she's my wife.

The Nonet was like a big dream, the chamber group I always wanted to have. It's a great pity that just when I was deepening the repertoire, when the musicians truly understood what I wrote, the economic realities imposed its dissolution. I had the support of the City of Buenos Aires for two years and then it was over. There was no foundation, no private or state institution willing to fund it. As in many other issues, in Argentina we are also going the wrong way culturally. In any country with a well-defined cultural policy, the Nonet would not have died. That's not what Piazzolla says, it's what comes through in the compliments we received everywhere we went. But rather than becoming a national treasure, it was dumped in the garbage can.

There are a couple of records as testament and several pieces that are very dear to me still in my current repertoire: "Tristezas de un Doble A," "Onda 9," "Vardarito," and a special arrangement of "Ver-ano porteño." It was a very productive period as a composer; I wrote like a madman and smoked almost a hundred cigarettes a day. I was on my way to a heart attack, and I was not forgiven. I ran into it in 1973.

---

* Luna Park: The Madison Square Garden of Buenos Aires.

** Hugo Guerrero Marthineitz: Popular radio host.

The Quintet has two lives. One is born in the 1960s; the other, with a completely different lineup, in 1978. Both expressed a Piazzolla in constant evolution. The first communicated a music at times aggressive, at times melodic. The second one offered something better prepared, perhaps more intellectual.

Between them almost ten years had passed and in them experiences as disparate as the Electronic Octet, an album with Gerry Mulligan, and film music for several Italian, French, and Argentine films. That had to be reflected in the music. Ten years do not pass in vain for an artist. I believe the second Quintet is the sum of all those experiences.

Not everything I did in Europe is of the same quality. The pieces I wrote for *Libertango*, *Piazzolla '77*, and *Piazzolla '78* (the titles

Piazzolla with ample beard at the time of his Nonet, 1972.

under which they were released in Argentina) are silly next to the music I wrote for *María de Buenos Aires*, the Nonet, or *La camorra*, which was the last CD recorded by the Quintet. In the case of *Libertango* there might be a certain influence, a Quincy Jones vibe. The intention was to create a more international tango.

But it could not have been that bad. One day while I was recording at a studio in Milan with Italian musicians, the first violinist came to me and whispered in my ear, "*Astor, questa e musica e non la merda che facciamo tutti i giorni*" [Astor, this is music, not the shit we play every day].

It's not the same thing to have a concert with a grand orchestra in Milan today, one tomorrow in Paris, and another one ten days later in Buenos Aires as to play with the Quintet. There is something nice about knowing each other, sharing. We musicians need to talk about music. When people play looking at their watches, it drives me crazy,

Piazzolla with his first Quintet. Left to right: Antonio Agri, violin; Oscar López Ruiz, guitar; Piazzolla; Kicho Díaz, bass; and Jaime Gosis, piano.

Piazzolla on motor scooter with one of his great 1960s quintets. Left to right: Osvaldo Manzi, piano; Kicho Díaz, bass; Cacho Tirao, guitar; and Antonio Agri, violin.

With a 1970s Quintet formation that proved ephemeral but that also had great musicians. Left to right: Antonio Agri, violin; Kicho Díaz, bass; Piazzolla; Osvaldo Tarantino, piano; and Oscar López Ruiz, guitar.

Autograph score for "Pedro y Pedro," signed "Astor Piazzolla, Marzo 1981, Paris, a Maffia y Laurenz" (three pages). Piazzolla dedicated this work to Pedro Maffia and Pedro Laurenz and asked that it appear in this book. Courtesy Leopoldo Federico

"Pedro y Pedro" autograph score (continued)

it gives me a pain. That's what happened to me with the great orchestras.

The Quintet was about something else. I want to recognize the help and support by the musicians who were with me. In these past ten years it was easier, we had more than enough work, made good money. That's why I don't want to forget the first Quintet, the one with Antonio Agri and Kicho Díaz, Osvaldo Manzi, Jaime Gosis, Oscar López Ruiz, and Cacho Tirao. We went through hard times. We had to play anywhere we could, and there was never a lot of money. Without them the story of Astor Piazzolla would not have been possible.

I've always written thinking of the musicians I have with me. But I also gave them freedom to fly. I had pianists who improvised like gods: Osvaldo Tarantino, who came from tango; Pablo Ziegler, who was schooled in jazz; Gerardo Gandini, a scholar in contemporary music. In the Electronic Octet I had Juan Carlos Cirigliano, who was a big fan of Horacio Salgán. I used to tell him: "If you want to put in some Salgán stuff go ahead, but watch out because there's a limit. You are playing my music."

Gandini and I talked about the same thing. He enriched my scores with ad libs that really fit well. That's why I always called the best soloists: to enhance my music. The one thing I could never stand was that the essence might get lost. I wanted tango swing, not jazz swing or contemporary music swing. Piazzolla had to sound like Piazzolla.

4

Suite Troileana

I had stopped playing with Lauro and was spending every night at the Germinal, listening to Aníbal Troilo's orchestra. By then I had become a very good friend of Huguito (Little Hugo) Baralis, a violinist with the orchestra. During the breaks he would come off the stage and have a coffee with me. I once told him I knew the whole repertoire by heart, that I could play it without reading the music. Huguito gave me a "And where did this nut come from?" look.

I also confessed my dream to him: I wanted to play bandoneon in the orchestra. He said he saw me as too much of a kid, that Troilo liked to hire experienced players, and that the bandoneon section was full.

One day I arrived early and got a bad vibe. Toto Rodríguez* had the flu and that complicated the weekend performances. I went to Baralis and told him: "This is my chance. Go talk with Troilo. I'll go to the boarding house to get my bandoneon and I'll be right back." The boarding house was nearby. I went flying. When I went into the Germinal I didn't see Baralis, but I did see Troilo. Shameless as I was, I went up to him and he stopped me before I said anything. He knew my story. "So you are the kid who knows my repertoire? All right, go up onstage and play."

And behind me rose all those giants I had looked up to from below: David Díaz, Orlando Goñi, Pedro Sapochnick, and, of course, Troilo himself. I put my life into every note, and when we finished Troilo

*Juan Miguel "Toto" Rodriguez: Bandoneonist, composer, arranger.

59

came up to talk to me in that style of his, "Kid, we play in blue clothes, you know. Tomorrow we play before an audience."

I was so happy that I started playing "Rhapsody in Blue" by Gershwin. The other musicians looked at me weird, but Orlando Goñi was the only one who spoke up: "With that stuff you're not going to beat anyone. Leave that for the Americans."

When my dad found out I was working with Troilo, he came to Buenos Aires. He wanted to meet him. I remember we went over Troilo's house on Soler Street to eat spaghetti that his mother had prepared. My dad made the round trip in the same day* on a motorcycle borrowed from someone in the family. In Mar del Plata we were always known as the crazy Piazzollas: my grandfather, my father, and me. When he said his goodbyes to Troilo, he was tearing up. He hugged him and, in front of me, told Troilo, "Please take care of the kid. He is only eighteen and you know all about the nightlife, the cabarets, the women." Troilo teared up also: "Don't worry, Don Vicente, I'll take care of him."

That evening we did not have a show so I told the man who was going to keep me from all temptations: "Maestro, what do you say about us going to the Doble Tres, that dive in Avellaneda, and try to make a buck at the dice?" With Troilo I didn't use the informal *tú*. I didn't even call him by his nickname: Pichuco. I didn't do that because he was seven years older than I, because he was my boss, and because of the admiration I felt for him. He did use the *tú* [actually the more colloquial *porteño* form, *vos*] with me.

He was dumbfounded with my proposal. "And where did you learn to play dice?" he said. So I told him how, when I was twelve, I would sneak out of the house when we lived in New York to go to the gambling dens. Troilo moved his head as if to say "no way": "Gato, you are the devil incarnate. May God save you." We came back at five in the morning, both penniless. He nicknamed me "Gato" [tomcat] because I was always restless, going to and fro, nonstop.

---

* The elder Piazzolla lived in Mar del Plata, a seaside resort city about six hundred miles south of Buenos Aires, quite a distance to have made round-trip in one day.

I had five beautiful years in his orchestra, from 1939 to 1944. It was another tango baptism, like meeting Carlos Gardel or discovering the Elvino Vardaro Sextet. But in Troilo's orchestra I also found out about the worst sides of the tango world, especially envy.

El Gordo trusted me. I started to call him El Gordo (The fat one) many years later when we were colleagues and friends. Many times he felt tired and asked me to replace him in the solo parts. This created resentment in the other players and started a war that was underground at first. Later, when I was already married and very much into my studies with Alberto Ginastera, things got more aggressive.

Playing with Troilo one made good money—about eight hundred pesos [approximately $240] a month. That did not allow for a millionaire's life but one could live well: I could afford to get married, rent an apartment, and study music. The band that paid most in those days was Juan D'Arienzo's. It paid about a thousand pesos [approximately $300] a month. But I would never have joined that

Piazzolla with Aníbal Troilo at the recording of a bandoneon duet in 1970.

orchestra, of course, not even drunk out of my skull.* I had my personality and well-defined musical taste.

Between the anger that the cabaret world produced in me and the
problems I had with certain musicians, my enthusiasm began to
wane. My age and my studies may have had something to do with it.
Whatever the reason, playing with Troilo did not seem to me the
ultimate goal.

I would get to bed late, and three times a week I would travel an
hour from Parque Chacabuco to Barracas for my lessons with Ginastera. I did my homework in dressing rooms, rehearsing a quartet with
Huguito Baralis, Kicho and David Díaz. They were the only ones
who understood me and accepted the notion that a tango musician
might want to progress. When there was a piano around Orlando
Goñi joined in and we played differently, more elaborately. One day
Troilo caught us and got angry. He said people wanted to dance and
if I took my ideas to the orchestra it might undermine his style.

My affection for El Gordo never wavered. Perhaps there were a
few arguments—he got angry at me when I left his orchestra—but
we always loved each other a lot. My admiration for him never
diminished. To the contrary, as the years went by I came to value
everything he did. He didn't have a great output, perhaps twenty-five
or thirty tangos, but almost all of them are jewels.

I pick up a bandoneon and play "La última curda," and it touches
my heart. If Troilo had had more musical education he could have
gone much further. The proof is in the list of musicians, singers, and
arrangers he hired. He surrounded himself with the best. He himself
had a great birth certificate: he had started as a musician in the
Elvino Vardaro Sextet and with Osvaldo Pugliese.

I wrote my first arrangement for Troilo almost by chance. Argentino Galván was not available and Troilo wanted to debut "Azabache," a *milonga* by the brothers Virgilio and Homero Expósito, in
a show on Radio El Mundo. The program was called "Ronda de ases"

---

* D'Arienzo's style, very rhythmic, was great for dancing but resolutely conventional in
its harmonic and melodic language.

[A hand of aces]. Each orchestra had to play a new piece in its repertoire; the one that got more applause, won.

Hugo Baralis alerted me to the fact that Galván was not around, which was why I went to El Gordo to ask him to leave it to me. At first he said no. He told me I did not have enough experience, that it was difficult. I insisted and he gave it to me. I had to write it overnight. I had the violins doing a scale in the upper register, something not common in the orchestra, but it came out great. We won first prize. Still, Troilo did not like it much.

From that moment on, he became the censor of all my arrangements. I would write down two hundred notes and he would erase half of them. Some would tell me it was jealousy. I don't think so. He

---

Aníbal Troilo (1914–1975)

Aníbal Troilo, also called "Pichuco" and "El Gordo," was a superb bandoneonist, composer, arranger, and bandleader. After Gardel, Troilo was perhaps *the* iconic figure in classic tango. He was a *porteño* through and through—he was born and died in Buenos Aires.

Troilo both consolidated and furthered the styles of his elders, establishing the sound many consider to be classic tango. While not a virtuoso, he was an expressive player with a distinctly bright and light sound. And while he was somewhat of a romantic with a knack for melodies, he also opened his orchestra to innovators like Astor Piazzolla. Piazzolla played in and arranged for his *orquesta típica* from 1939 to 1944.

Some of Troilo's own tangos, including "Sur," "Barrio de tango," and "Che bandoneón" written with poet Homero Manzi, "María" and "La última curda" with Catulo Castillo, and "Garúa" with Enrique Cadícamo, are now part of the canon. Just as Gardel became a legend in part because of his debonair persona, Troilo himself became a character larger than life, a man seen as embodying the tango ethos. In tribute after his mentor's death, Piazzolla wrote his four-movement *Suite Troileana*.

Piazzolla and Troilo, above, with Troilo's wife, Zita, who gave Piazzolla one of Troilo's bandoneons after his death. At right, backstage at the Teatro Colón in 1972. Piazzolla featured his Nonet, Troilo his orchestra.

was past such pettiness. He just wanted to defend his style. He didn't want the orchestra to sound like Piazzolla when I arranged it or like Galván when Galván arranged it, which I think was fair. Besides, he was right. To make him mad I sometimes used complicated chords. Everything I studied with Ginastera I wanted to try out in the orchestra.

The second tango I arranged was "Inspiración," and I gave it a cello introduction that was pretty long. Troilo didn't like this one either: "No, Gato, we need to give people other stuff. They want to dance. They don't pay their ticket to listen."

But he left it almost untouched, and it ended up sounding like a piece for listening rather than for dancing. Soon after we did the carnival dances at the Boca Juniors* stadium, and something really nice happened there. We started playing "Inspiración" and noticed how people gathered around the stage to listen. No one moved until the last note was played. That was my small revenge. I looked at El Gordo and told him, "You see, it's already a success. People also pay for listening."

Life in the orchestra was getting hard. My friends understood what was happening to me. Others would mess up the homework I did for Ginastera or would fill my bandoneon case with garbage. My reaction was to joke for joking's sake: mischief, throw *pica-pica,*** lock in the dancers when they were ready to go onstage. I also threw firecrackers into the reserved areas when I saw the curtains drawn, a sign that a client was making love with one of the hostesses, the call girls who worked at the club. Then someone went to Troilo with these stories, telling him I was behind all those things, and El Gordo got furious. He wanted to fire me.

What really upset me was that I was being dumped on. Cabarets were real whorehouses and some unusual things happened, but I

---

* As part of the carnival celebration, clubs in Buenos Aires traditionally had big dances at night with top orchestras. Boca Juniors is perhaps the most popular soccer club in Argentina. The stadium is located in the working class neighborhood of La Boca.

** *Pica-pica*: An herb that causes itching.

was not the only bum in the place doing those things. That's why I spent a week trying to think up some evil thing to create confusion. Finally I thought of buying a mosquito-killer spiral.* I cut a piece off and timed how long it took to burn.

It gave me a twenty-minute lead. I lit one on the end with a firecracker and placed it in a reserved area where a couple was, and I went to take my place onstage. When it blew up, the orchestra was playing. There was a deadly silence. First thing Troilo did was to look daggers at me, but there I was, sitting in the bandoneon row. So I put on a dumb face and made a gesture as though to say, "I have nothing to do with it."

I told him the truth much later. Troilo caressed my face, a typical gesture of his, and said, "Gato, I never had a doubt about it. I knew you did it. But at that moment I didn't have a gun handy or I would have shot you."

Even today I continue to joke, although now my jokes are more naive. Laura, my wife, says that one of these days I'm going to scare a guest to death because I open the door with a Frankenstein or a werewolf mask on. It's the Piazzolla family heritage: we have always been a little *crazy* [in English].

Cabarets are a peculiar institution in Buenos Aires nightlife. There were regular customers, people who truly enjoyed dancing a tango, as was the case with my friend Victor Samson, an attorney and former judge. The cabaret is also a place where great composers and lyricists got together, people like Enrique Santos Discépolo, Homero Manzi, Catunga Contursi, Enrique Cadícamo. They were all very close Troilo friends. They would come to hear the orchestra, and then we, the musicians, would stop by and chat with them. It was the nicest thing about the evening. It enriched us.

The people who frequented the cabaret were generally well to do. And there was a little bit of everything: money made on the up and up and the other kind. And you could see a lot of what the tango

* Mosquito-killer spiral: *Espirales*, as the name suggests, are spiral-shaped strips that are lit and burn slowly and create smoke that keeps mosquitoes away.

lyric says: "an old creep who spends his money getting Lulú drunk with his champagne."

In contrast, the audience at cafés such as the Germinal or the people who went dancing on weekends were from another, purer class. They were workers, middle class people, students. Tango was everybody's big love affair. I think Buenos Aires lived dancing and whistling tangos.

Troilo had many friends. Besides his illustrious gang, which included musicians, poets, and artists, there were the other ones, those from the racetrack, the numbers, and various gambling dens. I think they took advantage of El Gordo's infinite kindness. At the end of his life, when there was not much left in his generous pockets, some of those friends disappeared. But I never heard him complain. Troilo truly lived it up. He liked to live like a prince, wore the best clothes, and was an exquisite gourmand. The latter is a golden rule: great musicians know how to enjoy a good wine and savor a great meal.

In 1944 when I told him I was leaving his orchestra, he got mad. His mother even called my house and spoke with my wife, Dedé,* in a harsh, almost threatening tone: "How dare you do this to El Gordo?"

The tango world was shocked. People said this was a betrayal, that I was only twenty-three, and that away from Troilo I was going to starve to death. In truth I wanted to play my music. I was fed up with his crossing out my arrangements and with the cabaret life. But the anger passed quickly for both of us. He loved me a lot and I loved him. When I put together my own orchestra, he came by to wish me luck. El Gordo was a fan of the Quintet. He liked to listen to us. Afterward he would come by the dressing room, hug me, and tell me, "Gato, you never miss a note."

As the years went by some people spoke of a rivalry: Troilo or

* Dedé Wolff (b. 28 January 1923): Piazzolla's first wife. She studied painting in Buenos Aires with Vicente Forte and Juan Battle Planas and in Paris with André Lhote. She has shown her work in Buenos Aires, New York, and Mexico. Astor and Dedé had two children, Diana and Daniel. Wolff lives in Buenos Aires.

Piazzolla. Neither one of us added fuel to this. One time he sent me a beautiful little note:

Dear Gato:

I have always honored your friendship. Much more now that so much water has gone under the bridge. Now, I repeat, I'm only left to ask God that He gives you peace and He does not forsake me. We have done some things to deserve it.

> Affectionately,
> Pichuco
> 19 June 1967

Shortly afterward, Horacio Ferrer and I wrote a song that is now a classic for many singers: "El Gordo triste." It was my first tribute to a living Troilo. When he died, 18 May 1975, I was in Rome. I felt the news like a mallet blow. A few days later all the affection I felt took me to the piano and I wrote *Suite Troileana*, a work which has El Gordo's great loves: "Bandoneón," "Zita" [his wife], "Whisky," and "Escolaso" [gambling].

When I got back to Buenos Aires I played with the Electronic Octet for the opening night of a beautiful new place called La Ciudad. One evening Zita came by and gave me one of El Gordo's bandoneons. It was one of the most moving moments in my life.

5

Nadia of Paris, Alberto of Barracas

I had two great teachers, as I have said: Nadia Boulanger and Alberto Ginastera.* They taught me all the secrets of musical technique.

I place Nadia a step above in my acknowledgment because she was the one who put me on the path: she was the one who made me discover the real Piazzolla, the one who ended my confusion.

Dedé and I went to Paris in 1954. We made the trip by ship, with many dreams and little money. The year before, I had won the Fabien Sevitzky Award with my *Buenos Aires* Symphony, and one of the prizes was, precisely, a scholarship to study with Nadia in the classes she taught at the Fontainebleau conservatory. I wanted private lessons, but that would have put us in a very uncomfortable financial situation.

Dedé backed me up as always, and we went to live in a small room at the Hotel Fiat, on the Rue de Douai, that was being rented by Héctor Grane, an Argentine musician and good friend of ours. He was going on tour so he lent it to us.

The neighborhood where we lived, Montmartre, and the money,

---

* Nadia Boulanger (1887–1979): Illustrious French composition teacher and mentor to a generation of classical composers, including the Americans Aaron Copland, Virgil Thomson, and Elliott Carter.

Alberto Ginastera (1916–1983): Important twentieth-century Argentine composer who displayed a poetic imagination in wide-ranging genres, including ballet, opera, and instrumental works.

which was good enough for us to be able to eat every other day, put us in a beautiful and unforgettable bohemia. Nadia's house was a few yards from our place, on Rue Ballú. Nearby was the studio of André Lhote, with whom Dedé furthered her studies in painting which she had started in Buenos Aires.

There was something that alleviated our situation. In Paris I discovered that my song "Prepárense," written in 1952, was in the repertoire of the tango orchestras playing in France. Those royalties were like manna from heaven.

I arrived at Nadia's house with a suitcase full of scores, the complete classical oeuvre I had written to that point. Nadia spent the first two weeks analyzing the work. "To teach you," she said. "I first must know where your music is going."

One day, finally, she told me that everything I had brought with me was well written but that she could not find the spirit in it. She asked me what music I played in my country, what I wanted to do. I had not told her about my past as a tango musician, much less that my instrument, the bandoneon, was in the closet in my room in Paris.

Piazzolla with Nadia Boulanger in her Paris apartment where he studied with her in 1954–55.

I thought to myself: if I tell her the truth she will throw me out the window. Nadia had been a classmate of Maurice Ravel, teacher of Igor Markevitch, Aaron Copland, Leonard Bernstein,* Robert Casadesus, and Jean Françaix. By then she was already considered the best teacher of music in the world. I was a simple *tanguero*. But after two days I had to tell her the truth. I told her I made my living arranging for tango orchestras. I told her about Aníbal Troilo, about my own orchestra, and how, tired of all that, I thought my future was in classical music.

Nadia looked into my eyes and asked me to play one of my tangos at the piano. So I confessed to her that I played bandoneon; I told her she shouldn't expect a good piano player because I wasn't. She insisted, "It doesn't matter, Astor, play your tango." And I started out with "Triunfal." When I finished, Nadia took my hands in hers and with that English of hers, so sweet, she said, "Astor, this is beautiful. I like it a lot. Here is the true Piazzolla—do not ever leave him." It was the great revelation of my musical life.

I was with Nadia almost a year, studying a lot, especially four-part counterpoint, something that drove me crazy. I believe I once cried in anger because it was so hard. Besides, I was in the presence of a teacher who knew absolutely everything. She would give me forty or fifty exercises, and because I could not always find a solution I would repeat some, which was a form of cheating. But Nadia was a computer. She picked them out in an instant: "Astor, numbers 4 and 14 are repeated," she would say.

Counterpoint is something that I use a lot in my music. Counterpoint is to get four or five musicians to play different lines with a harmonious result. For this the talent of the composer is of fundamental importance. I could have studied twenty years with Nadia Boulanger, but without talent, that knowledge about counterpoint would not have been of much use. You can study a lot of classical music, but

---

* Although Bernstein was not himself a Boulanger student, his own teachers had studied with Boulanger, he revered her for having taught Copland, and he invited her to guest conduct the New York Philharmonic, which she did on 11 February 1939.

intuition is valuable, very valuable. Technique helps and enriches the product as long as there is some raw material to work with.

Teodoro Fuchs* marveled at the fugue in *María de Buenos Aires*. He once told me that no tango musician is capable of writing a fugue. Someone might say, "You can do it by studying." The opposite happened to me.

When I studied with Ginastera I could not come up with a fugue even if I pulled with a mule. Now I can write one in ten minutes, and it is something complicated, a mathematical exercise, pure intuition.

When I met her, Nadia had just celebrated her sixty-seventh birthday. She lived in a big apartment with an enormous organ and a concert piano. There were signed pictures of Igor Stravinsky, André Gide, Paul Valéry, and André Malraux on the walls. She was a very nice woman.

At five in the afternoon the maid would come in with a tray with all the elements for afternoon tea, but she would leave them on the table. Nadia served the tea. It was like studying with my mother.

I saw her again twenty years later at the Fontainebleau conservatory. She was almost blind then, but her musical ear, despite her age, was still perfect. I came up to her, took her hand, and said, "Hello, Mademoiselle Boulanger."

She recognized my voice and quickly answered, "Hello, my dear Astor. Congratulations, now you are very famous."

Alberto Ginastera was my first teacher and I his first student. I arrived at his doorstep by chance in 1941, through the efforts of Arthur Rubinstein and Juan José Castro.** Ginastera was the teacher who

---

* Teodoro Fuchs (1908–1969): Conductor who led concerts in all the countries of South America. Born in Chemnitz, Germany, Fuchs studied in his native country, fleeing Hitler in 1937 for Istanbul and later Argentina, where he conducted the Córdoba Symphony Orchestra, the National Radio Youth Orchestra, and the National Symphony Orchestra.

** Juan José Castro (1895–1968): Eminent Argentine composer and conductor who led orchestras in Buenos Aires, Cuba, Uruguay, Australia, and elsewhere. Castro composed in all classical genres, including opera, ballet, and works for orchestra.

Alberto Ginastera. His first student was Astor Piazzolla.

gave me the foundation. With him I learned orchestration, still one of my strong points, and everything that I would further develop with Nadia Boulanger in Paris. I spent almost five years with him, and I remember that time not only because of the technique I learned but the humanism he taught me.

Alberto used to say that a musician could not just stay in his scores. He would say that a musician has to know about painting, literature, theater, film. For me this was like getting an electric shock. In those days I was playing with Troilo, and with the majority of my colleagues I could only talk about soccer and gambling.

Alberto lived in Barracas, at 844 University Street, his parents' house. He was five years older than I, but when we were young we never spoke to each other with the informal *tú*. Only as adults, when I went to visit him in Geneva, Switzerland, could I find the Ginastera capable of joking around. The one I knew in Barracas was very introverted, always dressed in black. He looked like a Protestant pastor. I believe his life changed after his marriage to Aurora Natola.* Then he broke through his shell and renewed everything, even his music. He is the most important Argentine composer in history. Everything he did had worldwide transcendence.

* Aurora Natola: Argentine cellist and Ginastera's second wife. He dedicated his Concerto for Orchestra No. 2 to her.

With his revolutionary Buenos Aires Octet, already suggesting an idiosyncratic tango chamber group. Left to right: Hugo Baralis, violin; Aldo Nicolini, bass; Enrique Mario Francini, violin; Atilio Stampone, piano; José Bragato, cello (he would be also a member of Piazzolla's Sextet, his final group); Leopoldo Federico, bandoneon; Piazzolla; and Horacio Malvicino (who was also a member of his last Quintet), electric guitar. Note Malvicino's amp on the chair, a novelty in tango circles.

6

New York, New York (Second Movement)

The Buenos Aires Octet that I put together in 1955 had great artistic impact, but the work did not last. It was a great effort. We even gave up our royalties in exchange for recording our first disc. Today that work keeps going around the world: it has been released a hundred times, filling the pockets of the bums who live off the true creators, in this case the musicians of the Octet: Enrique Mario Francini, Hugo Baralis, José Bragato, Juan Vasallo, Atilio Stampone, Horacio Malvicino, Leopoldo Federico, and me.

Because of that, because I didn't have a dime, because I was married and had two kids, I decided to take a chance just like my father had done once. It was 1958. I wouldn't live the rest of my days in New York, but that city always gave me the courage to point the boat in the right direction.

Just as Nonino had done thirty something years before me, I traveled first. I settled in my cousin Bertolami's house and went out to find an apartment for Dedé and my children. When they arrived I didn't have good news to give them. Things were going badly, but I had made my move and now had to move forward.

One of the trump cards I had was a card of one George Greely, a man who had been in Buenos Aires as artistic director of The Platters. He came one night to hear the Octet. He liked it, and in the dressing room he told me he had an important position in the music department of Metro-Goldwyn-Mayer. He left me his phone number with the express request that I call him whenever I decided to go to work in the United States. One thing led to another and three years had gone by.

Once in New York I called the MGM offices in Hollywood, as the card said. A secretary answered, I asked for George Greely, and she

In New York, 1959, during a difficult time, Piazzolla playing a Piazzolla he hated in a promotional picture: the stereotypical *compadrito*, the tough guy. On the left is Juan Carlos Copes; at center is María Nieves.

said, "Oh, he died last month." I thought, "This lady is pulling my leg." But I also started to worry. I lived many years in the United States and people don't make this kind of joke, much less by phone, even less so to someone they don't know.

Just in case, I called again and told the secretary, "Ma'am, I've come from very far away, from Argentina. I need to speak to Mr. Greely." And she said the same thing again: "I am so sorry, Mr. Greely died last month."

I discarded the idea of miscommunication about the name because I spoke good English. It knocked my socks off. I did not have work as a film music composer, which was my ambition and what Greely had offered me in Buenos Aires.

I started to look for other work, and I was seconds away from signing up as a translator in a bank. I say seconds because I already had accepted the salary and terms. It was a very hot day in New York. The shirt, the tie, the jacket bothered me. I believe I also could not stand myself.

I got to the bank, looked at the faces of the employees, and at that moment felt I was making a fatal mistake. I turned around and left. I had decided that I'd do anything about music except leave it. That I would not do.

There was an opportunity to back a singer, and I formed my own group. It was a monstrosity featuring bandoneon, electric guitar, vibraphone, piano, and bass. It had a certain success, but I still consider it a sin. That was the Jazz Tango Quintet. The repertoire had a little bit of everything, from "El choclo" to Duke Ellington's "Sophisticated Lady," from "La cumparsita" to "Laura." In the music there was a kernel of Piazzolla, but there were certain things that went against my principles. I did it to eat.

With that in mind, I agreed to do a show with Juan Carlos Copes, María Nieves,* and a ballet directed by Ana Itelman. What they did have was class, but I was not very happy with the music.

---

* Juan Carlos Copes is perhaps tango's greatest dancer and choreographer. María Nieves was his longtime partner.

And to close that very bad year of 1959, one day the phone exploded like an atom bomb. I was performing with Copes in Puerto Rico, in the Club Flamboyán, when I received a call from Dedé, who had stayed back in New York with the kids. Nonino had died in Mar del Plata. It was too much.

When I got back to New York a few days later, I asked to be left alone in a room in the apartment, and in less than an hour I wrote "Adiós Nonino." And then I cried as I had few times before in my life. On the trip from the airport to the house on 92d Street, the image of Nonino appeared to me on every wall in New York. In that piece I left all the memories I had of my dad.

It was time to get back to Buenos Aires. I think God has the destiny of each of us written out. I say this because that tale in 1958 continued many years later, in 1989 when I went to Los Angeles to play with the Sextet. The day of the opening night I got a call in the hotel from one George Greely. I didn't know who he was. I did not remember the telephone incident with MGM. The man insisted [in English], "*Astor, do you remember me?*" He told me about Buenos Aires and The Platters. Then I realized who he was, and a chill went down my spine. I said, "George, you are going to live many years. I was once told you were dead." I told him about the call, and he didn't know what to say. He was as confused as I had been thirty years earlier, and too much time had gone by to find the truth.

He came to hear the concert, and afterward he came by the dressing room and told me one of the most sincere and painful things one musician can tell another: "Astor, I'm still at MGM. I made quite a bit of money, but I'm a frustrated artist. I am not who I wanted to be. Today I envy you: you are playing your music and with it you have triumphed around the world." It must be the same destiny that steers "La bicicleta blanca."*

---

*"La bicicleta blanca": A song by Piazzolla and Horacio Ferrer about the eternal, lone cyclist.

7

For Fans Only

NATALIO GORIN: *I want to dedicate a chapter to the people who have followed you for thirty, forty years, the fans, the first Piazzolla diehards.*
ASTOR PIAZZOLLA: Those are the ones who know me well and who sometimes understand my work better than I do.

With your permission, I am going to be a bit fresh. One time you said you had written two thousand pieces, and there are those who say you have written the same piece two thousand times.
I believe that's from some bullshit artist who copied it from a phrase some credit Stravinsky with in relation to Vivaldi. I could not care less. My musical response is that they confuse works with style. With ill will you could apply the same line to Gardel, Pugliese, Troilo, and Piazzolla because, luckily, I do have a style.

Astor, who would be in the lineup of the ideal quintet?
The violinist would be Fernando Suárez Paz.

Damn, just like that, without anesthesia, you left Antonio Agri out.
Suárez Paz is more modern, more contemporary. Let's put the human qualities aside. Talking violinists, Suárez Paz is *number one* [in English]. What's the difference? Only we musicians can see this. The common people wouldn't. Agri had been with me many years, had really caught on to my style. But one day he picked up, formed a Viennese-style string group, and got stuck. He didn't stop being a good violin player, he just got stuck.

Suárez Paz not only plays well, he is very expressive. He is very intuitive about adding things; his phrasing enhanced my music. I still have a very nice relationship with Agri.* In this sense he is a ten and the other guy a zero. There is no comparison. But on the other hand, you don't always judge someone by his personal conduct. No one wonders if Beethoven or Brahms were good or bad guys. They are valued for their work.

Now comes a position with several candidates: the piano chair.
No, I don't have any doubts. The best pianist in Piazzolla's history is Jaime Gosis.

Gerardo Gandini did not play with the Quintet, but I would like to know if Gosis is above Gandini.
No, he was not a better pianist than Gandini, but there never was and never will be anybody with Gosis's *touch* [in English]. Gandini is a different thing; his technical level cannot be surpassed. He alone was able to play piano in the Sextet. I wrote very hard stuff for him.

Gosis's history with me has a secret. He had played with Pedro Maffia, and I knew what music he liked. So I started writing things for piano as if it were a bandoneon. Gosis caught on quickly. He played the piano with a sound I really never heard anyone else get. I was lucky with almost all my musicians. Some loved money more than music, others were more lyrical, but all put their shoulders to the wheel. There are unforgettable things: Vardarito would play two notes on the violin that would sound like two notes from El Gordo Troilo, same thing with Agri. Or when Tarantino—another great soloist I had in my groups—let himself *tanguear*** on the piano, he was a marvel to behold.

On this no one can go wrong: the best bass player was Kicho Díaz.

---

* Antonio Agri died in 1998. See "Piazzolla's Musicians and Singers."

** *Tanguear*: Play in tango fashion.

Without a doubt. Many times people have asked me what it was about Kicho. I don't know. I think he is the father of all bass players. He was a sort of elephant carrying the whole Quintet on his back. His ease in playing was always a delight.

Throughout its history the Quintet had only three guitar players: Horacio Malvicino, Oscar López Ruiz, and Cacho Tirao. Who is the top guy?
The one who better understood my music was Malvicino, perhaps because he is the more *tanguero* of the group, perhaps because he's of my generation. López Ruiz is more modern—he came from jazz and pushed me to do strange things without taking the taste of the audience into account. He would tell me, "Astor, let's do 'Coral.' It's so nice." And that was a dense piece, hard to digest. He was a true pal of mine. He probably dealt with the worst part of the story, the part when we played in clubs for two people.

Now we have to pick the better pieces in Piazzolla's body of work.
The number one piece is "Adiós Nonino." I challenged myself to write a better one and I couldn't. It has a very intimate feel, almost funereal and yet it blew everything up. The day we premiered it with the Quintet, the musicians and I said, "This one isn't worth shit. No one is going to like it." And yet there it is. It was a period in the Quintet's life in which all the pieces had the spunk of "Calambre," "Los poseídos," "Lo que vendrá." "Adiós Nonino" ended wrong but like life: it just fades away. People liked it from the start, perhaps because it has a mysterious air, a melody that plays off a very strong rhythmic foundation. Then it changes key and finally that glorious ending with a sad resolution. Perhaps that's why people liked it: it was different from everything else.

How many different arrangements are there of "Adiós Nonino"?
Something like twenty. And life can be so odd sometimes. If I have to pick one I'd choose the arrangement for the Electronic Octet. It's strange. That group does not bring up the best memories for me. There are two other arrangements I like: the one for the Nonet and

the last one I did for the Quintet, which sometimes I think is perfect in sound and craftsmanship.

We need to pick more songs. We got stuck on "Adiós Nonino."
I would have to jump from period to period. "Tristezas de un Doble A" is one of my most important pieces. I feel the same about "Calambre" and "Los poseídos."

I am not setting a ranking, I'm just calling them off as I remember them: "La camorra," "Mumuki," "Revirado," "Lunfardo," and all the songs I was playing in the spirit of "Tanguedia."

"Retrato de Alfredo Gobbi" is not on that list, for example.
It's not that I forgot about it. That's a piece I stopped playing because of the challenges it presented. When I wrote it I was thinking of the musicians of that Quintet, the one featuring Antonio Agri on violin and Osvaldo Manzi on piano. We got to the point of playing an impeccable version of it. But when we passed it on to Suárez Paz and Pablo Ziegler, we realized that it was an arrangement from another era. This doesn't mean these musicians were better than the other ones. I want my musicians to enjoy what they are playing, and I write the arrangements thinking of the individual style of each one of them. I know that López Ruiz has a different harmonic taste than that of Malvicino, for example. I know that Console plays the bass a certain way. I know Gosis came from tango and Ziegler came from jazz.

Which is the best recording in Piazzolla's history?
La camorra, the last thing the Quintet recorded. The recordings with Gary Burton and Gerry Mulligan are also very good, although in Mulligan's case we had a sorry orchestra behind us. There is one album I hold apart for its technical and artistic achievements: *Concierto para bandoneón* with Lalo Schifrin's orchestra.

What does the Electronic Octet represent in your career?
A false step. It had a good moment when it comprised Horacio Mal-

vicino, Adalberto Cevasco, El Zurdo Roizner, Juan Cirigliano, my son, Daniel. Later, with a lineup of rockers, very young, we did a tour of Europe and played fifteen days at the Olympia in Paris. It was a total success. But the French, who know my work well, questioned me: "What's up with you, Piazzolla? What are you doing with this group? The world is full of electric guitars and basses, synthesizers and organs. Doing this you are only one more in the bunch. But with the acoustic instruments you have one of the best groups in the world. Go back to the Quintet." I thought about it and concluded, these people are right. I am Piazzolla. My music is related to tango. What do I have to do with jazz-rock fusion?

It looked like a search for a young audience. Others thought it was part of your musical evolution. As long as there was a bandoneon in the group, the tango sound was secure.
The group sounded nice, true, but it was not true Piazzolla. In those days Chick Corea's electric band, Return To Forever, was in fashion, and I got carried away—I wasn't the first and I won't be the last. Even Igor Stravinsky had his moment of weakness. During Stravinsky's last years, Pierre Boulez was coming up as a composer and twelve-tone technique was the rage. Stravinsky wanted to get on the bus and wrote the worst music of his life. Wanting to copy, he stopped being Stravinsky.

It is already said that Piazzolla is a tango classic. Is that at odds with your revolutionary aura?
Not at all. Don't they say today that Stravinsky is a classic? Who sets the limits of artistic revolution?

Your having crossed paths with Nadia Boulanger, Alberto Ginastera, Carlos Gardel, and Aníbal Troilo makes one think they touched you with a magic wand.
And I almost took some lessons with Olivier Messiaen, the only musician of this century who might have been at Nadia Boulanger's level as a teacher. That is to say I have always been restless about get-

Above: Piazzolla in front of the poster announcing the performance with his short-lived Electronic Octet at the Olympia, Paris, 1978. Facing page: The group comprised young Argentine rock and jazz musicians and featured Daniel Piazzolla (second from left) on synthesizer. Courtesy Víctor Oliveros

ting better. It wasn't about luck. The Gardel encounter was chance. I was very young. But I did want to play with Troilo. Destiny is controlled by someone high above, but one's good taste is also important. I wanted to record with Gary Burton and Gerry Mulligan. I never thought of Charly García.* I would have liked to do something with Miles Davis or Chick Corea, but there are problems with that.

Why should it be so hard to do something with Miles Davis?
I believe he is crazy, very crazy. If I speak to his producer I am sure

---

* Charly García: Argentine rock star.

we would do a record right away. What I don't like is to be billed second. I always want to be first or, at the very least, share the bill, as with Gary Burton and Gerry Mulligan.

There is a "Tangazo" in your—shall we say—erudite music, but it has been relegated to a second tier within your work.
The Ensamble Musical de Buenos Aires did a good version. Perhaps it lacks some spice. Classical musicians are like that. They are from Buenos Aires, Argentines, and yet it seems that they are embarrassed about tango.

It's an old feud between the classical and the popular music worlds. The musicians who play at Teatro Colón* look down on tango musicians as if they were garbage. And it shouldn't be this way. It's a big lie. Some musicians from Teatro Colón deserve to play in the worst nightclub in Buenos Aires. I had to deal with some of those places; I know them first hand.

You were luckier with the tango orchestras.
Always. El Gordo Troilo and Pugliese played my music very well. Troilo was number one, but the version of "Verano porteño" by Pugliese is a little jewel. On the other hand, the best "Adiós Nonino" was by Leopoldo Federico.

In 1969 in Alberto Speratti's book** you said, "The only female singer I like is Amelita Baltar. And of the male singers the only ones who come to mind are Edmundo Rivero and Roberto Goyeneche." Twenty years later, what do you think?
I think the same about Rivero and Goyeneche. Erase my opinion about the female singer. I was in the middle of my infatuation‡ with

---

* Teatro Colón: The historical opera house of Buenos Aires.

** Alberto Speratti, *Con Piazzolla*. Buenos Aires: Galerna, 1969.

‡ Later on Piazzolla would also claim, "I was never in love with her."

her, and I didn't realize what a voice she had. They say love is blind. In this case, it was also deaf.

Who was the female singer who best interpreted your music?
Milva. Now, she is formidable.

Piazzolla and Milva with the Quintet in 1985. Over the years Piazzolla and Milva recorded and did several tours of Europe together.

We selected a Quintet, and we didn't choose a singer for it.

Héctor De Rosas was the neatest of them all, the most careful. He didn't have what is called a hot voice, but this never bothered the music I wrote. He was one more instrument, a flute, in the Quintet. He put his voice right where it should go. He was the singer for that time. Later, to interpret Piazzolla-Ferrer, came José Ángel Trelles and Raúl Lavié. The former has a very nice voice, the latter this booming baritone. Lavié is perhaps *the* Buenos Aires singer of the 1980s. Another singer I like, although he never sang with me, is Ruben Juárez. He has swing and he phrases very well because he is a musician.

I put Goyeneche and Rivero in the category of classics, the best tango had after Gardel. Rivero was *el payador.** Goyeneche was *el porteño.*

There is a poet associated with an important period of your career: Horacio Ferrer.

I believed a lot in Ferrer. The poet who wrote *María de Buenos Aires* with me moved me. From that work on, we became very good friends and worked well on a series of ballads and preludes. I believe we have left a great body of work. Horacio has some marvelous pieces: "El Gordo triste," "La última grela," "Chiquilín de Bachín," "La bicicleta blanca," "Balada para mi muerte." Horacio Ferrer was the best poet ever associated with Astor Piazzolla's music.

*You wrote music for movies associated with the left—such as "Llueve sobre Santiago"—and a piece in tribute to Los Lagartos, the navy group led by a repressor like Captain Astiz.** It looks like political incoherence.*

---

* *El payador*: The comment alludes to a rural flavor in Rivero's style, which evoked the style of traditional folk singers or *payadores*.

**Navy Captain Alfredo Astiz: An infamous character in Argentina's modern history reviled for his role during the military dictatorship of 1976–1982 and, specifically, his role in the so-called Dirty War against dissidents. Astiz, who has been convicted to life in prison in absentia in France for the disappearance and death of two French citizens, lives in Argentina, free, because of a presidential amnesty. In the events leading up to the Malvinas-Falklands War, Astiz led a navy commando group called Los Lagartos which briefly took control of several islands in the South Atlantic. They surrendered to English troops without firing a shot, however.

I did a lot of music for film and never asked the director or the producers which side they were on. The only thing I asked for was freedom to create, to do my thing. Regarding Los Lagartos, I have to admit that is true: I was wrong. I was doing some concerts at the Teatro Regina a few days before the Malvinas-Falklands War and their taking the South Georgia Islands touched me. It felt like a very heroic thing to do at the time. I didn't know who they were. I only saw a group of Argentines going all out for their country. I dedicated a piece to them that was written but didn't have a name. A few days later Julio Cura, a friend with many contacts in Franja Morada,* comes up to me and says, "What did you do, *loco*?" and told me everything. Then I learned who Captain Astiz was. That very day I erased the title and the dedication from the repertoire. I didn't erase the song because it was very nice. It became "Tanguedia" in *El exilio de Gardel*, the Pino Solanas film.

A year before this story with Los Lagartos you had gone to have lunch with President Videla at the Government House. You accepted his invitation.
And what an invitation. They sent for me, which is very different. Two guys dressed in black came to my door carrying an envelope with a card saying President Videla expected me on such a day at such a time. Somewhere in the house I have the book with the pictures taken that day with all the other invitees as you call them: Eladia Blázquez, Daniel Tinayre, Olga Ferri, the composer Antonio Tauriello—there were painters, actors, and I don't know who else, everybody.

Are you sorry now you accepted that invitation?
I don't want to play the hero in retrospect. I have great courage in certain things, but at that moment I realized that trying to play the macho was useless.

---

* Franja Morada: Radical Party. Despite its name, the Radical Party is a moderate, reformist party. Franja Morada represented the university-based, left-of-center wing of the party.

The infamous lunch

General Jorge Rafael Videla was the leader of a military junta that overthrew the constitutional government of Argentina on 24 March 1976. Once in power Videla's junta became one of the most repressive regimes in Latin American history. In 1984 a blue-ribbon commission certified more than 9000 disappearances. The victims are presumed dead. Human rights advocates estimate that more than 30,000 people were murdered.

The invitation Piazzolla could not refuse apparently went to many artists and intellectuals. Only one, actress Thelma Biral, did not attend because she was working in Uruguay. The dinner on 4 April 1979 was attended by, among others, Eladia Blázquez (musician, poet), Daniel Tinayre (movie director), Olga Ferri (dancer and choreographer), and Antonio Tauriello (composer), as well as actor Walter Santa Ana, poet Alberto Girri, singer Víctor de Narke, novelist Adolfo Bioy Casares, sculptor Libero Badi, and folk singer Julia Elena Dávalos.

You also went to Chile to play when Pinochet was in power and other artists such as Serrat did not go as a gesture of repudiation.*
I don't make that kind of political trouble. I am a musician. They hire me and I go and play because that's my livelihood. Serrat utilizes his art as a means of making a political statement. I do not agree with this. And after all, Pinochet did not leave his presidency because Serrat was not going to Chile to sing.

What did you think of Pinochet?
I thought that we lacked a figure like Pinochet. Perhaps Argentina was lacking a little in fascism at one point in her history.

---

* General Augusto Pinochet: Chilean dictator from 1973 to 1990.

Joan Manuel Serrat: Catalonian singer and songwriter associated with progressive politics.

This is being said by a man who lived many years in Italy and France where people live in and enjoy democracy.

Perhaps I exaggerate my fascism. Others have had philosophies that changed quickly without much blushing. I was in France when Mitterrand took power with a very socialist message, and in a few years he moved to the center. It was the same thing with Felipe González in Spain. Politics is in the head. Real life is in people's pockets. In France they have socialist discourse, but when it comes time to pay up they are very free market. And what happened to so many communists in Argentina and the world over? Isn't Horacio Guarany* saying now he didn't know if he was a communist? That's worse than fascism. That's why I admire Osvaldo Pugliese so much: he never reneged on his past. Because of that lunch with Videla I was called a fascist in Paris. It cost me my friendship with Julio Cortázar.** One day we crossed paths at the Mexican embassy in Paris and he turned his face away. Later, some mutual friends explained to me why. I thought it was idiotic on his part. Before taking such an attitude he should have asked me under which circumstances I went to the Government House.

Let's get back to the music. Was the Sextet an artistic failure?

Those are the risks any creator runs. The Sextet was a search for something new. I wanted to test myself after the quadruple bypass in 1988. I could play and compose, and I sat down to write like a madman, nonstop. I wrote all those pieces that are more than half an hour of music and adapted certain things by the Quintet. I transcribed the violin parts to cello. The lineup with two bandoneons, cello, guitar, contrabass, and piano was audacious. I thought it was going to work out great, but suddenly I found the whole thing went out of balance, especially after Console and Bragato left. The sound

* Horacio Guarany: Argentine folk singer long associated with the communist party of Argentina.

**Julio Cortázar (1914–1984): Prolific Argentine novelist, poet, playwright, and translator, outspoken in his opposition to the Perón regime. He moved to France in 1951.

was too dark; the violin was missing. It was a mistake, like the one with the Electronic Octet. If I had been smarter I would not have formed this group. An artist has to go through all these things.

You don't realize something like this at a rehearsal?
No. It all fell apart when I had to call two emergency substitutes after Console and Bragato left. Besides, Daniel Binelli did not assimilate my style of playing. I wanted two bandoneons sounding as one, as with Piazzolla and Leopoldo Federico in the Buenos Aires Octet. But Binelli and I were two distinct players playing because each of us has a distinct temperament and Binelli is even more aggressive than I am. It did not work out. The Sextet was a mistake. It was God's signal to say "Enough—it's over." Now I play as a soloist with orchestras or with someone else's quartet. I don't have to hear complaints from the musicians about schedules, hotels, and all those dumb things that cause such wear and tear.

In spite of all that wear and tear, could you swear that never again are you going to call the Quintet's musicians?
No, I could not swear to it.

8

Aria for Chorus

Nonino and Nonina

My parents were the nicest beings I've known in my whole life. Nonino, Vicente Piazzolla, liked everything I did, and on top of that he understood it. He died in 1959 while I was performing in Puerto Rico, so he did get to catch some of my evolution. He was a great fan of the Buenos Aires Octet.

Nonino wrote some basic tangos, and in certain notes, as they sit in the score, I see myself. It is as if there was a genetic code that was passed on. In New York I saw him get teary eyed with Julio De Caro, with Carlos Gardel, or when he listened to me playing Bach's Two-Part Inventions on the bandoneon. He had good musical culture and a very lovable character: he had permanent good humor.

He called me Astor for one of his best friends, Astor Bolognini, who had been the first cello in the Chicago Symphony. It was like a premonition: my dad always wanted me to be a musician, a tango musician, and for me to play bandoneon. Both dad and mom were born in Mar del Plata. My grandfather Pantaleón—my middle name is for him—was a *tano* from Trani, from Puglia, just like my grandmother, Rosa Centofanti, which means that from my father's side we come from lower Italy.

My father was a tall man with nice features. I, on the other hand, came out short and with the Manetti nose. My mother was Asunta Manetti. Her other family name is Bertolami. They are more refined. They are from Tuscany, the most chic region in Italy. When I was born, on 11 March 1921 at two in the morning, my mother decided to have no more kids. She told me this once. She spent the night crying because I was born with a foot—the right foot—twisted inside out. They told her that it could have been infantile paralysis during her pregnancy, but she was never entirely clear about what happened.

They operated on me several times to correct the problem. I suffered a lot as a kid. But the improvements never were complete. The right foot grew to normal size, but the lower leg, to the knee, is thinner than the other one.

I inherited everything from them: the good humor from my father, the strong temperament from my mother. Nonina always supported Nonino. He packed his suitcases twice to go for the adventure of the United States, and there and here she worked hard by his side. Mom was also a fighter. And don't even think about speaking ill of her Astor. Once the mailman came to her house in Mar del Plata and jokingly said, "So your son is in Paris running after French women? In the magazines they say he is the boyfriend of Jeanne Moreau." That's all he had to say. My mother, who by then was an elderly woman, chased him all over Avenida Colón.* They are no longer of this world, and I miss them both.

George Gershwin

We never ran into each other in our lives, but I always felt there was a certain affinity between George Gershwin's work and mine. Perhaps it is because his music represents New York and mine Buenos Aires. Perhaps it is because both of us, starting out with very traditional styles—jazz for him, tango for me, wanted to raise the level of what we liked.

What separates us, or perhaps brings us together, is the path each took. Gershwin was practically an intuitive, capable of creating fabulous melodies from studies that were little more than elementary. When Gershwin went to Paris—this is something Nadia Boulanger told me—he wanted to take lessons with Maurice Ravel, and in a sort

* Avenida Colón: A main thoroughfare in Mar del Plata.

of aside, Ravel asked him how much he was making from his songs. Gershwin told him the truth: an astronomical sum. So Ravel turned the situation around: "Wouldn't it be better if I studied with you?"

The story must have been improved over the years. It has a lot of humor and some truth. In fact Ravel did not take him as a student. He was afraid of dumping on Gershwin a load of harmony and counterpoint for which he was not prepared. It would have been like telling Gordo Troilo, "Look, let's fix 'La última curda' a little bit, just a nip here, a tuck there, to improve it." No way. That's a jewel that should be left just as he wrote it. Technique is not applicable in all instances.

Carlos Gardel

My contact with Gardel was brief. The only pleasure I had was to film some scenes in *El día que me quieras* with him—I played a news-

Piazzolla (left, as a newsboy) in a classic still from *El día que me quieras* starring tango singer Carlos Gardel (third from left).

paper boy—and accompany him on certain occasions playing bandoneon, which I was just beginning to study. To understand and love
Gardel one has to have been in Buenos Aires, have lived a few years
—have lived a little—and I was just a boy of thirteen living in New
York. I didn't even play the bandoneon well. That's why when Gardel hears me play for the first time, he tells me in good humor, "Kid,
you play the bandoneon like a *gallego*."* If I allow myself to fantasize,
I think I would have liked to accompany Gardel today, as a grown-
up. I am sure my fingers at the bandoneon would tremble because he
remains the best.

When Gardel came to New York, my father made a wooden statuette for him—woodcarving was one of his loves—and he and my
mother wrapped it as a gift. They dressed me up—blue jacket, white
flannel pants—and they sent me to the Beaux-Arts apartments at
Broadway and 48th Street where he lived. The doll was a gaucho
with a guitar. I arrived at the place very early but didn't get into his
apartment through the door. There had been a domestic accident.

In the elevator I ran into Alberto Castellanos, a musician who
worked with Gardel and was taking up two bottles of milk. I asked
him in English were he was going, and he let me know he didn't
speak the language. So I said to him [in Spanish]: "Ah, you speak
Spanish." He told me he was Argentine and hugged me when I told
him I was from Mar del Plata: "Kid, you came just in time. I went out
without keys. Do me a favor: go into the apartment through the fire
escape and wake up the gentleman sleeping inside."

I did, but I did not wake up Gardel but rather LePera,** who was
in the next bed and had a bad disposition. He growled at me. After I
told him what I was doing—he had taken me for a thief—and asked

---

* *Gallego*: Galician, referring to Galicia, the region in northwest Spain from which many
Argentine immigrants came. Over time the name became synonymous with *foreigner*,
so that the implication here is, "You play the bandoneon like a foreigner."

** Alfredo LePera (1904–1935): Lyricist who collaborated with Gardel in some of his
most famous titles such as "Mi Buenos Aires querido," " El día que me quieras," "Arrabal amargo," and "Soledad." He died in the same accident in which Gardel lost his life,
in Medellín, Colombia, 24 June 1935.

him to open the door for Castellanos, Gardel woke up and we all sat down to have breakfast.

I gave him the statuette my father had sent him. Of course, he was surprised when I told him I played bandoneon, and he opened his eyes wide. We became pals. Gardel was always in a very good mood. He had a permanent smile. At least that's how I remember him. I became his guide; because he spoke English badly, I became his interpreter in the department stores—Macy's, Gimbels, Saks. I even took him to Santa Lucía, a very good Italian canteen in Greenwich Village.

One Sunday Gardel came to my house, invited by my parents. He came to eat ravioli and an apple doughnut dessert, all made by my mother. He ate it all. He was very fat then and was not taking care of himself at all.

Until the day I took my father's statuette to him, I knew little about Gardel. Dad had some of his records, but I was not interested. My head was on the streets of New York, and the music I adored was Bach's as played by Béla Wilda.*

But between Gardel and me there was a nice relationship. He was in New York for about a year, filming and making appearances at the Campoamor Theater, where I accompanied him several times on the bandoneon. There were fewer times than what we planned because I was a minor and the Musicians Union of New York objected.

Gardel had signed a contract with NBC to do three radio shows but did only one. It was not very successful. Gardel was not a Hollywood star. He produced his own movies for a Latin American audience.

Today, from a distance, I value those days a lot. I believe they were like a pill that magnified my love for tango. I remember his charm, his *arrabalera*** manners, and the sound of his voice: he spoke like a Uruguayan. He wanted to take me on tour, but my parents didn't

---

* Béla Wilda: Hungarian pianist and teacher, former pupil of Sergei Rachmaninoff, Wilda was the Piazzollas' neighbor who became Astor's teacher.

** *Arrabalera*: Of the *arrabal*, the rough, tough, poor outskirts of the city.

let me go because I was too young. It was written that this was not my destiny. Soon afterward, Gardel died in Medellín, Colombia.

But the story of my father's wooden figure does not end there. It seems like a master's tale. Many years after the accident—by then my parents and I had returned to Argentina—my first bandoneon teacher, Andrés D'Aquila, saw a wooden figure on sale for twenty dollars in a small shop in New York. It was burnt, but the signature of my father was clearly visible: Vicente Piazzolla.

Moreover, under the price there was a sign: "This belonged to an Argentine tango singer." D'Aquila went in, but because he didn't have the twenty dollars in his pocket he agreed with the shop owner that he would pick it up the following day. The man did not honor his word. The following day the puppet was not there. It had been sold.

It is hard to believe how that figure left New York, went to Medellín, was found among the wreckage of the plane, and was picked up and returned to almost the same place where it had taken shape in my father's hands. Because of it, because of the enormous spiritual value it has for me, I never lost hope that I would find it and that whoever has it some day would call me.

Alfredo Gobbi

One of the first pieces I recorded with the Quintet was "Redención," a tango by Alfredo Gobbi.* He was at the RCA studios the day of the recording and liked my version a lot. I even respected the bandoneon solos. It is not by chance that I included that piece in the Quintet's first album.

To me, Alfredo was the father of all of us who played modern tango. He was a great intuitive but wrote highly refined music. I always say Gobbi ingrained his style on Pugliese and Pugliese did the same on Gobbi, and of those comings and goings many beautiful things were born, things that later exploded in the 1940s.

* Alfredo Gobbi (1912–1965): Tango pianist, violinist, composer, and bandleader.

What destroyed me was Gobbi's end, because being who he was, he ended up in a shabby nightclub in the netherworld, beaten by alcohol and other things. Once I had the fortune to hear a recording someone had made of him playing in that club. I say fortune because even in that world he had entered, in that madness that made him say such things as "I dedicate this page to Jesus of Nazareth," one could hear his genius.

He would play the piano with three fingers and beautiful things would come out, like a little waltz he had dedicated to me. Once Alfredo came to my house. I wasn't in, so he left the score for that waltz under my door. It was written in an elementary way, in pencil. When I started studying those scribblings I thought, what a beauty. I would love to write like this man. The tragedy is that I lost that

Alfredo Gobbi was among Piazzolla's preferred tango musicians.

page. I will never forgive myself. Soon after, he died. So I wrote a piece as a tribute: "Retrato de Alfredo Gobbi."*

Roberto Di Filippo

I never heard anyone play bandoneon like Roberto Di Filippo. Only Minotto** might have come close in terms of technique, but he never equaled him. Di Filippo was with me in my 1946 Orchestra, which means we have been friends since we were almost kids. My friendship with him, Hugo Baralis, Chupita Stamponi, José Bragato, and Enrique Mario Francini was born of common interests.

Tango musicians usually talked about soccer, horse racing, babes, and getting drunk. We were happy talking about music. With Roberto, whenever we had a free Saturday morning, we'd go to the Gran Rex Theater to hear a rehearsal of the National Symphony Orchestra. Roberto was also capable of singing arias—but I mean singing them. Every time we meet I kiss his hands. He knows what I mean: how much I admire him. He retired from Teatro Colón playing oboe. Later he got very sick and as part of his therapy started playing bandoneon again. My Lord, he's playing better than before.

Every time we meet he reminds me of an anecdote about Alejandro Barletta, a musician who has many dummies hoodwinked by playing Bach on the bandoneon, which is what I used to do as a kid in New York. Life is like that: a couple of journalists made a little noise and he believes he discovered the world.

One time this Barletta stopped by Radio Splendid. He came on very smug, he listened for awhile, and then said he was a concert player on the bandoneon and that's why he never played tangos. I knew him because once I had been stuck at a concert of his. Finally

---

* "Retrato de Alfredo Gobbi" (Portrait of Alfredo Gobbi) first appeared on record on the album *Piazzolla en el Regina* (RCA, 1969), played by the Quintet.

**Enrique "Minotto" Di Cico: Bandleader and composer who achieved mythical status as one of tango's best bandoneon players. Minotto is Italian for "tough hand" (*mano brava*).

*la tanada** came to the surface and I said to him, "You want to know how the bandoneon is played?" I didn't wait for him to answer. I asked Roberto to play a tango, any tango. A minute later this Barletta guy was as white as a sheet. Never again did he cross my path. He even has an ugly way of playing: he opens and closes the bandoneon as if he were knitting.

Di Filippo should be declared number one in Argentina. His technique is unmatched.

Orlando Goñi

I used to adore listening to Orlando Goñi** play certain pieces he claimed as his own, and one day, later, I discovered they were by Alfredo Gobbi. We were never friends. I believe Orlando didn't have any friends except, perhaps, a bunch of drunkards like himself who hung out near the Tibidabo.‡

He had been a student of Vicente Scaramuzza, the great teacher of the great Argentine pianists. Goñi had beautiful hands, hands I've never seen on any other pianist. He was one of those strange characters in tango. His face was pale as befitted a man and a musician of the cabaret world. It was the color of tango in the 1940s. He did not like classical music and detested jazz, but playing tango he was something supreme.

I have always thought the original Troilo sound was an invention of Goñi at the piano and Kicho Díaz on the contrabass. I had to sub for him at the piano, an instrument I played badly, but in an emergency there was no other solution. The bus would be leaving for some club date and Orlando would not show up—he was drunk. So

---

* *La tanada*: Like *tano* (Italian), *la tanada* is *porteño* slang for some characteristics considered typical of the Italian heritage.

**Orlando Goñi (1914–1945): Notable pianist and bandleader, member of the bands of Aníbal Troilo and Alfredo Gobbi.

‡ Tibidabo: Fabled nightclub on Corrientes Avenue, torn down in 1955.

I would play "Comme il faut," "Tinta verde," and a few others, and with that El Gordo [Troilo] saved the day.

Goñi left Troilo's orchestra to form his own, and at one point he let me hear a couple of pieces he had been preparing for his repertoire. Everything was top notch. But soon afterward he died, a victim of alcohol. At the piano he was a genius.

Osvaldo Pugliese

My dad, Nonino, used to say: "Astor, the great tango musicians come from lower Italy." The Piazzollas came from Trani, in Puglia, from

Piazzolla in 1989 with maestro Osvaldo Pugliese, the great tango composer and bandleader.

which, obviously, also came the Puglieses. Was it just chance or was my dad right? When I was eighteen and I was with Troilo, in between sets I'd go to the Moulin Rouge because that's where Pugliese* played. The rhythm of his orchestra drove me crazy.

Osvaldo is someone one values all one's life. To be in Paris, get together with Argentines, and play his records means to have a pleasant moment, come close to Buenos Aires. Yet we must also recognize his evolution within his traditional style. He never became stuck in time.

Pugliese and I have had mutual respect at a distance. We haven't had many opportunities to sit down and chat. It was as if He from above had ordered, "You guys each do his own thing." Sometimes people ask me why I haven't done things with Salgán** or Pugliese, and in truth, it's not easy. Not long ago, I shared the stage with Pugliese in Holland. I wrote a special arrangement of "Adiós Nonino," and Osvaldo looked clueless—he couldn't play a note. Later I tried to play "La yumba" his way and I couldn't. I felt bad, as if I had dirtied his music. It seems our destiny that our roads must go separately.

What will always remain unshakable is my appreciation of him as a human being and my admiration for him as a musician.

Jorge Luis Borges

There is an album in my oeuvre that will endure because of the music and the poetry of Jorge Luis Borges. It is called *El tango*, and it features "El hombre de la esquina rosada."‡

For me it was a true honor to work with such a figure of world-

---

* Osvaldo Pugliese (1905–1995): Among the most important composers, bandleaders, and pianists in tango. A modernist working within a traditional framework, Pugliese transcended tango schools. A long-time member of the Communist Party, he once even ran for a seat as a representative for that party.

** Horacio Salgán (b. 1916): Pianist, composer, and bandleader. An influential modernist, Salgán can be seen as a transitional figure between the classic tango of the 1940s and Piazzolla's revolution.

‡ "El hombre de la esquina rosada" (The man in the pink corner) is a famous short story by the noted Argentine writer, poet, and essayist Jorge Luis Borges (1899–1986).

With poet Jorge Luis Borges in a meeting brought about by the magazine *Gente* in 1965. Their collaboration, a collection simply titled *El tango*, had rich, at times brilliant, results. But their personalities did not quite match. Photo by Ernesto Carreño

Piazzolla with Jeanne Moreau backstage in Paris in 1984. Moreau used Piazzolla's score of 1975 for *Lumière*, her first movie as director. The photo was probably taken by Piazzolla's wife, Laura Escalada.

wide stature. Still, when the work came out we had some differences. Borges even said I didn't know anything about tango, and my response suggested he didn't know anything about music. He was an authoritarian man, even boorish in some things. I remember inviting him to my house so he could hear all the work before we went into the studio. I sat at the piano and played "Jacinto Chiclana," "A don Nicanor Paredes," "El títere," and the rest of those pieces for him.

When I told him I had composed all the music in a 1900s style except "Oda íntima a Buenos Aires," Borges told me that he didn't know anything about music, and besides, he didn't care. But then he tossed out opinions like a big expert. I believe he was a magician of the written word. I have never read more beautiful poems than his. But regarding music, he was deaf.

Jeanne Moreau

I see Jeanne Moreau* often. She is a sensational woman. She knows about music. She also has an exceptional collection of paintings, Paul Valéry's notebooks, Le Corbussier's furniture, and the most incredible record collection from Gregorian chant to the Rolling Stones. She has great charm. I feel like I'm dreaming. I am with the woman of my dreams. What a nice adventure—and besides I am writing the music for her first film as director, *Lumiere*.

I have had the luxury of spending almost three hours with her by the Champs-Élysées. We went into record shops, bought for me one by Jean-Luc Ponty, did some window shopping, and talked about a thousand things. We ended up in a Vietnamese restaurant, feeding ourselves with delicacies and hot sake. My head was spinning like a spinnin' top. I felt like Gerard Philippe.**

---

*Jeanne Moreau (b. 1923): French actress and director who starred in such films as *Ascenseur pour l'echafaud, Jules et Jim*, and *Going Places*. Piazzolla was introduced to Moreau by publisher Aldo Pagani in Paris. This text is from a letter from Piazzolla to Natalio Gorin, Rome, 7 August 1975.

**Gerard Philippe: Popular French actor.

After dinner we went to her place. She walked around barefoot, and we listened to records until early morning. Everybody must be expecting me to say that I took her in my arms and gave her a big wet kiss. Not at all. First of all, she is a lady, and secondly I am not a sportsman of love. Moreover, I am shy, not some Sir Lancelot. Besides, if I am rejected, she might take away the film and then it's goodbye Charlie. She saw me a bit down because of my emotional problems* and was concerned. With a woman like her I accept feminism; the other ones can stay home cooking.

Lalo, Waldo, and Astor

I could say it like the tango says: three friends we always were— Lalo Schifrin, Waldo de los Ríos,** and I. One went the jazz way: Lalo. Another chose folk music: Waldo. And I got into tango.

I was the first to emigrate, in 1954. Lalo I believe left in '58, also for the United States. Waldo ended up in Spain in the 1960s. We had many things in common. None of us got stuck in the sentimentality of the nostalgia for *dulce de leche*,‡ the café, or the barbecue. We went looking for a destiny that was closed to us here.

Lalo was drowning in weekend dance gigs. Today he is a figure on a worldwide scale. Three years ago [1987] we reunited to record my *Concierto para bandoneón y orquesta*, something that was a thrill for both of us.

Waldo studied with Ginastera. He was a remarkable arranger. But

---

* By August 1975 Piazzolla was alone in Rome. Singer Amelita Baltar, his companion since 1968, had left him the year before.

** Lalo Schifrin (b. Boris Claudio Schifrin, 1932): Argentine pianist, composer, and arranger. He came to the United States at the invitation of the great jazz trumpeter Dizzy Gillespie who heard him in Buenos Aires. Renowned for his work in film and television, in 1955 Schifrin played piano with Piazzolla's String Orchestra in Paris, which is why Piazzolla says that they "reunited."

Waldo de los Ríos (?–1977): Argentine pianist, composer, and arranger.

‡ *Dulce de leche*: Typical Argentine caramel.

certain people started to hate him for his version of Mozart's Symphony No. 40. He once told me he had sold five million records and that his share was a dollar a record. When he did the second album in that so-called classical line, he sold much less and that bummed him out. He had gotten into money madness.

One night in Madrid he played with me, and I heard some catcalls when he took the stage. They censored him because of his Mozart. What was Waldo's sin? Nothing. The important part was that Mozart reached a lot of people. Classical composers are not the property of the Berlin or the Chicago Symphony. I felt that what Waldo had done was very worthy. The last time I saw him I found him very depressed. Soon afterward, on 29 March 1977, he committed suicide.

Alain Delon

Alain Delon* hired me to do the music for *Armaguédon*, which was a French cinema box-office hit in the 1970s. I know this well because in Europe the fortunes of the soundtrack composer go with that of the film: the more the film makes, the more the composer makes.

He let me know through one of his secretaries that he wanted to meet me. We arranged for a meeting at the studios outside Paris, and he received me in a trailer that was his office and dressing room. He did not make me wait a second after the appointed time. The first thing he said was, "Thanks for your talent and for working on my film."

Afterward we spoke about music, and I realized he knew what he was talking about. He knows his contemporary composers and told me his favorite was Béla Bartók. We must have spent twenty minutes together. He was booked full. He took me to the door and thanked me again. I left with the feeling that I had met a grand gentleman. He was the famous Alain Delon, and at no time had he made me aware of it.

---

* Alain Delon (b. 1935): French actor who starred in such films as *Rocco and His Brothers*, *Is Paris Burning?*, and *Borsalino*.

The dedication, presumably to Piazzolla's son, Daniel, reads: "For Danny, this rehearsal with Gerry Mulligan. Milan 74. Astor." Courtesy Víctor Oliveros.

Gerry Mulligan

Summit, the album I recorded with Gerry Mulligan* in 1974, is one of the nicest things of my life.

We first recorded the rhythm tracks with a Milan-based orchestra, something rushed. Then the two of us went into the studio by ourselves. The idea of doing something together was his, and I agreed immediately. For me there was a nostalgic reason, if you will. In 1955 in Paris, as I was listening to the Gerry Mulligan Octet, the Buenos Aires Octet started to take shape. Recording with Mulligan was my opportunity to record with one of the all-time jazz greats. That's why the

*Gerry Mulligan (b. Gerald Joseph, 1927–1996): Baritone saxophonist, composer, and arranger, an important influence in the West Coast cool jazz movement.

With Gerry Mulligan in Venice, 1975.

Piazzolla receiving the Sagitario de Oro award in Italy in the 1970s for his recording with Mulligan.

first piece I wrote was "Twenty Years Ago" and the second "Twenty Years After." The song that I liked best, the one that got most airplay, was "Años de soledad." But I believe the whole work is evenly good.

Gerry thinks so also. I like playing with him. The sound of the baritone sax is like a dagger in the heart. He had some trouble following the scores. He hadn't been reading a lot of music recently, and my rhythmic accents are not easy to play on the sax.

I believe our meeting will come to full bloom in future recordings. We both have the time and desire. This first record—and not taking into account the United States because there its release was delayed —is among the bestsellers of my life. When I speak of sales I'm speaking of fifteen or twenty thousand copies in all Europe. What matters is that later they remain in the catalog. The proof is in the record bins.

Nadine Trintignant

I've just signed with Nadine Trintignant,* Jean Louis's wife. I am writing the music for her film *Voyage de noces* [Wedding trip]. She is crazy about me. She just told me, "Write what you want. I will adapt the music to the image." How do you like that? I'm set with babes. The bandoneon is like a magnet. They hear my music and fly. Are they nuts or is it true? The only thing I can tell you is that I'm crazy with joy. And get a hold of this: I will be writing for just two instruments: violin, by Agri, and bandoneon, played by me. Yes, I know: how am I going to manage? Let me just tell you that I'm jumping in with both feet; I will just double up the work. I believe until now I haven't screwed up. This is a unique opportunity for me and if I fail, the bear will get me.** On 3 September I will begin recording music

---

*Nadine Trintignant (b. Nadine Marquand, 1934): French director. Once a film editor for Jean-Luc Godard, Trintignant directed a short and several television programs before directing features in the late 1960s. *Le voyage de noces* was her sixth film. This portion is from a letter from Piazzolla to Natalio Gorin, Rome, 7 August 1975.

**Piazzolla was also working on another film, Jeanne Moreau's *Lumière*. "The bear" is a reference to the saying, "Sometimes you get the bear; sometimes the bear gets you."

for both films, Jeanne Moreau's and Nadine Trintignant's. I can tell you that is she is a sensational director.

Besides she called me up and didn't let me catch my breath: "*Maestro* Piazzolla, I adore your music and right now I am listening to 'La mufa,' and this is what I want for my film, especially the sound of the bandoneon."

I told her I was traveling to Paris the next day. She waited for me at Orly and took me to the studio. We had lunch, saw the film, and without taking times [for the music sequences] she told me, "Now do what you want." I wrote down all the scenes, and that night I was back in Rome."* I must do a theme for each of the main characters: Jean Louis Trintignant and Stephania Sandrelli. This babe is Carlo Ponti's** latest affair. If I had his dough I would have myself a harem.

Arthur Rubinstein

Dedé and I were still going out so this must have happened in early 1941. For many, playing with Troilo must have been the golden Mecca. I also lived it like a dream. But by the time I was twenty years old the bug bit me: I wanted to do new things, see what else there was outside tango. Then I wrote a piece for piano and went to ask Arthur Rubinstein[‡] for his opinion. He was then in Buenos Aires. This might seem complete madness, but nothing ever stopped me, and besides I was twenty. I found out the maestro was staying at the Alzaga Unzué residence and off I went.

---

* Piazzolla was living in Italy. As happened at other times throughout his career, for this film he composed fine but unusable music because he would not conform to the length of the sequences. Trintignant eventually called on film composer Michel Legrand. Piazzolla's soundtrack for *Le voyage de noces* was released in Argentina under the title *Viaje de bodas*. Ironically and wrongly, the release promotes the music as the soundtrack from the film.

**Carlo Ponti (b. 1910): Italian film producer who married Sophia Loren in 1957.

‡ Arthur (Artur) Rubinstein (1887–1982): Great American pianist. Born in Poland, Rubinstein was a supreme interpreter of Chopin. He was also revered in Spain and South America; one of his four children was born in Buenos Aires.

I rang the bell and Rubinstein himself opened the door. He had a napkin in his hand, and I believe the napkin had spaghetti sauce stains on it. It was lunch time, and he must have been eating. I apologized and offered to return later. He said he was just about done and asked me who I was. After my explanations he invited me to come in.

He was extremely polite, very casual. I told him why I was there, I told him about my concerto, and five minutes later, to my surprise, he began playing it on this impressive Steinway. He finished and then I had my first big embarrassment. He asked me where I had the orchestra part, "because you told me you had a concerto and here I only see a sonata."

I confessed that that was all I had. So Rubinstein asked me if I wanted to study. He had seen something there and wanted to help. He picked up the phone, called Juan José Castro, told him he was with a young man of interesting aptitudes, and while he winked at me asked him if he could take me on as a student. When he hung up he told me Castro did not have time and that he recommended another teacher: Alberto Ginastera.

Even then, before leaving, I shamelessly asked him to play a few bars of Ravel at the piano. I wouldn't have done what he did. If a guy came over to my place and asked me to play "Adiós Nonino," I'd throw him out the window. Rubinstein took me to the door and gave me an autographed photo. I never saw him again. But that number to call Ginastera began changing my life.

Gil Evans

The first news I had about Gil Evans* was in 1958, in New York in Dizzy Gillespie's house. He told me, "I will have you listen to the best musician in the world today, and the best arranger." And he played me *Miles Ahead*, a record by Miles Davis with the Gil Evans

---

* Gil Evans (1912–1988): Arranger, pianist, and bandleader, best known for his collaborations with trumpeter Miles Davis, most notably his orchestral arrangements on *Miles Ahead* (1957), *Porgy and Bess* (1959), and *Sketches of Spain* (1960).

Orchestra. And I had to agree with Dizzy. It sounded heavenly. Many years later, in 1984, Gil came to hear my Quintet in New York, and from then on we saw each other on every trip.

Unfortunately, Gil died last year, 1989, at age seventy-five, in incredible poverty, living with a son on the five hundred dollars a month an ex-wife gave him.* For the last ten years of his life he played every Monday at Sweet Basil, a club in New York. The best musicians in New York would go and play for free to be able to play with Gil. I was there once and left with a stomach full of music.

It reminded me of Piazzolla in clubs, places where we would play for coins just to play. Gil's case makes me think that not only in Argentina are there injustices with great musicians. Here they happen because there is no work and there because an artist like Stan Kenton had to write jingles to live decently.

Gil also wrote arrangements for several rock groups, among them Sting's,** which explains why some rock groups sound so good. Behind the big sound systems and the light shows are people of great talent making good products.

Gil died amid great sadness, in a small room‡ where he had a bed and an electric piano. It was all he had. That, and an enormous talent.

Igor Stravinsky

I have met many people. But for a musician, one of the most important things in life is to meet other musicians, the greatest ones, the ones one admires. And if there is some reciprocity, better yet.

---

* This is Piazzolla's version of the story.

** Sting (b. Gordon Sumner, 1951): Rock bass player and songwriter, best known for his work with the Police in the early 1980s. Later he embarked on a solo career, collaborated with Evans, and commissioned Evans's arrangement of Jimi Hendrix's "Little Wing," featured on Sting's *Nothing Like the Sun.* In turn, Sting is featured on *Sting and Gil Evans: Last Session Live at the Peruggia Jazz Festival July 11, 1987* (Jazz Door).

‡ Piazzolla talks about Evans's death in his "small room" in a figurative sense. Evans actually died away from home, in Cuernavaca, Mexico.

It filled me with pride to know that when great musicians came to Buenos Aires, they asked to see my Quintet. I'm speaking of Aaron Copland, Salvatore Accardi (who was such a fan of Antonio Agri that he lent him his Stradivarius to record two pieces with the Nonet), Dizzy Gillespie, Stan Getz, Gary Burton (with whom years later we would record a fantastic record), and all the Brazilian singers and

Piazzolla at the piano with Brazilian poet and singer Vinicius De Moraes, left, and singer Amelita Baltar, 10 July 1980. Courtesy Agencia O Globo

musicians who landed in Buenos Aires, from Maysa Matarazzo to Joao Gilberto, from Vinicius de Moraes to Milton Nascimento.

In 1958, while living in New York, I had a very special thrill because I met Igor Stravinsky. It happened one day after I got a call from Albino Gómez: "*Che*, Astor, tonight I have to go pick up Stravinsky and take him to a party. Do you want to come with me? And by the way I can introduce you." Albino is a very good friend—now he is the Argentine ambassador in Sweden and at that time he was an aide at the Argentine consulate in New York. When he called I was not in a good mood and put him off: "Albino, stop screwing around. It's too early to be joking. I gotta work." Shortly afterward Albino insisted: "Astor, I'm serious. Come with me." I told him to bug off and hung up.

That night we had a cocktail at the Waldorf Astoria to honor Victoria Ocampo,* but I didn't see Albino anywhere until I saw him walk into the room—with Igor Stravinsky on his arm. It was true. I kicked myself for the missed opportunity. I didn't take my eyes off him. To see Stravinsky was like seeing God. He was elderly then: his hand trembled as if he suffered from Parkinson's, but he drank whisky like a cowboy.

A bit later Albino came over with an ironic look and told me: "Come with me; I'll introduce you." I gave myself another shot of whisky (I am a bit shy about certain things), went up to him, and confessed: "Maestro, I have been your student from a distance. It is an honor to meet you." It was the only thing I dared to say. He shook my hand with great kindness. And it was true. I was before a teacher-at-a-distance. During my studies with Alberto Ginastera, the score for *The Rite of Spring* was my bedside book.

* Victoria Ocampo (1891–1979): Argentine writer, founder and director of *Sur*, an influential literary magazine in Argentina.

Piazzolla and Dedé Wolff on their wedding day, 31 October 1942. They had two children, Diana and Daniel, and separated in 1966.

9

Love Theme

NATALIO GORIN: *Astor, we should have an entire chapter dedicated to love.*
ASTOR PIAZZOLLA: Yes, I agree.

And how would you start it?
Talking about Dedé Wolff, my first wife. She was a good companion, loyal. She raised our kids, Daniel and Diana, very well. I have a great love for her. Besides, she helped me a lot in anything that had to do with my career. I would be a low life if I said a word that could hurt her.

How did you meet?
I believe everything started in Hugo Baralis's house. He was a dear friend, perhaps the best I ever had. We had just finished eating ravioli made by his mother, Doña Manuela, and he asked me what was happening with me because he saw I was a bit down. And then I told him I couldn't stand the loneliness at the boarding house any more. Huguito looked at me and a bit later came up with something unexpected: "I believe I have the girl right for you. She's a friend of my sisters'. She's very nice, a bit serious, has blue eyes. But I warn you, Astor. No fooling around. This is for a gentleman."

And that's how we met, 21 September 1940 at Hugo's house. I wanted a real woman. I was not into hanging out with late-night babes and even less so with those at the cabaret. Besides, I was scared about the [venereal] diseases of the day. My dad had talked to me so much about it that he made my head spin.

My parents came from Mar del Plata to meet their future in-laws, everyone got along very well, and all approved our marriage. Dedé and I were truly in love. She studied painting. We also had artistic affinities. We married on 31 October 1942 at the church on Belgrano Avenue and Lima Street. The following year Diana was born. Daniel was born in 1944.

I'll read for you, word for word, something you said in Alberto Speratti's book of 1969: "If we separated after such a long time, twenty-four years, it was because of me. She deserved more than what I was giving her. I'm a selfish guy, someone who only thinks about his music. I don't want anyone to touch my things. It is like a treasure no one should handle. I'm a guy isolated from everything, and if you scratch the surface a bit you find that deep down I am neither interested in politics, nor the economy, nor the motivations behind contemporary societies." Are you still the same Piazzolla?

Yes. Exactly. It's a sort of *menefreguismo.** Deep down the only thing I'm interested in is my world—with a change. When I met Laura, my current wife, I was capable of saying things like: "If you put music on one side of the scale and love on the other, music will always be more important." Now I think the opposite: I care more for Laura. I do because of all she has meant to me these past fifteen years we've been together. Laura brought me good luck and love. With her beside me, life started to go right. She cared for me and accompanied me with great love. I believe she even helped me perfect my composing. Because she knows a lot about music, we discuss my playing, my arrangements. Laura is the only one who catches on if there are changes in the sound of the bandoneon from one concert to the next.

If one was to simplify, one could say Dedé represents the young love, Amelita Baltar the infatuation, and Laura Escalada the definitive love.

---

* *Menefreguismo*: From the Italian *me ne frega*, a rather coarse expression loosely translated as "I don't care." *Menefreguismo*, then, can be understood as "I-don't-give-a-damn-ism."

It might be. But I was never in love with Amelita. I never liked her. She needed me and I needed her. Deep down it was a musical partnership that started with something called "love," in quotation marks. Laura, on the other hand, was different. I learned to love, to live. Now I am completely happy. I have everything a man might desire: love, a woman who takes care of me, who cooks special meals for me to keep me healthy. Laura is something special. She keeps me alive. If not for her, I'd be underground.

Singer Amelita Baltar entered Piazzolla's life as a last-minute replacement for singer Egle Martin in *María de Buenos Aires* in 1968. The stormy relationship between Baltar and Piazzolla spread over six years and two continents.

Was the separation from Amelita very conflictive?
I suffered a lot. It hurt me. Something I can't stand is the betrayal of a friend or a woman, especially a woman. It seems to me the saddest, the lowest thing a human being can do: betray the person beside him or her.

Given your big tanada,* *did you ever think of killing Amelita?*
Several times.

Then it means there was love.
There was anger. The six years we spent together were like living inside a volcano. God wanted the end to be as it was: violent. She left Italy, where we were together, and I never heard from her again.

Then Laura Escalada enters your life.
Yes, and it was the best thing that could have happened to me. This is my world, the love I've been looking for. Before I lived by going from flower to flower, as the tango says. Now I don't need any of that.

You haven't said how you met.
It was 11 March 1976. It was my birthday, and I had gone to Channel 11 [a television station in Buenos Aires] to do an interview on a show she hosted. Between commercial breaks she told me she liked my music. I was surprised that a TV host knew that much about Beethoven, Bach, Gershwin. When she told me she was a lyric singer I almost fell over backward. When we said goodbye I invited her and her coworkers to one of my concerts. She came, and that night we ended up eating stew at El Tropezón. There began a relationship that in time became love. Eventually, after talking many hours, we decided to live together.** We got married after the divorce laws changed in Argentina. We married on 11 April 1988.

---

* *Tanada*: In this case *tanada* would mean an Italian-style blow up. "I asked about killing Amelita because that's a theme that appears often in tango," Gorin said, "especially considering he had just spoken of betrayal."

** Piazzolla and Escalada actually moved in together two months after that encounter.

I'd like you to talk about your children.

They were raised by Dedé because, as I told you, I lived only for my music. I can't say I was a good father, and my separation from their mother created a tense situation between us. Later we began to understand each other and the relationship improved. I encouraged Diana's poetry and her literary work, and Daniel played with me in the Electronic Octet. Both got married and gave me beautiful grandchildren. We love each other a lot.

With Laura Escalada, singer and television personality. They met on 11 March 1976 on a television show she hosted. They married on 11 April 1988.

10

Love Theme (Encore)

Getting letters is the only thing that helps me endure this terrible Italian summer. I know: I'm not good at being by myself. I believe your position is a bit cozy. You don't know Rome or the Italians. I'm alone in a neighborhood of thieves and, more often than not, eating by myself at home because I can't find anyone to go have dinner with. To this, add thousands of things. You'll also say your perennial line: "You have your music." Shit . . . . Music is only useful when you are in the mood to write it or hear it. Everything else is false. There is only one thing that does you good: peace of mind. If I have to pay dearly to get it, I will, whatever happens. Of course, I will not be such an idiot as to stop being Piazzolla, stop writing, playing. I don't think you will understand all this noise. I've always been alone, even when someone went with me, but I need to have someone with me who makes me happy, who makes me feel like a man and young. One can look for a companion, but love is not a sport, at least for me. Many people are bothered by Piazzolla's happiness. Given that they can't defeat him musically, they want to defeat him spiritually. . . .

Love is blind and, in my case, deaf. There are many who do not accept her* at my side. But do they know what she means to me? Do they realize that even if she sang backwards she would be beside me because I'm in deeply with a babe who makes me feel like a kid? Now I am losing her because of stupid things. She wants to work,

This chapter is from a letter from Piazzolla to Natalio Gorin, Rome, 21 July 1975.

* Amelita Baltar.

123

and there is nothing happening here. Besides, she misses her son. That's my loneliness, these women are deadly. . . .

Being alone does not mean for me being afraid of having no one here, in Rome, if I fell ill. Imagine that many times, when I have gone over my limit in my alcohol dose, I felt really badly without knowing whom to call on. All my friends are in Baires.* I could croak any moment, at least that's what happens to people with a bad heart. Perhaps I'll live to be one hundred, but there is always room for doubt.

Loneliness

Natalio Gorin commented: "In some of his persecution fantasies —and he had many, perhaps a residue of his struggles in the tango world—Astor blamed everything and everybody for his emotional problems. The Amelita issue is a complex one. When he says 'I am losing her because of stupid things,' it is because Amelita is leaving him. She wasn't working in Italy, Piazzolla was barely making it, and she had just had a big hit show in Buenos Aires with fellow singers Susana Rinaldi and Marikena Monti."

He was, in Gorin's words, "a famous man who didn't have anyone to talk to." These lines about Piazzolla's loneliness are especially poignant given the circumstances of his falling ill in Paris in 1990 far from his beloved Buenos Aires and his friends. When the unexpected that he feared finally happened, Laura Escalada was with him.

---

* Baires: Buenos Aires.

11

Self Portrait

I discovered music when I was eleven years old. The apartment building where we lived in New York City was very big. In the back there was a hall and a window. One summer afternoon I was hanging out, without much to do, and I heard a piano playing Bach, although that was something I learned later.

At that age I didn't know who Bach was, but I felt as if I had been hypnotized. It is one of the great mysteries of my life. I don't know if it was Johann Sebastian Bach or one of his sons. I believe I have bought all Bach's recorded works, but I could never find that music again. That pianist practiced nine hours a day: three hours of technique in the morning, three hours of Bach in the afternoon, and three at night, trying out repertoire for his concerts. He was Hungarian. His name was Béla Wilda, and soon he became my teacher.

My father and I went over to knock on his door. I'll never forget that moment. I was dazzled by the grand piano and the Camel cigarettes he smoked, which gave out a deep tobacco smell. Neither my parents nor he had much money. We had common problems. So I started studying with my teacher thanks to an arrangement: my mother gave him free manicures and twice a week would send him an enormous bowl of pasta. Hunger also knocks at the doors where good music is heard. I never went hungry, I was that lucky, but I know a lot about going around without a nickel in my pockets.

The first notions about the bandoneon were passed on to me by Andrés D'Aquila, an Argentine musician living in New York. I also studied for a bit with Homero Pauloni when we returned briefly to

Mar del Plata. But it was Wilda who made me get the bandoneon out of the closet and taught me to play Bach by adapting the music written for piano.

Months later the Hungarian moved away, but the inoculation had taken. My thing was "a rare mixture of Museta and Mimí."* I played bandoneon, the fundamental tango instrument, the music my father liked, but I had become a Bach fanatic.

The bandoneon was a rarity in New York. Playing it was a big deal, and to give myself airs, I started to take it to school. Mother Superior didn't like it one bit, but that was at first. Later she asked me to play at a party. They put a music stand in the middle of the school yard with the scores of two marches I had studied on previous days. I was surrounded by boys in black shirts, and I played "Giovinezza" and "Camicia nera," two fascist marches. When I finished, amidst everyone's applause, Mother Superior kissed me and told me God had forgiven all my sins.

The Latin American community in New York was not that large then. Among those people I was a child prodigy. I played anything on the bandoneon: classics, Spanish music, Mexican songs. Sometimes they dressed me up as a gaucho, and I would play folk songs from Argentina at festivals or radio shows. When I met Gardel, to accompany him in some of his presentations I had to learn some tangos on the run.

When my parents decided to return for good to Argentina, in 1937, I was sixteen years old with a rather murky future. I made a few bucks playing with a trio—drums, bass, and bandoneon. The repertoire was by request: *rancheras, pasodobles,*** a tango.

---

* Piazzolla quotes the tango "Milonguita" by José González Castillo and Enrique Delfino, about the women who danced for money in clubs and worked as prostitutes on the side. The line alludes to Mimí, a working girl, reminiscent of the seamstress of Puccini's *La bohème*, and Museta, a socialite, perhaps like Puccini's Musetta, the heartless flirt.

** *Ranchera*: Popular Argentine song and dance.

Pasadoble: Popular Spanish dance in double time.

Piazzolla, still a kid and dressed as a gaucho, played in festivals for the Latin community. This is a 1933 family picture.

I also remember a small stage in a sort of Munich beer hall that my father patronized in the summer. A trio played there that must have inspired some of the scenes that Federico Fellini shot years later. Pocholo played the piano, Rolando the bass, and I played the bandoneon. Pocholo and Rolando were much older than I, and they were both blind. They adored me and I adored them. Pocholo was a marvel doing Francisco De Caro's tangos. He had a style that years later I would discover in Jaime Gosis.

In New York I brought a pair of shoes with aluminum points, and I did a couple of tap dance numbers. These blind guys were on their way back from everything, and every buck they made they spent on whisky. But they have a special place in my heart. Playing the music of De Caro, Maffia, and Laurenz with them gave me a warning: I was getting into tango madness.

I got a big bang out of hearing the Elvino Vardaro Sextet when it came to play Mar del Plata. By then I was playing in local groups, and I felt like making the push and told myself: I want to play this music. The same thing happened later when I went to Miguel Caló's debut. I felt shaken just as I had the time that Béla Wilda was playing his piano.

Of course, there was a difference. Now this was not a kid. I had become a man who was starting to battle for his life. That same year, my dad lent me two hundred pesos [about $60] and I took off for Buenos Aires. Mario Sasiaín, a friend of the family, accompanied me right up to the door of the rooming house where I was to share a room with Líbero Pauloni, Homero's brother.

Líbero took care of me—he was a good guy—but I got bored with drifting around town aimlessly. It was then that I felt loneliness for the first time in my life. It wasn't easy to get into the tango world and even tougher to get a job. I did go straight from Mar del Plata to Aníbal Troilo's orchestra. I went through some very bad experiences. I had bad moments. The anguish I felt made me cry more than one night. I'm not ashamed to admit it: I missed my parents.

Perhaps because of this loneliness I married young, in 1942. Dedé, my wife, studied painting and encouraged me in my music studies. By then I only played tangos. I had abandoned everything I had learned with Béla Wilda, Bach and Mozart on the bandoneon. I started listening to Stravinsky and I even wrote a piano concerto—without orchestra—that out of pure nerve I showed to Arthur Rubinstein.

From that I ended up in Alberto Ginastera's house. I would go to bed at five in the morning after playing with Troilo, sleep two hours, and from Parque Chacabuco take the bus to Barracas [the other side of town] to study with Ginastera. Dedé helped me a lot. She did not want me to work at night, but she wanted me to be a serious musician. Things started to happen. I stopped working with Troilo and formed an orchestra to back Fiorentino. That lasted about two years.

The big day was 1 July 1946. That's when I, Astor Piazzolla, could form my own orchestra. I was a tango man and to be able to form my own orchestra, doing my own arrangements without asking anybody for permission, put me on another level in Buenos Aires. By then I was listening to as much music as I could.

I had become a fan of Stravinsky and Béla Bartók. I would take Roberto Di Filippo, a great pal, and go to the symphony orchestra rehearsals. I wanted to know about the oboe, the clarinet, the French horn. I was developing the notion of writing erudite music. Under Alberto Ginastera's wing I wrote a piano sonata that still today is used as a model at the National Conservatory. Every time I hear it I realize it has little to do with Piazzolla and a lot with Stravinsky, which shows where I was at the time.

I studied piano with Raúl Spivak.* I wanted to play piano at the top level. But it was to go *contra natura*, because I have my thumbs pointing outward, out of whack, from the bandoneon playing. I didn't waste my time with Spivak—to the contrary. I did all my work, including the arrangements, on the piano, not the bandoneon. The piano has an advantage: it is easy to imagine the whole orchestra. I also did a conducting course with Hermann Scherchen who

* Raúl Spivak: Argentine classical pianist.

was also the teacher of Pedro Ignacio Calderón and Simón Blech, among others.*

I started to feel more secure about what was mine. Musicians of the stature of Aaron Copland and Igor Markevitch passed through Buenos Aires, and these two had the same praise: both came to tell me that my orchestra, the 1946 Orchestra, played a tango at a high musical level.

I kept studying like crazy. In addition I would go to see exhibits at every art gallery. I did not miss an opening night of modern theater. I felt like an intellectual, but more likely I must have been an intellectualoid. My thing had a snobbish tinge. In time I learned that thanks to other snobs I was able to do a great part of my career: they were the ones who applauded from the first row.

In 1949, because of lack of work, I disbanded the orchestra. Again the bandoneon went into the closet. We had entered into conflict again, the bandoneon and I.

I dedicated myself to writing arrangements for other orchestras. I wrote music for films. I won the Fabien Sevitzky award for my *Buenos Aires* Symphony, which Sevitzky himself came to conduct. It premiered 16 August 1953 at the Buenos Aires University Law School auditorium. It was an evening I don't remember as quiet because I had an audience that was both for and against me, and the thing ended up in a fistfight.

Even Carlos Montero, who years later would become the director of Teatro Colón, fought, umbrella in hand, for my piece. Sevitzky invited me to the stage and hugged me. I was a little shaken, and he told me something very nice: "I have never seen such fistfights at a premiere, but relax, this is all publicity. Don't forget they whistled down Stravinsky's *Rite of Spring* and Ravel's *Bolero*. You start the same way."

In the middle of that melee a short man came to congratulate me. He introduced himself as a violinist of the National Symphony Or-

---

* Pedro Ignacio Calderón: Important Argentine orchestra director, conductor of the National Symphony Orchestra.

Simón Blech: Orchestra director.

chestra. He congratulated me and asked, "You have no relation with the Piazzolla who plays tangos, have you?" When I told him it was the same person, it was like the earth had swallowed him. The part of the audience who applauded the work was mostly students. They were the first to understand my music.

That Fabien Sevitzky award took me to France to study with Nadia Boulanger. For Dedé it was also an important trip, as her studies in painting with André Lhote perfected her skills. The kids stayed in Buenos Aires in the care of my parents, Nonino and Nonina, and

At the premiere of Piazzolla's three-movement *Buenos Aires* Symphony on 16 August 1953 in Buenos Aires. The piece won Piazzolla the Fabien Sevitzky Award which took him to France and his lessons with Nadia Boulanger. Sevitzky himself, left, conducted, but some in the audience were scandalized and the evening ended wildly.

with that kindness they always had, they also would send us a few bucks because they knew things were hard.

My biggest income was the eight hundred pesos [approximately $240] a month that the producers of *El patio de la morocha** wired me to Paris. That was what we had agreed for me to write the arrangements of El Gordo Troilo's music. That trip in 1954 was crucial in my life. It marked a boundary. It was when Nadia Boulanger found the key to the true Piazzolla.

I started writing like mad: "Chau París," "Bando," "Nonino," "Marrón y azul." All that repertoire was recorded on an album featuring Lalo Schifrin on piano. In Paris something different was also born. One night Luis Sierra, an Argentine friend living there at the time, and I went to hear the Gerry Mulligan Octet. We came out charged. We had a coffee afterward and right then I told him that something like that, but featuring the best tango musicians, should be put together in Buenos Aires.

I finished my scholarship, said goodbye to Nadia, and returned to Buenos Aires with the urge to explode it all. The Buenos Aires Octet in 1955 was an artistic success, but work didn't last long. To record we had to make certain concessions, practically give away our rights.** Something similar happened to me later with a record that is still popping up all over the world: *Tango in Hi Fi*, recorded with a string orchestra. It features "Tres minutos con la realidad," "Melancólico Buenos Aires," "Tango del ángel," and a lot of other nice things.

People don't know and don't care about who is the producer of a record but do know and admire the artist who made it. The truth, after these many years, is that there was a dummy, me, who took the money out of his own pocket to pay most of the musicians while

---

* *El patio de la morocha* (The patio of the dark-haired woman) was a tango-based musical comedy series featuring Aníbal Troilo and his orchestra with arrangements by Piazzolla. In the shows a series of musical tableaux, tied together by a flimsy storyline, were set up to showcase the orchestra, singers, actors, and dancers. The shows were a hit in Buenos Aires in the 1940s and '50s.

**In fact, he had to sign all royalties away in order to record.

someone else made the profits. We are still in litigation. But who cares to defend artistic creation? I made similar mistakes regarding [publishing] rights later on, I was duped many times, and in other instances I was naive. But I don't regret anything. In the long run I reaped what I sowed.

It seemed it was written that I had to go back to New York. I traveled first and told Dedé to sell everything we had in Buenos Aires and then join me with the kids. If I had thought it through, most certainly I would have done it differently, but that's how I was—impulsive, daring. Only these past few years have I taken my foot off the accelerator. My project of writing music for film in Hollywood collapsed like a house of cards. Then Jazz Tango, the J-T Quintet, was born. It was a hybrid, although it had a seed of Piazzolla. The proof of the crime is on an LP somewhere. In it I mix some of my own things—"Triunfal," "Para lucirse"—with jazz pieces—"April in Paris," "Sophisticated Lady." And there is one that's even worse, one that does not appear in any catalog. I gave the only copy extant in the country to Pipo Mancera,* and he told me he lost it. Sometimes I get the urge to hear it again. One must own up to his own atrocities.**

To return to the United States with my family I had to sign a leonine contract,‡ but I had no other way. I didn't even have enough money for the tickets. People came to see me from Universelle, a French publisher, and I accepted their offer for an advance of twelve hundred dollars. In that package came fantastic pieces like "Adiós Nonino" and everything I'd later write for the Quintet, pieces like "Calambre," "Los poseídos," "Nuestro tiempo," "Verano porteño," and many others.

---

* Nicolas "Pipo" Mancera: Argentine television host and producer, very popular and influential in the 1960s.

** Perhaps indeed "one must own up to his own atrocities," but still, vibraphonist Gary Burton, who in the 1980s toured and recorded with Piazzolla, was surprised when told of the maestro's experiments with jazz tango and the vibraphone. Piazzolla, perhaps still ashamed, had never told him.

‡ Leonine contract: Lopsided, in which one party receives the lion's share.

Piazzolla with Italian producer Aldo Pagani, his champion and European agent who would be essential to his international fame. But from the day Piazzolla signed Pagani's contract in April 1974, they were joined in a story of mutual affection and contempt.

It would not be the only complicated moment in my life. After *María de Buenos Aires* (1968), after creating the Nonet (1971), I had a heart attack (1973). When I recovered, I had to face reality. I had left behind a very creative period, but I was nearly ruined financially.

I was past fifty, and I had to start over again.

That's when I got a proposal from Aldo Pagani,* an Italian producer, a partner in Curci-Pagani Music. He offered me a fifteen-year contract, the rent of an apartment in Rome, five hundred dollars a month to eat, and, most importantly, the opportunity to record anything I would write from then on. This is the period that starts with *Libertango* and continues with *Suite Troileana*, *Summit* with Gerry Mulligan, and many others.

*Aldo Pagani (b. 1932): Music publisher. A musician by training, he started his company in 1961.

Piazzolla in Buenos Aires during the late 1960s. Courtesy Víctor Oliveros.

The contract with Curci-Pagani was much more beneficial to me than the one I had signed with Universelle. Every time "Adiós Nonino" is played around the world I get twenty-five percent of the royalties. What I did with Curci-Pagani is fifty-fifty. The live performances were not included.

I remember César Luis Menotti* came to my apartment in Paris—by then I was already living with Laura—and to walk in he had to bend down. He didn't say anything, but I am sure he was thinking, "And this is how Piazzolla lives?" Truth be told, it was a very modest place, the reflection of many hard years. It was a great challenge: either I would take a leap forward or get stuck in place forever.

The J-T Quintet was the precursor of the one I would put togeth-

---

*César Luis Menotti: Soccer coach who led the Argentine national team that won the World Cup in 1978.

er in Buenos Aires in 1960. And when I presented it on "Welcome, Mr. Piazzolla," a television show on Channel 9, the lineup still featured a vibraphone. But such are things in the life of a musician. Sometimes a change is made for circumstantial reasons. I added a violin to the Quintet because I couldn't find a vibraphonist with the spunk needed to play my music.

Then begins a period of bohemia. We played very small dives. Jamaica could only fit thirty people. Afterward comes the period at the 676. A lot of work, little money. Sometimes we got paid, sometimes we didn't.

What was nice was the applause of the audience and the great musicians who came to hear us: Isaac Stern, Frederich Goulda, Stan Getz, the Tommy Dorsey band. Someone who was always there was a Buenos Aires character I appreciated a lot as an artist and friend: "El Mono" Villegas.*

Later, along with Pipo Mancera, we opened at a place called La Noche where I experimented with a new Contemporary Octet. But it was a very brief thing because of lack of money. I had to work, and in exchange for being allowed to play my music, I was capable of going onstage naked. I did television, tours around the country with [comic] Tato Bores. And always with the same struggle everywhere.

It got me angry, but deep inside it also made me happy because I was a fighter, and when the time came I also provoked people. One time in Río Hondo,** a guy sent me a little note onstage. It said, "A lot of noise, too little tango." I responded with something boorish. That same night, an older gentleman looking at the amplification for the bandoneon said out loud: "*Che*, nowadays they don't even respect the *fueye*."‡ It made me laugh.

I played everywhere, out of conviction and also because I often

---

* Enrique "El Mono" Villegas (1913–1986): Argentine jazz pianist.

** Río Hondo: Córdoba, a north-central province of Argentina.

‡ *Fueye*: Porteño for the Spanish *fuelle* (bellows); *tanguero* shorthand for bandoneon

didn't have much choice. I went from playing a whorehouse in Tucumán—the owner was filthy rich and wanted to have the pleasure of having Piazzolla play for his clientele—to the Philharmonic Hall in New York.

My life had many up and downs, successes and disillusionment. I've also known great artistic success accompanied by economic disaster. That was the case with *María de Buenos Aires*. I sold an apartment and a car to put it on stage and was left with nothing. It was a total loss. But I enjoyed myself, and that *operita* I wrote with Horacio Ferrer was among the most important pieces I've ever composed. It was colossal for its time. Today I wouldn't be able to write something like *María de Buenos Aires*. I don't have what it takes anymore.

Piazzolla, caught with his eyes closed, second from left, with collaborator and lyricist Horacio Ferrer to his right and the orchestra and singers of *María de Buenos Aires*. Back row: Néstor Panik, viola; Antonio Agri, violin; Kicho Díaz, bass; Cacho Tirao, guitar; Víctor Pontino, cello; Hugo Baralis, violin; Arturo Schneider, reeds and flute. Front row: Héctor De Rosas, singer; Piazzolla; Ferrer; Amelita Baltar, singer; Jaime Gosis, piano; and José Correale, percussion. Not in the photo: Tito Bisio, vibes.

I left Rome in 1975 because it was full of bad memories. I always preferred Paris, which is a continuation of Buenos Aires, or vice versa. The difference is that in Paris you breathe art everywhere. Paris is also the city where more of my records are sold, and this is where the Society of Composers and Authors (SACEM) is based, an organization that received me with open arms after I wisely left SADAIC, the composers' society of Argentina.

In 1978 I founded a new Quintet and for many reasons I finally had the feeling I was winning the war. *María de Buenos Aires* and the Nonet had left my head full of music and I could pour it into the Quintet, in a more elaborate music. I believe we all grew with that group, me writing new pieces and the musicians playing the new music.

Those were the best ten years of Piazzolla. I can't say my work is as popular as Sting's, but my music did spread all over the world and

The European look, 1977. Photo by Giovanna Piemonti

Piazzolla recording his *Concierto para bandoneón y orquesta* with the St. Lukes Orchestra, directed by Lalo Schifrin, in the Richardson Auditorium at Princeton University, September 1987. The recording was released in 1988.

at the same time I could develop my erudite music, if you'll pardon the expression. When I recorded *Concierto para bandoneón y orquesta* with Lalo Schifrin in 1987 in the United States, the musicians stood up and applauded us, something very hard to get in a recording session because of the coldness of the situation, the isolation.* It was very nice recognition.

I don't know how much longer I will keep playing. The fingers have the last word: if they can handle it, so can I. The doctors who did the quadruple bypass in 1988 assured me that I had a heart for another twelve or thirteen years. In truth, I can't complain. To make it to eighty-one, eighty-two, would be great news. As long as I have my family, my children, my six grandchildren, my wife, my dog, my bandoneon, what else can I ask for?

The only thing I fear is a bad illness, the suffering. That I couldn't take.

* Here Piazzolla refers to the isolation of sections and musicians for acoustical reasons.

12

Bandoneon

My first bandoneon was a gift from my father when I was eight years old. He brought it covered in a box, and I got very happy because I thought it was the roller skates I had asked him for so many times. It was a letdown because instead of a pair of skates, I found an artifact I had never seen before in my life. Dad sat down, set it on my legs, and told me, "Astor, this is the instrument of tango. I want you to learn it."

My first reaction was anger. Tango was that music he listened to almost every night after coming home from work. I didn't like it. I knew that the bandoneon cost nineteen dollars and that he bought it at one of those places in New York that sells used stuff, a pawn shop. We never found out whose it was.

My first teacher, Andrés D'Aquila, was actually a pianist who had some notions about the bandoneon. What he taught me was elementary: the placement of the notes on the buttons. Today I understand my reaction as a kid: it's hard to fall in love with the bandoneon. The keys are on the side; they are a bit of a mystery. One can't see them. On the piano, the keys are right in front of the player. The violinist looks constantly at his hands. It's the same thing with the bass player, the percussionist. With the bandoneon you barely see the fingers.

Many things happened in my life since that gift my father gave me. The bandoneon has become for me something more than a musical instrument. Sometimes I think it is my psychoanalyst: I start playing it and I blurt everything out.

141

That interplanetary travel starts when I discovered Béla Wilda, when Bach's music hits me hard. Bach is the first thing I played on the bandoneon. It was Wilda who adapted some classical pieces so I could play them. The rest has to do with my experience with Carlos Gardel and the discovery of the Elvino Vardaro Sextet. By then I already had a Double A that my father had bought in Casa Emilio Pitzer in Buenos Aires. It cost him three hundred pesos [about $100], and for me it was like going from an upright to a concert piano. I was enjoying tango, the bandoneon. I was a self-taught player.

For many years I played it sitting down, like most of my colleagues, until I became a soloist. Then I felt the need to look for a different position, more in tune with my personality. Sitting down I felt tied down.

I stood up, nailed the left leg to the floor, and put the instrument over the right one. Since then I play with my guts over the *fueye*. Sometimes I even think we dance together, the bandoneon and me. Sometimes I feel I'm crying while I play a solo, but without tears. Same thing happened to Gordo Troilo playing "El motivo." It's called the electricity of the artist.

Tango had great bandoneonists. There is a Maffia style, a Laurenz style. The first was more intimate, the latter more effusive. El Gordo Troilo was something else. He wasn't dazzling, but he was a marvelous interpreter, incomparable just playing two notes.

Technically you had Minotto. And the greatest of all of us—but an unknown to the greater audience because one day he got sick of tango and joined the Teatro Colón orchestra as an oboe player—was Roberto Di Filippo. Leopoldo Federico should not be missing from the top of any list. In the later generation there are two very good ones: Dino Saluzzi and Néstor Marconi.

I am different from everyone. I am not saying better or worse than Troilo or Federico. What no one has is my *touch* [in English]. Perhaps someone might surpass me, but no one can play like Piazzolla. But I wasn't born in a vacuum, nor is my sound a rarity that fell from the sky. Everything is connected. I say so in my music.

In the first section of *Suite Troileana*, titled "Bandoneón," El Gordo is always beside me. At times I play like Piazzolla, at times like Troilo. Something similar happens in "Tristezas de un Doble A." In the Quintet version I include a bandoneon solo that can last ten, fifteen minutes depending on how I'm feeling. In it I go on a trip and take with me Maffia, Laurenz, Di Filippo, Federico, Troilo, and I have the feeling I'm playing with them.

The worst thing that can happen to a bandoneon player is to be timid. We of the union call it playing inward. That's not good. You can't be afraid. If one makes a mistake, it doesn't matter.

Several young guys, bandoneon players, have asked me how many hours a day I practice, and I think my response disappointed them. I can be talking with a group of people and at the same time going over the bandoneon parts in my head. The human brain allows for that kind of thing. Arthur Rubinstein did the same thing. He didn't practice like crazy. I take the bandoneon out of its case fifteen days before a concert, go over everything, and that's it. That allows me to have my fingers in good shape. That's my system. Other players maybe need to be with the instrument in their hands the whole day.

Every bandoneon has its history. The last time I was in Brazil, a lady came to see me. She had been widowed recently and her husband had left four bandoneons, and she came to offer them to me. Of that lot only one was worth something: a Double A in unbelievable mint condition. It still had the factory smell.

Now these instruments cost between one thousand and two thousand dollars, depending on the shape they are in. With the one I bought in Brazil, now I have seven, of which four are playable. Three are in Buenos Aires, and a friend of mine in Paris has the other one. It's a backup for my European touring.

The bandoneon that Zita, the widow of Gordo Troilo, gave me is not playable, at least for me. It's like a car that has been driven by an old aunt at forty kilometers [25 miles] per hour. When you push the accelerator it does not respond. The same thing happens to me with Troilo's *fueye*. I have to play it softly. And I caress nothing. My fingers are like machine guns. The times I played it in public it died on me after two minutes, and that's the way it will be until judgment day. It's *achanchado* [out of shape]. Of course, I care for it like a relic.

There are two bandoneons I would never give up for anything in the world: that first one my father gave me, which is now in the custody of my grandson Daniel Astor, who is a drummer and a rocker. The other one I would never give up is Troilo's bandoneon.

I talk to the bandoneons. That's why I swear that at one time El Gordo's *fueye* cried "Ay!" I think I hurt it. Maybe I banged a button with my finger. I play with violence; my bandoneon must sing and scream. I can't conceive of pastel tones in tango. I speak to him (the bandoneon) so he doesn't stand me up in the middle of a concert. Sometimes I beat him up.

Those hits to the box in the middle of a piece are often a part of the music, a percussion effect. But now and then there is also a blow when I hear something go wrong. It's one of those mysteries, like what happens when the television sets go wrong and you bang on the box and it somehow gets fixed. With bandoneons it's the same—until they break down completely. Luckily there are still a pair of *tanos*, Romualdo and Fabiani, on Martín de Gainza Street, who are still fixing and tuning bandoneons.

Nearly twenty-five thousand bandoneons of the Double A brand were sold in Argentina—but not all were of the same high quality. The 20,000 to 25,000 series is the best. It has to do with a good moment in the factory, when the Germans had gotten a handle on how to manufacture them. It was artisans' work. Today it would be unthinkable, especially because there is no great market for such instruments.

A certain Mr. Muller, a bandoneon player in a German tango orchestra, came to see me while I was on tour in Germany. He told me he had worked in the Arnold company that made the Double As. Actually Double A is a nickname we gave them in Argentina because the *fueye* simply said A-A, for Alfred Arnold, the founder of the establishment.

He told me that almost all the production before World War II was for Argentina. After the war, the factory was taken over. It was on the communist side, and that was the end of it. When the family tried to revive the brand in the 1960s, there was no real market for it and least of all in Argentina.

I hope that in fifty years the bandoneon will not have turned into a museum piece. For that there would have to be a new Laurenz, a new Maffia, a Troilo. I am not optimistic, but I don't lose hope.

Handwritten note from Piazzolla to his young audience of rockers: "I was born the 11th of March 1921 in Mar del Plata. I've been leading popular music groups for exactly 30 years. I started with an *orquesta típica* in 1946. I did away with that type of group in 1955 and I've struggled against my detractors ever since: Buenos Aires Octet, String Orchestra, Quintet, New Octet, Nonet, and, today, this Electronic Octet that has nothing to do with the others. I call on you, the young musicians of Argentina, who are the only ones who can achieve the continuity of this music I love. Thanks. Astor Piazzolla, Buenos Aires 76."

13

500 Motivations

1989

Recently* I gave some rock guys an arrangement of "500 motiva-ciones," a ten-minute-long piece that I wrote for the Electronic Octet in 1976. They told me they were going to do it without bandoneon so I don't know how it came out.

For me it is something of the past, something that, I accept and acknowledge, I wrote influenced by Chick Corea even if it sounded like Piazzolla. They could question those "500 motivaciones," but not the rest of the repertoire of the Octet. That was my music. It smelled of tango, not rock. I have never believed in that madness called *rock nacional.*** It doesn't exist. It's rock. Period.

From that point of view I dare argue the issue with anyone, not as someone from "across the street" but as a musician who accepts rock as a natural thing. I understand it, and depending on who plays it, I like it.

If I were eighteen today I also would wear a black shirt with a skull, ripped-up blue jeans, and would hole up for a month with three or four good musicians and then would go out to blow every-thing up. It's easy to be a winner. Most Argentine groups play crappy stuff. I believe one of the gravest problems in Argentine music is that it lacks an identity. I speak of today. What happened fifty years

---

* The conversation was taking place March 1990. Piazzolla is probably talking about 1989.

** *Rock nacional*: Term used in the 1970s in Argentina for indigenous rock 'n roll, sung in Spanish and influenced by local styles.

ago belongs to the past. In that environment, tango advanced further than folk music. The reason is simple: because it had and still has better musicians.

An intuitive artist like Atahualpa Yupanqui,* the best at what he does, cannot be considered an artist of the vanguard. But his music, or better yet, his songs, are very authentic, very Argentine. Cuchi Leguizamón** did some very nice things I thought important, but he can't seduce the kids today. Argentine folk music is stuck in time. When they wanted to move on from the *bombo*‡ to percussion, it sounded false. Waldo de los Ríos might have changed history. There is also Manolo Juárez, but he is more a complete musician than just a folk artist.

Perhaps folk music has room for an opening similar to what happened in tango. I don't dare. There has to be a musician who would take the place of Waldo de los Ríos. He or she has to come from the popular field. The things that some so-called erudite composers have tried sound like a disaster to me. Besides, at this point in our sound culture, at this point in our universal culture, to speak in those terms is not appropriate.

Neither what Atahualpa nor what Waldo did is conventional folk music. Theirs are products developed from traditional folk music, just like my music is a development from tango. What Leda Valladares§ does is true folk music. That's musical archeology in the best sense.

What bothers me about Argentine rockers is their lack of curiosity. That four or five kids get together in someone's garage and start

---

* Atahualpa Yupanqui (1908–1992): Perhaps the most important twentieth-century composer and singer in Argentine folk music.

** Gustavo "Cuchi" Leguizamón (1917–2000): Folk song writer from Salta in Argentina's northwest.

‡ *Bombo*: Traditional two-headed drum.

§ Leda Valladares (b. 1912): Argentina's most important folklorist and researcher, best known for her compilations of indigenous music of the Argentine northeast.

out by playing crap I feel is fine. It's part of the growth cycle. But if the final result, when they are all grown up, is Soda Stereo or Charly García, then we are screwed.

They should follow the example of Queen, U2, Pat Metheny, Sting, or Emerson, Lake & Palmer. Keith Emerson is a conservatory-trained musician, a world-class pianist. Sting went and knocked on Gil Evans's door. The world does not accept ugly music. It wants something more elaborate, quality. And here [in Argentina] I don't see it. Lito Vitale* is doing some interesting stuff. I follow him. Alejandro Lerner has some very nice melodies. And that's about it. The rest of the rock scene is poor and poorer.

I am not afraid of rock. I like to get into that world. In Paris, with Pierre Philippe,** the same one who wrote the lyrics for the opera *Gardel*, we did *Crimen pasional*. It was an hour-and-a-half play for Jean Guidoni.† We went to premiere it at a festival, and we found the amplification was for a soccer stadium. I was with my bandoneon and Guidoni was singing and both of us were surrounded by great musicians who played rock to make a living. People went nuts. People recognize the good stuff.

I like the Beatles. Period. I can't say I'd kill myself for them. I don't think they invented gunpowder. Many who came later did surround rock with good music; they did get together with great arrangers. To play like Pink Floyd or Weather Report you have to have put in many hours in the studio. Mick Jagger is a fan of Stravinsky, Béla Bartók. I know this through Jeanne Moreau who is good friends with him and sent him all my records.

I still don't lose hope of playing with some of them, be it Pat

---

* Lito Vitale: Pianist, composer, arranger, and producer who fuses contemporary folk, jazz, classical, and New Age music.

** Pierre Philippe: French songwriter. Piazzolla was going to compose the opera *Gardel* in the Southern Hemisphere during the summer of 1989–90, but he never wrote a note. He was spent both physically and creatively.

† Jean Guidoni: French rock musician.

Metheny or Al Di Meola. It's a matter of setting the dates. With Di Meola the idea has gone pretty far. He wants me to write music for a duet, with him on guitar and me on bandoneon. It will be a beautiful challenge. My beloved Gil Evans told me once that he became young again when, at seventy-two, he did some arrangements for Sting. I also want to get back the kid Piazzolla.

14

Triunfal

I worked all my life for tango; now I hope tango works for me. It's not that I'm thinking of retiring or anything like that. My destiny has been written, and one day it will tell me it's time to stop.

I think it's a right I've earned. I didn't sit down to wait for fate. I'm about to celebrate my sixty-ninth birthday, so I think I still can make a few more bucks. And if that's not the case, there are no complaints. I took my chances for what I believed in, my music, and thank God I never went hungry. History has many examples of great musicians who lived and died in misery and never suspected that one day their music would be appreciated.

I got that recognition during my lifetime. I can enjoy it. My music is being played everywhere. I also continue to play it. In April I return to Europe, settle in Paris, and start a series of concerts in Italy, France, and Germany. That's just to finish the season in Europe.

Now I get good rest between concerts. I'm only playing eight or nine a month. That's it. The madness of taking a plane, arriving, rehearsing in the afternoon, playing in the evening, then taking a plane the next morning and doing it all over again, week after week, is over.

I am not possessed by the god of money. I don't want twenty houses, five cars, and a yacht in Puerto Banús. I am ready to confront the future, the end, as one would say. One does things for the companion by one's side. My wife is much younger than I am, and if something happened to me, she should be at peace. It might sound necrophilic, but it's reality.

I have been a very controversial artist in my country and, on the flip side, well regarded abroad, where no one cared to wonder if my music was tango or not. I am not a popular artist. I do not attract crowds. At the Opera Theater in Buenos Aires* I could do two sold-out shows, maybe three—never a whole week. This is not to be unless some government entity supports it and we could make tickets very cheap. I am an artist of a great minority compared to the rock groups that fill up soccer stadiums.

Someone said recently that I was famous but not popular. That was a nice compliment. When in Argentina people read that Piazzolla was successful in Italy, in France, in Germany, in the United States, in Japan, I am certain many of my compatriots say to themselves, "Damn, this guy plays a music I don't like, but it must have something."

It is what has happened with Jorge Luis Borges: few have read him, everyone knows of him. In Europe, besides the recognition, I am in fashion. I go to any city and people come to hear me. Piazzolla's music caught on in all circles, the intellectual and the popular. This year I am going just by myself, with my bandoneon. There I will join a string quartet or a symphony orchestra, depending on the repertoire.

I am a music worker, now a member of the French society of composers and authors, which is itself an honor. It means I am among the two hundred most prolific composers there. In Argentina, while I was a member of SADAIC, I was scuffling all the time. In France I am placed at the same level as Ravel, Debussy, Michel Legrand, Michel Colombier, and all the great French composers. An Argentine is among those names.

Tango is a fashion in the world today, but people come to hear me because of my music, which is related to tango. The ballets in the great theaters around the world are dancing my music. Julio Bocca and Maximiliano Guerra** are not the only ones. I get asked

---

* Opera Theater: Seating 2500 persons, the Opera Theater in Buenos Aires is among the largest in Argentina.

**Julio Bocca and Maximiliano Guerra: Top Argentine classical dancers.

for scores from the strangest places, places I would have never dreamed of for Piazzolla's tango.

I was also surprised by the phenomenon in the United States, especially for how the music got in. *Playboy* magazine had a feature on me which ended by saying that before making love, you have to hear my music. It seems to be exciting for them, puts them in the mood.

It never occurred to me that it had such sensual appeal. I tired myself out explaining why, but they still didn't want to hear of it. That's why the recordings in the United States point in that direction, as in *Tango apasionado*. What's important is that as they go past that sensuality, they start to learn about the work I did in Europe, *Libertango*, the album with Mulligan, with Gary Burton, and all the rest. Someone who is very happy is Mulligan. The last time we spoke he told me the record we did fifteen years ago in Milan was still giving him good money in royalties.*

Now I'm by myself. I got tired of having a group, the hassles, and the wear and tear. But I would be unfair if I didn't acknowledge how much the Quintet meant to me in the past ten years, from 1978 until I dissolved it. What I had sown in *María de Buenos Aires* and with the Nonet was harvested by the Quintet. Its sonority gained in heft with my arranging and we all started to fly. That's where the Piazzolla phenomenon grew in Europe. I believe the greatest success for Argentine music abroad was by the Quintet.

In the past twenty years two artists have represented Argentine music around the world: Astor Piazzolla and Mercedes Sosa. The truth is in the bins at the record stores. Last year in the main cities of Germany, you could find twenty-three Piazzolla titles. In Paris there were twenty, all different, all original.

In these past ten years I have played a lot with the Quintet, but in terms of composing, I've aimed toward erudite music, as it is now called. I think classical is the right term, even if avant-gardists might

---

* Publisher Aldo Pagani told Natalio Gorin that Piazzolla's recollections of Mulligan's talking about great sales were "pure foolishness." "Reading that paragraph made me smile," wrote Pagani to Natalio Gorin, 7 December 1998.

get annoyed. Stravinsky is a classicist even if he's almost a contemporary of ours. I wrote *Concierto para bandoneón y orquesta*, *Suite Punta del Este*, *Three Tangos for Bandoneon and Orchestra*, and *Five Tango Sensations*, which is what I am going to play in Europe with the Salzburg and Mantova String Quartets.

The violinist of the Mantova is Anahí Carfi, an Argentine who is also the first violin of the orchestra at La Scala in Milan. She told me that in the first part of the program—I join them in the second—they are going to play a string quartet by Alberto Ginastera, which makes me think about the turns of fate: my music and that of my first teacher performed the same evening. The only thing that will be impossible is a big hug because Alberto died in 1983. But his memory will be onstage.

I have played *Concierto para bandoneón* in many places around the world, but there is one very special night: 11 June 1983, when the

The last Quintet during a European tour in 1986. Left to right, standing: Héctor Consols, Piazzolla, and Horacio Malvicino. Seated: Fernando Suárez Paz and Pablo Ziegler. Courtesy Pablo Ziegler

Teatro Colón opened up to my music. The Colón is a special place for an Argentine musician, the gold prize, and I couldn't escape the feeling. For a moment I felt like that Piazzolla who studied with Ginastera and who went on Saturday afternoons with Roberto Di Filippo to catch the symphony orchestra rehearsals.

Another joyful moment was the concert with the Sextet at the Opera Theater on 9 June 1989. That evening has its own particular story.

I have never hidden my anti-Peronism. I did not like the reverences one had to make to Perón and Evita to be able to work, and I didn't like their methods. I am talking now about the first presidency, in 1946, when I had my first orchestra. There were other musicians, such as Mariano Mores, who took advantage of the situation. I, on the other hand, in my rebelliousness, resisted singing "Los muchachos Peronistas."*

What I must acknowledge is that during Perón's administration Argentine music was supported and encouraged. It is not by chance that tango had its great moment right up until 1955, the end, to my mind, of the 1940s, the golden era of tango. When the Liberating Revolution** triumphed, many got revenge, and I didn't like that either.

Before the last elections I made some rather strong pronouncements. I said that if [Carlos] Menem won I would leave Argentina forever. Nothing personal against Menem, but I had him identified with the worse segments of Peronism, the labor bosses who have done so much damage to the country. Menem's answer took me by surprise.

---

* General Juan Domingo Perón (1895–1974): A crucial figure in Argentine politics. Elected in 1946 and re-elected in 1952, he was overthrown by a military-civilian coup in September 1955. María Eva Duarte, his second wife, became the almost mythical Evita. She died of cancer in 1952 at the age of thirty-three. Perón returned from exile in June 1973 and was elected president. He died in office in 1974 and was succeeded by his third wife, Isabel, whom he had chosen as vice-president.

Mariano Mores (b. 1922): Tango pianist, composer, and bandleader.

"Los muchachos Peronistas" (The Peronist boys): The Peronist party anthem.

** The Liberating Revolution or Revolución Libertadora: The military-civilian coup that overthrew Perón on 16 September 1955.

Rather than get angry and tell me to go to hell, as was his right, he said I was Argentina's deluxe musician. And he ratified it after he won the elections. Days after his victory, I was playing with the Sextet at the Opera Theater, and he came to hear me. Afterward we had a glass of champagne in my dressing room. The same man I had so disqualified was the first Argentine president (then elect) who came to hear my music. I don't know if he understands what I do.

He told me he was a fan of Aníbal Troilo, which I liked because we share that appreciation. But then he said the same thing of Héctor Varela,* and my soul dropped to the floor. I don't think President Menem knows a lot about music, but he showed me he knows a lot about politics.

Just like at the Colón years before, that night at the Opera Theater gave me a special feeling: I felt recognized in my own country, which is most important. I was born in Mar del Plata, grew up in New York, found my way to Paris, but every time I go up onstage people know I am going to play a very Argentine music, the music of Buenos Aires.

That's the card left behind by Astor Piazzolla, the son of Nonino and Nonina.

---

* Héctor Varela: Bandoneonist, composer, and bandleader, Varela led a popular but musically pedestrian tango orchestra.

POSTSCRIPT

Program cover from the Teatro Lirico of Milan, 1982.

Astor Piazzolla, publisher Aldo Pagani, and composer, arranger, and baritone saxophonist Gerry Mulligan at the console reviewing material for *Summit*, the only
recording that brought them together, Milan, 1974. Mulligan's Octet and his sophisticated cool jazz inspired Piazzolla in Paris in 1955. The result, in part, was Piazzolla's
revolutionary Buenos Aires Octet. Courtesy Aldo Pagani

The Penultimate Goodbye

NATALIO GORIN

"Who is Piazzolla? Onstage he is God, offstage a son of a bitch."

I don't remember the following seconds. Perhaps there was silence, hot like a fire unleashed by these few words, quiet because the speaker is no secondary character in this story. He is Aldo Pagani, the man who had so much to do with the crowning of Astor Piazzolla's music, first in Europe and later throughout the world.

Perhaps the Piazzolla-Pagani relationship, which always treaded a thin line between love and hate, was not at one of its better moments. But Pagani never recanted his bold phrase, tossed off like a throwaway line one summer afternoon in Milan in 1978. We have met on several occasions since, on some of his rare trips to Buenos Aires and most recently in Rome in 1995 at the presentation of the Italian translation of this book. At every encounter I would remind him of his words, and Pagani would ratify their authorship with a gesture, very certain, very northern Italian, very arrogant.

That talk in Milan took an even more surprising turn. Pagani would claim to be the man with the idea for *Suite Troileana*:

> I called Astor, who lived in Rome at the time, and asked him, "Are you going to write something in tribute?" And he responded rudely: "No. Leave me alone. I've already written 'El Gordo triste' with Horacio Ferrer and that's enough." And he hung up on me. Four or five days later—I had already forgotten about it—Astor calls me at my house in Milan. "Aldo, get the orchestra and the recording studio ready. I wrote a great piece.

It's going to be called *Suite Troileana*. It has four movements, the great loves of Pichuco: 'Bandoneón,' 'Zita,' 'Whisky,' and 'Escolaso.' One thing, though: I need to have Antonio Agri come from Buenos Aires. He's the only one who can play the solo violin parts." He didn't say a word about his earlier refusal. Piazzolla is a difficult man. He's always against whatever you say at first.

The story is a starting point for walking the crossroads of the artist and the man, the musician and the character. Like all stories, it can start in any corner; in this case, it begins at the intersection of Piazzolla Street with Troilo Avenue.

Suite Troileana offers three moments in which to approach the good Piazzolla: first, the bandoneon solo in the first movement, when Astor seems to whisper in Pichuco's ear: "This is the way you played the *fueye*; this is the way I play it"; second, the jam by the whole group in the second half of "Bandoneón," which has irresistible tango power; and third, the romantic musical encounters between the bandoneon and the violin in "Zita." According to Astor these allude to the last tender conversation between Troilo and Zita when death was already waiting outside.

Piazzolla loved his friend, respected him, and always acknowledged the opportunities and artistic support Troilo gave him. First Troilo had him debut in his orchestra, and then he premiered Piazzolla's early works as a tango composer, pieces such as "Tanguango," "Triunfal," "Prepárense," and "Para lucirse."

Troilo also loved his friend and respected him, but he had a weakness: at the worst points in the battle, he winked at those who said that what Piazzolla did was not tango. His reasons are inexplicable. Deep down, Troilo knew Piazzolla was going to go farther than he as a bandoneon player and as interpreter of the sound of a Buenos Aires looking toward the year 2000. Jealousies, including artistic jealousies, come without warning. They arrive, find their place in the heart, and are usually stronger than the will.

Destiny brought them together when it was time to say goodbye. Both were felled by strokes to the brain, but Troilo had a better arrangement with destiny or with lady luck, who as we all know is blind. Astor, who did not fear death but did fear a long agony, had to carry a heavy cross until he found his final peace. Everything carried a high price for Piazzolla, not only succeeding with his music but also dying.

Suite Troileana goes back to 1975, a year that seems to mark a dividing line in Piazzolla's work. It is a line that also divides many opinions. Several studies published in Argentina and abroad discovered Piazzolla in the 1980s, the authors mesmerized by the sound of the second Quintet or by Piazzolla's classic pieces.

It is never too late to approach Piazzolla, and one can enter his world through any period. But those who go back to the Buenos Aires Octet, the first Quintet, or the Nonet have a better grasp of Piazzolla's history.

While Piazzolla, the composer, in his later years did suffer the natural wear and tear that comes with age, Piazzolla, the bandoneon player, was brilliant until his last breath. In this book there is a moving testimony by Anahí Carfi. And if there are any doubts, one can listen to his performance of *Concierto para bandoneón y orquesta* of 3 July 1990, barely thirty days before his stroke and in the midst of his physical decadence, as Carfi also relates.

At one point it was said that the last Piazzolla group, the Sextet, had two bandoneons because Piazzolla was insecure about his own stamina, but reality proved otherwise. The quadruple bypass of 1988 did not result in a fearful performer. To the contrary, several discs by the Sextet support this notion, and so does a noncommercial recording of the last performance by Piazzolla in Argentina, June 1989, at the Opera Theater. There one can hear clearly how Daniel Binelli yells to him "*sangre!*" [literally "blood!"], a call for more gutsy playing, during an improvisation, and how Astor takes up the challenge with the vitality of the kid who fifty years earlier had taken his test as a player for Aníbal Troilo. Obviously, fifty years later the player had arrived at such a level of refinement that everything he played sounded heavenly.

Suite Troileana, besides being our lookout point, belongs to an uneven but rich portion of Piazzolla's discography. This judgment applies to *Suite Troileana* and to *Summit*, the other classic of this period. In both albums, as was the case earlier with *Libertango* (1974) and afterward with *Piazzolla '77* and *Piazzolla '78*, the strings and the rhythm parts are elementary. The players were Italian and for them Piazzolla wrote very simply, without much ambition; even the composer seemed to be under the effect of a Europeanized tango virus.

Are those records bad? The most fanatical supporters of Piazzolla must accept the fact that not all Piazzolla's oeuvre is brilliant, although his work always has brilliant moments. Perhaps a comparison with Picasso would be appropriate: not all his oils, his sculptures,

The Sextet in Scottish garb, Glasgow, 1989. Left to right: Daniel Binelli, bandoneon; Héctor Console, bass; Piazzolla; Horacio Malvicino, guitar; and José Bragato, cello.

his ceramics show the same degree of beauty and creativity, but one cannot be indifferent to any of them. It is the same thing with Piazzolla's European records of the 1970s: you cannot remain indifferent to Piazzolla's sound.

In his live performances Astor played only two movements from *Suite Troileana*—"Bandoneon" and "Zita"—as if to acknowledge that those were his most representative pieces. "Whisky" and "Escolaso" were not part of the regular book. Those were the days of the Electronic Octet, the days of a search for a younger audience, and the time of the press conference during which he was going to announce a major concert at the Gran Rex Theater* set for 3 December 1976.

Piazzolla was not enthralled by large theaters and much less so in those days. He had only dared to perform with the Quintet at the Regina Theater, a cute, small hall in the most elegant part of Santa Fe Avenue (the Fifth Avenue of Buenos Aires). In Buenos Aires his audience didn't give him any illusion of massive success.

Those were also days of change and renewal in popular music. Musicians such as Luis Alberto Spinetta and Gustavo Moretto looked at tango from the rock side. On the tango side, tango-rock fusion seemed possible in the work of musicians like Astor Piazzolla, Rodolfo Mederos, and Daniel Binelli. The movement was the indigenous Argentine version of the jazz-rock fusion in the United States that was led by such mythical musicians as Miles Davis and Chick Corea with his group Return To Forever, featuring guitarist Al Di Meola and bassist Stanley Clarke.

At that press conference I introduced Astor to a young rock writer who asked him, among other things, why he didn't play "Escolaso," a piece which the writer, with great authority and gall, said had a rockish feel. Astor was always faster than the speed of light in certain things: he said nothing but his eyes lit up. A few nights later, before a full Gran Rex sold out at popular prices, hot with music fever, "Escolaso" reappeared on the music stands as the first encore.

---

* Gran Rex Theater: The largest movie theater in Buenos Aires with capacity of 3300 persons. "But that night," Gorin recalled, "there were 3500 people in the place."

That was a special night for Astor, one that almost became a turning point, a hinge moment of dramatic change in his artistic life. But he didn't dare. He thought about it, took a look, felt it was a jump into the void, and chose to stay on this side of the line.

For that concert he wrote "500 motivaciones," a tune he played that night for the first and only time, a piece in which not even the bandoneon, also for the first time in his life, could connect him with the tango feel. He had come that far in his bold incursion into the country of rock. He had put on the tee shirt with the skull in front; he was ready to let it rip. But at the noise of the first window crashing, he decided to hide the stones in his pocket forever.

He would tell me many years later, in March 1990 in Punta del Este, that it was the French who aborted his idea. They convinced him that the true Piazzolla was in the Quintet, not in some electric experiment. But it wasn't only the French who thought that.

After the show at the Gran Rex, as he had so many times before, Astor wanted to know his gang's opinion. Quito González Azcona and I—and I believe we were not the only ones—told him the best part of the evening was the new arrangement of "Adiós Nonino." Such was the confusion unleashed by the great novelty of "500 motivaciones." Astor was part of that confusion.

By the way, that arrangement of "Adiós Nonino," the same heard later on *Olympia '77* (*Piazzolla en el Olimpía de París*), recorded in Paris with a different group, gets many votes—including Piazzolla's —as the best arrangement of that piece in Piazzolla's history.

How far could the Electronic Octet go? Did Piazzolla want to become a musician for the masses, the leader of tango-rock fusion in Argentina, or did the adventure scare him? He had talent to spare if he wanted to move in that direction. But he also had a commitment to a Piazzolla whose education had taken him a lifetime. He was not a kid. "500 motivaciones" was the road not taken. He didn't want to say "Adiós" to Nonino again.

I once asked him about the ending of *Concierto para bandoneón y orquesta*, where, suddenly, all the erudite language vanishes and in its place emerges a tango, streetwise and danceable, his very own "Flaco

Aroldi." "Actually, I didn't know how to finish it," he said. "And then I told myself: I give 'em a tango so the erudite know that when I want I can write like them, and when I want I can do my thing."

"500 motivaciones" had a similar spirit. It showed Piazzolla the *provocateur*: "I can write and play like Chick Corea; now let's see if Chick Corea can play and write like Astor Piazzolla."

And right then and there he froze his romance with those young audiences and musicians committed to fusion, but he had to pay a price for it that even today cannot be quantified. Some of those rockers never forgave him for backing down. Astor had played with their feelings in good or bad faith. That secret he never revealed. The truth can only be guessed.

Suite Troileana leads to a penultimate reflection. In a show called *Between Borges and Piazzolla*, seen in Buenos Aires at the Astral Theater in 1997, an old pal of Astor's from the 1950s and a great specimen of the *porteño* breed, Juan Carlos Copes, danced the second part of "Bandoneón" every night with his daughter Johana.

Copes had choreographed the whole show, but that piece had a distinctive feature: he danced it alone, carrying Johana, asleep, as Borges would say. That symbiosis of dance and music, that jam in "Bandoneón" translated by Copes without arabesques, with his clean elegance, filled me with emotion but also with anger, and it revived an old question: how is it possible that in Argentina someone once said Piazzolla's music was not tango?

It is clearly not just a question asked by some people acting like jackasses—forgive me for a not very academic expression—although there is a lot of that. What is worrisome is that behind the ignorance there was also ill will. That combination is lethal. From this notion the innocent—the regular audience, the people—are exempt.

The charge here is against certain musicians and certain people in the media, some famous, some not, who meddled in tango all their lives. They committed the crime of hypocrisy with the sole purpose of protecting their own interests.

This alone would be a fair argument against the second half of

Pagani's statement. Astor shot in self-defense, with the dangers of being trigger-happy. Also, trigger-happy or not, he did say some silly things, sometimes fully aware that he was doing so, looking for scandal to promote his music.

Jorge Luis Borges and Astor Pantaleón Piazzolla did not have much in common. They were not "brought together by the horror," as Borges might have written, but by an open spirit, generous, vital. Both were true creators.

The 1960s were a very special time in Piazzolla's life, a time of new intellectual and artistic paths in Argentina, a time when all the music he carried within began to explode. Astor crossed paths with a Borges sitting on top of his world, his masterpieces already written.

Literature was the magical habitat of Borges. Nothing was strange to him and everything surprised him. No word, no line, and no verse in the universe was foreign to his intelligence. His literary knowledge was overwhelming. He suggested, word for word, the lonely reciter of encyclopedias he once wrote about. But Borges conceded his ignorance in many labyrinths, including music.

Music was the magical habitat of Piazzolla. But he also knew about the blues and browns of Picasso, the *nouvelle vogue* in Argentine cinema, and he knew about words. Looking for his Manzi or his Cadícamo* one day, Piazzolla opened his doors to Horacio Ferrer, the greatest tango poet since Homero Expósito at the turn of the century. In this he was not wrong.

Piazzolla's cultural sophistication was far above that of the average *tangueros*. He was fluent in two languages, Spanish and English, and could handle two others, French and Italian. This is why his encounter with Borges was not that uneven intellectually. And that partnership would result in a notable product: *El tango* is the best record in the history of popular song in Argentina.

But the relationship would short circuit. It's a given that such an

---

* Enrique Domingo Cadícamo (1900–1999): Author, lyricist, composer. He wrote such classics as "Anclao en Paris," "La casita de mis viejos," and others.

encounter would have such a fitting finale, given their personalities. Borges would claim Piazzolla did not understand tango. Piazzolla would respond that Borges was deaf. Piazzolla's knife was sharper. One had to be very deaf to hear tango as Borges did.

The fight was barely a sideshow. The people put the squabble aside and took the true treasures: "Jacinto Chiclana," "Nicanor Paredes," "El títere," "Oda íntima a Buenos Aires," and "El hombre de la esquina rosada."

"Luck pampered him," Borges wrote in one of those tales of tough guys he had neither met nor seen, as he once admitted, but about whom he heard stories in his neighborhood, Palermo Chico.

Did luck pamper Piazzolla? Not always. The magic wand put him, still a boy, in the Aníbal Troilo orchestra, and there was no bigger prize in tango. But if we are talking luck, we will have to agree that his founding of the Buenos Aires Octet in 1955 did not happen at the best point in Argentine history.

It was a time when Buenos Aires lived by, breathed, sang, and danced the tangos created by the 1940s generation. The Argentine cinema was still about white telephones answered by stars like Mirtha Legrand and Zully Moreno. Literature, a matter for elite, small warring groups, never reached the masses. Piazzolla, as a great defender of Argentine music, acknowledged the administration that fell in 1955. But the Juan Domingo Perón regime was also part of the intellectual and artistic obscurantism of the postwar world.

Meanwhile the Liberating Revolution that broke the constitutional order in the name of freedom also in the name of freedom sent innocents before the firing squad. Such actions were at the root of the violence in Argentina in the 1970s, the so-called Dirty War, brought about by the childish murdering tendencies of the guerrilla organizations and the worst terrorism of them all: state terrorism.

Into that landscape of Argentina in 1955 burst forth Piazzolla's Buenos Aires Octet, without doubt the most revolutionary group in tango history, at least until the end of the century.

The break with conventional form was such that even the members of the group were concerned about how far out they were. Gui-

_.... Horacio Malvicino once told me they invited maestro Osvaldo Pugliese to a rehearsal at the club Rendez Vous not only to give them a critique of the arrangements or of the sound quality but also to tell them if they were still within the boundaries of tango. Malvicino recalled that when Pugliese said, "It is tango," everyone breathed easier.

I suspect Piazzolla was the least interested in Pugliese's opinion, but the Octet worked as a cooperative and he had to hear the members out. (The twists and turns of history: thirty-five years later, in April 1989, Pugliese was among the invited guests at a rehearsal of the Sextet at the Club Italiano, although this time no one asked him if this was or was not tango.)

Piazzolla returned from France at full speed. Encouraged by Nadia Boulanger to continue his work in tango, he put into the Octet the principles he had learned from the great French pedagogue and what he carried in his blood. The result was an explosive formula, valid for all his work and crucial in 1955:

Troilo + Gobbi + Ginastera + Boulanger.

That's the great Piazzolla revolution. It featured new rhythmic and sound effects, string counterpoint, a violin that sounded like a drum, the cello and the bass as low drums, formidable soloists, and an aggressive electric guitar improvising in most of the pieces.

Some arrangements suggested disrespect. There was such boldness in those scores that years later Piazzolla would write a piece called "Extasis," based on the last minute of the arrangement he had written for Horacio Salgán's classic, "A fuego lento."

The hundred fans the Octet had, commanded by Víctor Oliveros, the best-known fan in Piazzolla's history, howled with pleasure wherever the group played. But they enjoyed it for a short time. The Buenos Aires Octet lasted only a year and a half. Those one hundred madpeople plus the few who played the music on the radio or bought it at the store were a decided minority compared to those who said no.

The rejection was to be expected because of the natural tendency against anything new and because of traditional tango's deep roots in the community at large. But there were also radio personalities who hosted tango shows and seeing Piazzolla's interests at risk committed a true fraud: they did not play the Octet's records.

Some students of Piazzolla's oeuvre—among them Carlos Kuri, who in his *Piazzolla: La música límite* (Corregidor) has done a remarkable job with Piazzolla's discography—question Nadia Boulanger's advice to Piazzolla in Paris in 1954, when she recommended that he return to tango. However, Mme Boulanger was not necessarily suggesting that her disciple leave his incursions into classical music. Piazzolla himself was a decisive factor in this key anecdote in his life. There are no two versions of it, only different shadings. And above all there is a musical truth. Piazzolla is who he is in the world thanks to a formula that is much more tango than classical music:

Buenos Aires Octet + Quintet + *María de Buenos Aires* + Nonet.

The *Suite Punta del Este* or the *Concierto para bandoneón y orquesta* are important works on the classical side of Piazzolla, but as a whole they are not the most important in his repertoire; these are not the pieces that imposed Piazzolla's music into the world. That's why when such great interpreters as Yo-Yo Ma, Gidon Kremer, or Daniel Barenboim play Piazzolla, they choose pieces from his *tanguero* side.

He says in this book that his music "smells of tango. That's why it is so attractive to the world," as if to erase any doubt. Many years earlier, a great Brazilian poet seemed to anticipate the same notion with words as simple as they were exacting.

Back in the early 1970s, I interviewed Vinicius de Moraes one afternoon in the lobby of the Alvear Palace Hotel. At the prearranged time, Vinicius, who like Piazzolla was very punctual, was waiting for me with a glass of whisky in hand. I could have stayed there a year, just sitting there, hearing his tales, his opinions. He had other business to attend to, and after two hours I began to pack up my notes. Everything Vinicius said had a particular charm. It wasn't just his great culture, his knowledge of Brazil and of the world, or his sense of humor, which he often used to make fun of himself and his eight or nine marriages. He spoke in a whisper that turned everything into a secret among friends. Finally I asked him about Piazzolla, and he started talking with the thoroughness of a true expert on his work. Until he put his hand over mine and said, "You Argentines, do you know Piazzolla is the best popular musician in the world?"

Good question, I thought. Many don't know, I told myself.

As we said goodbye, and perhaps concerned that his statements might have repercussions in his country, he added in that half whisper of his and without making it sound like a demand: "Do me a favor. In the story put that I say that the two best popular musicians in the world are Piazzolla and Antonio Carlos Jobim."

The 1960s offered Piazzolla new air. Luck started to pamper him, at least in that it helped his takeoff—his and that of many other creators.

Argentina returned to constitutional rule in 1958. In a period that was not totally authoritarian, José María Guido, representing a civilian-military coalition, completed President Arturo Frondizi's term, and President Arturo Illía followed him. His administration was brief, 1963–1966, but bright in terms of civil liberties, something little known by Argentines since 1930.

Into that landscape the historic and legendary Quintet of Astor Piazzolla was born. The country underwent an artistic revolution and discovered for the world *One Hundred Years of Solitude* by Gabriel García Márquez and the cinema of Ingmar Bergman. Argentina loved Federico Fellini and talked about a boom in South American literature. Plays by Harold Pinter were put on the stages of Buenos Aires while the Instituto Di Tella shook up the art world.

And Vittorio Gassman, in a celebrated moment on film, helped people laugh and talk about sex without the taboos in existence until then. It was in a scene in *Il sorpasso* by Dino Rissi that a lady, dancing very closely with Vittorio and feeling his charms, exhales an appreciative "oh-la-la," and Vittorio lowers his eyelids, raises his eyebrows, and offers his classic response, *"Modestamente"* [Modestly].

It was the decade of Pelé in his prime, a genius at soccer who, thankfully, did not go on about politics, religion, or drugs. He just played. That was all, and in the field he was a god.

These were years of intense and revealing polemics. In tango the argument was Troilo or Piazzolla. In cinema it was "Death to Lucas Demare; long live Leopoldo Torre Nilsson." On the larger national stage the challenge went all the way to Discépolo* and Luis Sandrini, a comic actor.

These were growing pains. Nations are not built in a day, a year, or a decade. Luckily, everything was questioned; everything was up for discussion. Thirty years later film directors Adolfo Aristarain and Eliseo Subiela, both fans of Piazzolla, celebrate Lucas Demare and Torre Nilsson. No one doubts Troilo and Piazzolla are key figures in the history of tango, and we know that without Armando Discépolo and Sandrini, an Argentine national theater would not exist.

The 1960s were lived intensely. Julio Cortázar and Marta Lynch led a new generation of writers. *Pajarito Gómez*, an essential film by Rodolfo Kuhn, premiered. Surrealism had a new flag: *Los compañeros* by Mario Monicelli. The moderns responded with Michelangelo Antonioni's *Blow Up*. The Beatles revolutionized popular music.

Many Argentines embraced the idea of change with conviction. Some lined up, without any guilt, out of snobbism. And Piazzolla knew about this bunk. In certain intellectual circles or in the financial establishment it was fashionable to say you'd go to hear his music. Astor allowed them into the orchestra seats. As the song would say, he needed not to be alone.

He was such an elite artist that he made the cover of a magazine, for the first time in his life, only on 25 May 1965. It was the now long-gone magazine *Primera Plana*, and not by chance. That publication, in language, style, and technique, also represented a turning point in Argentine cultural history. Many journalists working today are children of *Primera Plana*, as members of its newsroom or as readers (as was my case) who waited for every issue as if it would bring biblical

* Armando Discépolo (1887–1971): Author, composer, playwright, brother of Enrique Santos Discépolo.

truths. That cover seemed to put things in their proper place by saying simply, "Astor Piazzolla: The Music of Buenos Aires."

Those days were not Prague Spring. Then again the revolution was not in the streets as it was in Paris in 1968. These were hard times. Along with the new bright lights in the arts and sciences there were also mediocre artists like Palito Ortega and Leo Dan.

Also living under the protection of democratic rule were characters who undermined its very freedoms. Mariano Grondona, who later became a champion of democratic institutions, a welcome change, was then an aristocratic plotter against the legitimate administration of President Arturo Illía.

Culturally there were also outrages. At RCA Victor, a leading recording company of the day, a Colombian executive, Ricardo Mejía, sent to Buenos Aires by the headquarters and freshly installed in his position, would order, with absolute carelessness and ignorance, the destruction of master tapes that held Argentine musical treasures. There was no law on the books to stop him. In this way many recordings of the Alfredo Gobbi orchestra, for example, went into the trash can. It was years later, and by a miracle, according to guitarist Horacio Malvicino, that the original tapes of *Piazzolla at the Regina* were recovered.

Argentine popular music was in danger, unprotected for several reasons. First came an advance notice about globalization. The first product that crossed the oceans had a name that was short and punchy: *rock*. And second, besides being unprotected by laws, tango was paralyzed. The great creators of the 1940s were getting old, many had died, and others, like Troilo, were comfortable in their role as living legends.

It was in this context, still more favorable than the one that greeted the Octet in 1955, that the definitive lineup of the Quintet was born: bandoneon, electric guitar, piano, contrabass, and violin.

RCA opened its doors to Piazzolla but with one condition: to record an album of his own music he also had to record one that was more *tanguero*, with a more traditional repertoire. That's the reason for *Piazzolla bailable y apiazzollado* and *Piazzolla interpreta a Piaz-*

zolla. The former features Jaime Gosis (piano), Oscar López Ruiz (electric guitar), Kicho Díaz (contrabass), Elvino Vardaro (violin), and Piazzolla (bandoneon). In the latter, Simón Bajour replaced Vardaro and Horacio Malvicino took López Ruiz's place.

Against the opinion and the prediction of the company, the album with Piazzolla originals sold many more copies than the one with dance music. This was a personal triumph for Astor and a vital push to continue on his way.

Piazzolla interpreta a Piazzolla features some notable pieces, indispensable in any basic collection. The version of "Adiós Nonino" here has the freshness of the early arrangements; "Contrabajeando," another not-to-be-missed piece, is a compendium of everything Kicho Díaz could play in those days. It is only comparable to "Kicho," a piece that Astor would write eight years later.

Here one can also find "Calambre," a classic of the Quintet, and an incomparable version of "Lo que vendrá," unique in that no one in Piazzolla's career played the violin solo intro as Simón Bajour could do.

The other album, *Apiazzollado*, also has some musical riches. There are three pieces any Piazzolla fan can include in an anthology: "Chiqué," a piece by Brignolo* that Piazzolla used for many years as an encore in a joke on himself ("And now we are going to play a tango"); "Redención," a piece by Alfredo Gobbi at his best; and "Triunfal," in which the piano part by Jaime Gosis "sounds heavenly," as Astor would say of a Chopin sonata played by Arthur Rubinstein.

Piazzolla was a difficult character offstage. This is something acknowledged by people who were very close to him for many years. One need only to read the public statements of his son, Daniel, about the lack of communication and the fighting to get an idea of his father's personality.

He didn't have many friends. He had many acquaintances. And it is obvious that he knew almost all the musicians in tango history, the old ones as well as the new generation. In this landscape it is not

---

* Ricardo Luis Brignolo (1892–1953): Bandoneonist, composer, and bandleader.

hard to find caustic critics capable of repeating Pagani's un-Borges-like line word for word. Of course, it is also fair to ask how much of the rancor in these words is because of not having been selected to play with him. Or because, when the time came, they couldn't keep up with the hellish pace of a man who asked, wanted, and demanded from others things only he could do.

The artistic morality of Piazzolla was not that of a "son of a bitch." If he had stayed put, say, with his Quintet in *Piazzolla bailable y apiazzollado*, even today he would have been considered a successful *tanguero*. But he was a fighter. He took chances for his ideas. He didn't measure risk. First there was the music, then the money.

On a visit that friends and acquaintances made to the clinic where Piazzolla convalesced in Buenos Aires after his stroke of August 1990, I met Roberto Nievas, one of his representatives before Atilio Talín took over. The story Nievas told me is crystal clear and moving regarding Piazzolla's artistic principles.

Nievas said that a few weeks after forming the Quintet, at the beginning of the 1960s, he got a big offer to play the carnival dances at San Lorenzo de Almagro, an important soccer club. There was one condition: the organizers asked for Piazzolla to appear leading his 1946 Orchestra. Nievas passed along the request and was told no. There was no way to make Piazzolla change his mind. Nievas also told me that in those days, as in so many others in his life, he was not in a good financial situation. Only those with ill will could ever have accused Piazzolla of returning to the past, brief as it might have been, to remake what had been done, which in any case was good. He was going in one direction and did not want to lower the flag, not even for one week.

Any son of a bitch of the dimensions suggested by Pagani also would have profited from his experience with Carlos Gardel to the end of his days. And in Argentina we know a lot about this. Gardel has left many "widows" behind, the absence of a true will notwithstanding. Piazzolla did meet Gardel. A picture of them, and not one that happened by chance, united them for all time. He never thought of using the meeting for profit. He had everything served to him on a silver platter: Gardel could not challenge what he might say, the younger man's having walked the same tango circuits and having that photograph (from the film *El día que me quieras*, page 95) for which other *tangueros* would have given years of their lives. And yet Astor kept a low profile before Don Carlos, one of Nonino's idols—another strand for weaving a thousand fables. He told the story exactly as it happened. He respected the legend, and he especially respected himself.

Aldo Pagani is also a difficult character. In Punta del Este in March 1990, far from a tape recorder, Astor told me Pagani was a frustrated musician. He said Pagani had studied cello without much success, and apart from his peculiarities at the time of settling the accounting —a problem his heirs have also confronted, according to what they have said in several publications—there was a certain affection between them.

Astor acknowledged Pagani as a lifesaver at a difficult time in his life. On the other hand, when Pagani says, "Onstage he is God," he feels it. He is a true fan of Piazzolla's music. Of course, business is business, especially after Astor's death.

The last time I saw Pagani in Rome I asked him about a strange title I had seen, "Aconcagua," which he had used on a version of *Concierto para bandoneón y orquesta* recorded in Germany. And without moving a muscle in his face, he said it was so "because this is the peak of Astor's oeuvre, and the peak in South America is Aconcagua."* Pagani is no madman. He is quite a piece of work. *Aconcagua* is a hook to catch the naive fan who thinks he has discovered a new work.

The 1960s saw the best Astor Piazzolla, the best of Piazzolla the composer, that is. And just as he extended the 1940s in tango until 1955, his 1960s came to a turning point actually in 1975. It was a fifteen-year-long cycle that started with the formation of the Quintet and came to a close in three albums: *Libertango, Summit,* and *Suite Troileana.*

---

* Aconcagua: The highest peak of the Andes and of the Western Hemisphere, located in western Argentina near the Chilean border.

In this period Piazzolla wrote the bulk of an oeuvre still not surpassed by any other Argentine musician, popular or erudite. In fact,
in the last years of his musical life Piazzolla set out to recreate everything he had written in the '60s, as if he was updating and making a
clear copy of his life's work. Thus *La camorra*, especially the piece
"La camorra I," suggests a perfect tango testament. Besides, it is the
last recording by the Quintet (chance?) and it is recorded in New
York (chance?), the city where Astor grew up and began thinking
about his life.

From 1975 to the end, the peak moments of the composer are few:
the soundtracks for the films *El infierno tan temido*, *El exilio de Gardel*, and *Sur*; the album with Gary Burton; passages in *Tango apasionado* and *La camorra*; and pieces such as "Libertango," "Mumuki," "Tanguedia," "Biyuya," "Vuelvo al sur," "Regreso al amor,"
and especially "Oblivion," which is as beloved around the world as
"Adiós Nonino."

It's important to insist that this Piazzolla the composer, Piazzolla
the player, like Gardel's singing, plays better every day. With his second Quintet, Astor seems to be flying over his old scores with a different poetry. He also arranges old pieces and writes new ones
around old ideas. Knowingly or not, he is returning to his sources, as
if in a perfect tale.

Listening to "La camorra I," one has the feeling of hearing the
orchestras of Alfredo Gobbi and Aníbal Troilo—and, of course, the
Astor Piazzolla Quintet. This is not a figure of speech. As Roberto Di
Filippo and Leopoldo Federico say in "My Crazy Bandoneon," "Piazzolla's musical knowledge made it possible for the Quintet to sound
like a twenty-piece orchestra." Horacio Malvicino, another very *tanguero* character who took part in these recordings, has a similar feeling about "La camorra I."

In Piazzolla's home in Punta del Este in March 1990 during a
pause in our taping, listening to the piece, I asked Astor about a noise
that comes out of his throat (his soul?). The cry is a rare mix of
fatigue and ecstasy that can be heard clearly in the middle of a dazzling jam. He answered me with a characteristic line that reflected his

pride and his joy for having reached such a musical level with the Quintet. "I left my lungs in that recording," he said. That was Piazzolla. That's the way he was until 4 August 1990.

Each album after those first two of RCA Victor that opened the 1960s became a landmark in his history. Each album features two or three anthological pieces, an irresistible climb toward his peak, *María de Buenos Aires* (1968). It was a creative period that continued until his Nonet. Astor acknowledges this when he says, "*María de Buenos Aires* and the Nonet had left my head full of music."

In *Nuestro tiempo* (1962) he featured two pieces from the "Ángel" series: "Introducción" and "Muerte." Here the thread begins. In the slang of musicians and of many Argentines, it is called *yeite*, the equivalent of a "lick" that strings ideas together. Piazzolla was no exception. When some say of him—sometimes in bad faith—that he wrote the same tango two thousand times, they make a grave conceptual error. The truth is that there are two thousand moments of a life's work that, like any creative product, has its ups and downs.

Tango para una ciudad (1963) features the first version of Piazzolla's all-time classic, "Buenos Aires hora cero." And there is more: "Revirado" and "Fracanapa."

20 años de Vanguardia (1964) features two pieces that reappeared many times in his repertoire: "Lunfardo" and "Bandoneón, guitarra, y bajo." Besides, the Buenos Aires Octet reappears, if only in the studio, playing "Tango ballet," a piece that returned to the bandstand in 1989 in an arrangement for the Sextet.

Concierto en el Philharmonic Hall de New York (1965) seems to herald the upcoming peaks. For the first time a Piazzolla LP is pure Piazzolla, from the first to the last piece. It includes the "Diablo" series, "Todo Buenos Aires," "La mufa," and a piece that is crucial in Piazzolla's oeuvre, "Milonga del ángel."

That 1965 album shows the power Piazzolla was carrying around in his *sesera* [noggin], an ugly word, an academic would say, but well worn by Piazzolla perhaps as a bad habit from the 1940s when it was common in *porteño* slang. This was the year of *El tango*, the enormous work left behind by Borges and Piazzolla, and this was also the year of the first recording of "Verano porteño" perhaps the number two piece for Piazzolla fans only after "Adiós Nonino."

Then *María de Buenos Aires* finally arrived in 1968. It was a great artistic and critical success. But as if to underscore the fact that the feared critics do not write history, it was a box-office failure. That meant a financial disaster, especially for Piazzolla who had taken a big personal risk.

It was said then that the poetry of Horacio Ferrer was to tango lyrics what Piazzolla's music was to tango. The idea of the *operita*, the "little opera," as they called it, seems to me, even today, as bold as it is light. Piazzolla was reaching his creative heights. As Quito González Azcona, a fan and a Piazzolla scholar, used to say, "*María de Buenos Aires* does not need lyrics: you can understand it just by listening to the music." It is an opinion I fully share.

Ferrer was at the beginning of a career as a poet, a career that would later have notable moments in Piazzolla's music, but writing "short," writing songs. *María de Buenos Aires* should have been the culmination of the collaboration between Piazzolla and Ferrer. Ten years later, musician and poet were *jugando de taquito*,* such was the artistic understanding between them. That would have been the proper time for them to try an *operita*, but destiny had it the other way around.

Artistic society would have its revenge a year later—especially for Ferrer—with the success of "Balada para un loco." As an extraordinary symbol in the history of tango, to talk about the craziness of love the expression would no longer be "*rechiflao en mi tristeza*," but Ferrer's line, "*piantao, piantao, piantao*."** This was the second tango revolution Piazzolla was part of, this time with tango song, tango with lyrics, and this time luck coddled him.

---

*Jugando de taquito: Playing more or less by memory, by feel, the soccer equivalent of basketball's no-look passes.

***Rechiflao en mi tristeza*: Roughly, mad in my sadness, from the lyrics of a classic tango.

Piantao, piantao, piantao: Kooky, kooky, kooky.

His encounter with Ferrer was epochal in the history of popular music in the Rio de la Plata. As always, voices were raised to disqualify Piazzolla-Ferrer's tango until singer Roberto Goyeneche put things in their proper place, and no one from tango's conservative fringe bothered again.

It happened days after the world premiere of "Balada" by Amelita Baltar (at the Buenos Aires Song Festival at Luna Park, 1969). When asked if "Balada" was a tango, Goyeneche narrowed his eyes, searched in his book of *porteño* sayings, and settled the issue with one line: "*No, que va a ser un tango: es un tangazo!*"*

"Balada" is still rolling around in the world, like the moon down the avenue in Ferrer's lyrics, but Piazzolla-Ferrer left behind a repertoire that is far from being exhausted. It includes "Balada para mi muerte," "Chiquilín de Bachín," "La última grela," "Preludio para el año 3001," "La bicicleta blanca," "El Gordo triste," "Mi loco bandoneón," "Bocha," and "Milonga del trovador," and this is only a partial list. These are songs just as rich as or richer than "Balada," sometimes because of the music, sometimes the lyrics. But the public said "Balada," and popular taste often rules.

Piazzolla's head was full of music, and the quality of his work kept rising. After the "small opera," Piazzolla released a historical album titled *Adiós Nonino* (1969), the one with the black cover. It includes such classics as "Otoño porteño," the second part of the "Four Seasons" series; "Tangata"; and "Coral," a favorite piece of guitarist Oscar López Ruiz.

"Coral," a very difficult work, intellectual, not at all commercial, was like a rebel flag. That line, "Screw the people and let's play what we musicians like," a direct Piazzolla quote, was heard a lot behind closed doors with the first Quintet.

In this approach Piazzolla had the solid support of López Ruiz, who encouraged him to play that part of the repertoire. But the guitarist's influence also seemed to bother the other musicians. Bassist Kicho

---

* No, what do you mean it's a tango: it's a hell of a tango!

Díaz once told me that, in his opinion, one of Piazzolla's worst defects was how easy it was to manipulate his decisions. And in this, he pointed squarely to "the kid" López Ruiz. (López Ruiz was in his thirties.) "One time," he recalled, "I said to him, half jokingly, half seriously, 'Astor, for everything you do, you check first with this punk?' "

Kicho, who admired Piazzolla as a musician, was not the first, nor the last, to point out such a weakness in his character. Kicho also accused him of being an ingrate. "For Piazzolla, his musicians are the best in the world—as long as we are up there onstage with him," he said.

> But if one day, to be able to work, we decide we need a change of atmosphere, we instantly become a piece of shit. It happened to me. It happened to Antonio Agri. And I know of many faithful friends, such as Miguelito Selinger, who one day were pushed aside, I am sure, because someone filled Astor's head with trash. All those things pain me a lot. While I played with him, the phone rang all the time. After I joined the Sexteto Mayor I never heard from him again. He didn't call me even when I had a serious illness. All's forgotten onstage. There he is one of a kind—and I have played with all the greats.

Adiós Nonino is the only appearance of pianist Dante Amicarelli in Piazzolla's discography, but this is a high-voltage album, very demanding, because Astor wrote one of his best arrangements of "Adiós Nonino" for this recording.

The opening cadence played by Amicarelli has a story behind it, again told to me by Miguelito Selinger, that shows what might go into the making of a musical jewel. Amicarelli was not only a talented player but also a craftsman who could sight read the most demanding score. This seems to have hurt Piazzolla's pride, so one day, according to Selinger, Piazzolla called and said, "Come with me to Amicarelli's house. I wrote an arrangement of 'Adiós Nonino' for him that's going to lay him flat on his back. If he can sight read that, I'll slit my wrists."

They got there, Amicarelli took the score, set it on the piano, took a look, turned to Piazzolla, and said "Nice little arrangement"—little arrangement?!—and began to play it without missing a note. Piazzolla did want to slit his wrists. Luckily he didn't.

In the history of the Quintet there are two cadenzas for "Adiós Nonino": Amicarelli's and the one played by Ziegler in the second Quintet. Whether this was because the first one got lost or Piazzolla simply wanted a new one has never been clear to me. But they are different. The former sounds more *tanguera*, Ziegler's more technical. Both are impeccable, to be savored.

The quantity and the quality of Piazzolla's writing in those days was amazing. *Piazzolla en el Regina*, his first live album, features the debut of "Invierno porteño" and "Primavera porteña," closing the "Four Seasons" cycle. Also on that album are two pieces that would become important in his repertoire: "Retrato de Alfredo Gobbi" and "Kicho."

A year later he recorded the soundtrack for the film *Con alma y vida* by David Kohon, which comes with a footnote. From the frenetic tango, danceable and down-and-dirty, dedicated to the male character, el Flaco Aroldi, will later come the finale of *Concierto para bandoneón y orquesta*.

In 1970 he also recorded "Pulsación," a more intellectual attempt to put music to an art-documentary film directed by Carlos Paez Vilaró, so bad, apparently, that it has never been seen in Argentina, nor anywhere else in the world for that matter. Not even the music saved it.

Concierto para quinteto (1971) was the farewell on record to the first Quintet, a short intermezzo in the story. The Nonet was about to be born, named Conjunto 9 (Ensemble 9) by Astor in a rare moment of artistic self-consciousness. The same man who had overcome so many barriers once told me he had chosen Conjunto 9 "to avoid the kidding" that the classical-sounding name Nonet might bring; a tango group had never been called that before.

For some very respected Piazzollaphiles, the Nonet is the peak of Piazzolla's history, an idea supported by the second of the two albums recorded for RCA in 1972. It features pianist Osvaldo Tarantino who adds an energizing tango swing. Astor decided to dissolve the Nonet strictly for economic reasons. Without the funding provided by the City of Buenos Aires, which had helped found it, the group was impossible to maintain.

The two albums contribute some remarkable pieces to the story: "Tristezas de un Doble A"; "Vardarito"; a new arrangement of "Verano porteño," the best in Piazzolla's history; a new version of "Buenos Aires hora cero"; "Onda 9"; and at a lower level, "Oda para un hippie."

The Nonet also left behind some stories. "Vardarito" and "Verano porteño" were recorded with a Stradivarius violin that the great Italian violinist Salvatore Accardi lent Antonio Agri for that purpose. The gesture confirms Vinicius de Moraes's comment about what Piazzolla meant to great artists around the world. To Agri in particular it represented the acknowledgment of a prestigious colleague. What Accardi never knew—and Oscar López Ruiz tells the story with great humor—is that the Stradivarius, a priceless instrument, traveled to Agri's house in the Buenos Aires suburb of Adrogué one night in Agri's cheap and very suspect Citroen 2CV.

"Tristezas de un Doble A," contrary to what many might think, is not a meditation on the bandoneon brand used by most of the great players throughout tango's history. The notion indeed seems plausible after the arrangement for the second Quintet in which Astor's long improvisation seems to summon Troilo, Maffia, and Laurenz. But one afternoon back in the 1970s Horacio Ferrer told me that "Tristezas de un Doble A," the one written for the Nonet, had nothing to do with the instrument made by the Germans. Double A was Astor and Amelita, Amelita and Astor, wrapped in the sadness of a fight like the ones they used to have in those days. Following the melody, again in the Nonet version, the sadness suggests how true Ferrer's idea might be.

The story also says that *Concierto de nácar para nueve tanguistas y orquesta* was born on a night that was darker than dark. In the early morning of 22 August 1972 there was a bloody event in Argentine history that came to be known as the Trelew Massacre. That night it was the theme of conversation for everybody in the halls of the Teatro Coliseo where Piazzolla, the Nonet, and the Ensamble Musical conducted by Pedro Ignacio Calderón were to debut the work.

It was a tragic day, forever seared in the consciousness of Argentines. Investigations years later proved that it was not the result of a bloody escape attempt by a group of guerrilla fighters, as the military regime claimed at the time, but a true massacre.

Despite this beginning, however, *Concierto de nácar* took its place artistically among the best of Piazzolla's oeuvre. As he said, in those years his head was "full of music."

As in later versions, most notably the one at Teatro Colón on 11 June 1983 with the Philharmonic, the strings of the Ensemble did nothing more than frame the musicians of the Nonet, who offered a master class. The third and final section of *Concierto de nácar* shows how far Piazzolla's creativity reached in those days, what went through his mind and reached the music stands. It is a waterfall of notes, sounds that disperse and come together in a beautiful, explosive musical discourse, crying that the best Piazzolla is right in front of the Argentines. Of course, Astor would have to pay a price for it.

After the Nonet was dissolved there was a brief return to the Quintet, but a big event awaited Piazzolla and it was not about music. Around the corner, in 1973, he bumped into a thug that was not in any Borges story. He had a heart attack.

Piazzolla was running his life at three hundred miles an hour. In the preceding ten years he had written his best works, and he had played everything himself. He smoked an average of a hundred cigarettes a day. Amelita, his companion, was at that time starring in a Broadway-style extravaganza called *Tres mujeres para el show*, also featuring top singers Marikena Monti and Susana Rinaldi. She was making more money than he was. For an artist like Piazzolla, for a *tano* like Astor Pantaleón, brought up on fistfights in Little Italy in New York, this was a blow to his pride. Damn. And if this was not enough, his relationship with Amelita was faltering. From where they were to the final breakup was not a long road.

Astor could not complain. The bell rang on the right door. López Ruiz insists this change marked his life forever. "Ever since, he was not the same," he said.

Regarding Piazzolla, the composer, the observation seems to the point. Regarding the man, the character, the warrior, it is a different story. Piazzolla was several years past his fiftieth birthday, had a scar over his heart, and still he started a European adventure called for by Aldo Pagani's contract. He left Buenos Aires in 1974 with no money in the bank, and after returning from another blow, the one of 1990 to the brain, the one that was terminal, he left behind his name in the music books of the world. He also left behind a solid financial situation. Just from the royalties collected by the French society SACEM, his heirs receive around four hundred thousand dollars annually. The heirs are his widow, Laura Escalada, and his children, Diana and Daniel.

Lidia Pugliese, widow of Osvaldo, once told me a story about that tireless and vital Piazzolla. They were at a rehearsal in Amsterdam in 1989, one of the few times they shared a stage. Osvaldo worried as he watched Piazzolla run up and down the theater checking the sound and the set. "So finally," recalled Lidia, "Osvaldo calls him and says: 'Astor, why are you running so much? It's not good for you. We are grown men. C'mon, sit here, let's have a coffee.' Astor listened to him—for about ten minutes. We saw he was very nervous."

The stories about love belong to Piazzolla, and he was generous with his privacy. I just want to add two events to what he has already said and to the letter excerpted in chapter 10 in which Astor contradicts himself, although everything is understandable when one talks about love.

On his return from his first period in Europe (late 1974), he brought two albums in his suitcase—*Libertango* and *Summit*, the latter made with Gerry Mulligan—which had not yet been released in Argentina. A group of friends and acquaintances went to the airport to receive him. There were hugs, small talk, and a caravan of cars to Callao and Santa Fe, to a restaurant across the street from the Wilton Palace Hotel where he was staying.

Astor was anxious and kept looking at his watch. He seemed unable to stay in his chair. Someone, naively, not knowing where his head was at, was asking about the new version of "Adiós Nonino" (on *Libertango*, the Italian version) in which he had superimposed several bandoneon tracks for the first time.

Experience I. Technique? What technique?

Astor didn't make it to the after-lunch coffee. He picked up his Italian bag, put it over his shoulder, and headed to Riobamba and Arenales, where Amelita Baltar lived. That was what was going through the head of this jealous, hurting, *tano*. He was still looking for an explanation for why Amelita had slammed the door behind her and had left him in Rome, alone, with his music and the inopportune calls of Aldo Pagani who every day wanted to check on his investment.

Amelita was Piazzolla's great love affair.

Everything had a high price for Piazzolla, even death. That's why, with great respect, choosing my words carefully, I want to say that his true friends heard the news of his death with pain and relief. The agony was over.

Piazzolla nearly died in the Aerolíneas Argentinas plane that brought him and his breath-support equipment from Paris, such was the gravity of his condition. Astor, the true one, had been left behind in Paris, forever, on 4 August 1990. The news of 4 July 1992 only fulfilled what history had dictated.

One spring afternoon in Buenos Aires on a sunny terrace at ALPI, the Argentine association against paralysis, on the corner of Salguero and Soler where Astor was rehabilitating, his son, Daniel, Miguel Selinger, Quito González Azcona, Víctor Oliveros, Kiko Salvo (another great fan), and I began arguing with the passion of so many years.

Some spoke of the first Quintet or the second. Some said Agri, others Suárez Paz, Gosis, or Ziegler, the fear of Luna Park, the Buenos Aires Octet, this arrangement of "Adiós Nonino" or that. In the middle of that group, listening without listening, watching without watching, sat Astor Piazzolla in a wheelchair. Suddenly the words made no sense. We fell silent. It was a moment as terrible as it was magical, supreme, unforgettable. We all knew that it was time for the penultimate goodbye.

Experience II. I returned many times to several hospitals, and only once did I see a sign of life in his eyes. On a Saturday morning I found him sitting in a wheelchair in a corridor of Sanatorio Lesit. I said hello, sat on the floor right beside him, and talked to him. It was all in vain. Astor seemed concerned only by one thing, the noise of the elevator's metal doors, until on one of those trips the elevator brought Laura Escalada. Then I saw a spark of happiness. It was the only time.

Laura Escalada gave Piazzolla peace. She was his last love. She helped him organize his affairs, conquer the world with his music, find economic stability. Laura Escalada "was the best thing that could have happened to me," he says in this book.

We last spoke on 24 June 1990. Astor was in Paris, living in an apartment at Résidence Orion at Les Halles, a few yards from Pompidou Center, close to the Seine and the Louvre, a marvelous place to feel Paris. I was in Milan in the middle of the World Cup. I called him from the Giuseppe Meazza Stadium before a Germany-Holland match. We joked about our cities brought together by phone: "Let's see which one is uglier." I reminded him that we had an appointment in Buenos Aires in September to complete the "Bandoneon" chapter. He surprised me with a question to be answered by the expert (in this case, me): "Do we win today?" he asked.

In Turin, Argentina was about to play Brazil, but I couldn't imagine Astor glued to the television to watch soccer. He didn't understand the first thing about it. He was a street kid from New York where soccer was then as alien as the bandoneon his father gave him. I told him it was a difficult game, a way of saying nothing really. He responded by saying, "Maradona will win it."

And that's how it was. Argentina won thanks to a brilliant play by Diego Maradona turned into a goal by Claudio Caniggia. Astor had been right not for being a soccer-wise man but because he was a fan of number 10, Maradona. He admitted that he watched because of him.

Of course, we also talked about music. I told him I had seen a poster announcing a concert in Varese on 19 July—Astor canceled for health reasons—with the Mantova String Quartet. On the same

A poster announced Piazzolla's forthcoming appearance on 19 July 1990 with the Mantova String Quartet in Varese, Italy, along with legendary jazz musicians he greatly admired, but his health prevented him from doing it.

bill there were such greats as Wayne Shorter, Miles Davis, Michel Camilo, Tito Puente, and Dizzy Gillespie. And he told me, with customary excitement but his voice weakened, that he was about to record *Suite Punta del Este*. He never fulfilled his wish.

(Once Piazzolla died, good ol' Pagani, listening to his pocket, put out a version of *Suite Punta del Este* that is technically horrible. It was recorded live with minimal equipment at a Piazzolla performance in Caracas, and if that was not insult enough, the first bars are missing. The best version of *Suite Punta del Este* is by Camerata Bariloche featuring as soloist Daniel Binelli, the premier bandoneonist of his generation.)

To that memory of our last talk, of appearances canceled for health reasons, one must now add the words of Anahí Carfi, and the question remains: why was Piazzolla working in 1990? The answer lies with that man who never gave up, not even when wounded. If there are other reasons, only those closest to him in Paris know what they are.

Author Natalio Gorin with Diana Piazzolla, Astor's daughter, Víctor Oliveros, president of the Centro Astor Piazzolla, and Daniel Piazzolla, Astor's son, on 9 June 1995.

Sometimes I think his tale is nearly perfect. And if at one time the news was a relief, now I can feel his absence. Videos and records are not enough. I miss Piazzolla. That old ritual was unique: Piazzolla nailing his left leg to the floor, placing the black box over his right knee, a black box that was not about death but about life. Then he'd put his left hand up in the air, counting the beats for the *alevare*, and then came the magic of his music.

Up on the stage he was a god. Off it he was a human being like everyone else. He was born in Mar del Plata but loved other cities: New York, Paris, Buenos Aires. The tale closes almost perfectly. The Quintet's last rehearsal was in Buenos Aires (at Sham's, April 1988); its last recording was in New York (*La camorra*, May 1988; released 1989).

He was so different from the rest that he didn't stop dying. He died in Paris on 4 August 1990, and he died in Buenos Aires on 4 July 1992.

Some say this line is by Pablo Picasso, he of the blues and the browns: "It is enough, isn't it? What else is there left for me to do? What could I add? Everything has been said." It could have been signed by another genius, Astor Piazzolla.

Piazzolla, center, with poet and lyricist Horacio Ferrer and singer Amelita Baltar at the club Michelangelo in Buenos Aires, 1970.

Milonga for Four

Classical and universal music

HORACIO FERRER

In my adolescence when I met Piazzolla, the dominant ideas about the future of tango held by critics, musicologists, music historians, and concert audiences were contradictory, diffuse, and discouraging. Prestigious researchers and thinkers, Carlos Vega and Lauro Ayestarán among them, divided music into two fields, "classical" and "folk."

The first category included, by their criteria, works by such artists as Beethoven, Mozart, Verdi, Ginastera, or Fabini. The second included traditional pieces by anonymous composers. Between them was an indeterminate area they called "mesomusic," into which flow the derivatives of classical styles and the higher forms of folkloric invention. According to such criteria, tango is "mesomusic."

Since the mid 1930s, the period in which Vega and Ayestarán stated their theories, Cátulo Castillo, a young poet and tango musician, predicted that the future tango-song would be as refined as a *lied*, a chamber song. A Cátulo contemporary, Vinicius de Moraes, included among his complete works a group of *cancoes de camara*, chamber songs, with music by Claudio Santoro, separate from his "popular songs."

Milonga: Originally a genre of South American songs in question-and-answer format, the *milonga* is also an Argentine ballroom dance that preceded the tango in the early twentieth century.

In this conceptual landscape Astor Piazzolla began his life as a composer. In the summer of 1956 in Mar del Plata, in his own hand, he wrote me a list, which I have kept, of his classical pieces written since 1944 and numbered from Opus 1, Suite for Harp and Strings, onward.

His tangos, those already premiered with his orchestra, such as "Se armó," "El desbande," "Villeguita," or those played by Troilo, Fresedo, Basso, and Francini-Pontier, tangos such as "Para lucirse," "Prepárense," "Lo que vendrá," "Contratiempo," "Triunfal," were not on his list of works, this even though Aaron Copland praised the high class and polyrhythmic complexity of Piazzolla's orchestra, which he had seen and heard at Tango Bar on Corrientes Avenue.

In the musical environment, in the general teachings, in the conservatories, there was a segregation that remains unchallenged. That's why certain musicians and poets working in the popular field hope to enjoy erudite, cultivated, learned recognition. This is the same recognition denied not only to tango people but also to creators

---

Horacio Ferrer

Born in Montevideo, Uruguay, in 1933, Horacio Ferrer is a poet, lyricist, and distinguished author of ten books on the history of tango, most notably *El libro del tango: Arte popular de Buenos Aires*. In 1954 he founded the Club de la Guardia Nueva (New Guard Club) in Buenos Aires. Named illustrious Citizen of Buenos Aires, he also received the highest honor awarded by the Argentine Society of Authors and Composers.

"Horacio Ferrer is the best poet I ever had with me," Piazzolla said, and the work they created together was among Piazzolla's most famous. Ferrer also collaborated with Charles Aznavour, Julio De Caro, Roberto Grela, Mariano Mores, Osvaldo Pugliese, Horacio Salgán (*Oratorio Carlos Gardel*), Héctor Stamponi, Osvaldo Tarantino, Aníbal Troilo, and others. He founded and is president of the Academia Nacional del Tango in Buenos Aires.

such as the Cubans Armando and Chiquito Oréfiche, the Brazilian Arturo Dantas, or the virtuoso Andalusians working in Spanish song. In those days, at a bar across the street from Radio El Mundo, I heard an arranger of commercial orchestras say, "Listening to tango is like dirtying your hands with grease from a truck."

These are small resentments, family grudges and attitudes, because by then the originality of tango and its orchestras had been recognized by Rubinstein, Toscanini, García Lorca, de Falla, and Khachaturian, among other creators.

The year before our summertime together, Astor had arrived by boat from France with his wife, the painter Dedé Wolff. It was a rainy night and I had waited for him at Montevideo's port. Afterward he came to the cellar of the Club de la Guardia Nueva, where he premiered some of the tangos he had written and recorded in Paris—"Sens unique," "Río Sena," "Bando," and others.

That night and on many others we talked about the future and the fate of tango. He told me, with pride, of the lessons he learned from Madame Nadia Boulanger and the extended conversations after class. In particular he told me about the day in which he presents himself as a classical composer and she intuits his pedigree and his popular sensibility. And, because he's Argentine, she asks him to play one of his tangos. Astor plays "Triunfal," and the eminent teacher advises him never to leave the popular path, and to grow with his own tango.

A short time later and following her advice, Piazzolla creates and leads the Buenos Aires Octet. At his request I had to introduce the first concert by the Octet, to my mind the most revolutionary orchestra in the whole tango epic.

Astor has changed course. He would not dream of being the "classical" composer in a remote, romantic chalet by the ocean writing symphonic opuses. His great heart beat with absolute clarity: the way is not to grow outside but inside tango, being up onstage with his *fueye* of ten lungs, challenging, seducing, and fighting with the people whose lives he enriches—in spite of themselves.

Agustín Carlevaro, an unforgettable friend and guitar teacher, argued that the only rating possible in the music world would be "short music" and "long music," meaning quality pieces short or more developed, each in its own style just as beautiful: "Responso" by Troilo and "Bolero" by Ravel, Enrique Delfino's "Griseta" by the Astor Piazzolla orchestra and a long waltz by Chopin.

One night at the Teatro Coliseo in Buenos Aires, before the premiere of one of his "long" pieces, Astor told me: "We the café guys have won," alluding to his history as director of an *orquesta típica*. I also remember Astor, when both of us were in Madrid, buying clothes in the most elegant shops of La Gran Via and Virgen de los Peligros Street. I remember he picked a black overcoat with velvet lapels and his comment was "This is to *cajetillar** by night in Buenos Aires."

He was a café and late-night man, and that was the material of which "Buenos Aires hora cero," "Lunfardo," "Decarísimo," "Retrato de Alfredo Gobbi," and "Balada para mi muerte" are made.

The early morning light terrified him because he was a first-rate worker, a musical fountainhead that needed every hour of his day at the piano. There he would compose, writing the notes with his left hand with a stunning certainty and speed.

In 1971 while we were at Saarbrücken negotiating the television premiere of an oratorio we had written that year in Paris, a musical analyst at the station was examining the score for *María de Buenos Aires*, the little opera we had written earlier. With a disdainful gesture he said, "This is not avant garde music."

Then very angry and beating on the originals with his hands, Piazzolla screamed indignantly, "It might not be avant garde, sir, but it is mine, all mine, all of it, all written by me!" From then on, when he and his groups stop playing the music of his favorite composers in favor of his own music, Astor and his stubborn inspiration enhance nightclubs, stadiums, concert halls, and theaters without the old prejudice of his music as symphonic or tango.

---

* *Cajetillar: Cajetilla* is slang for dandy, so *cajetillar* can be understood as "to play the dandy."

Each of his ideas, each of his feelings, finds the length and instrumentation it deserves. Whether pieces for solo guitar, his formidable solo cadenzas for bandoneon (as in "Tristezas de un Doble A," "Le grand tango" for bandoneon and cello, and other duets), his series *The History of Tango*, "La camorra" in its several versions, *Suite Punte del Este*, his *Concierto de nácar para nueve tanguistas y orquesta*, and his *Concierto para bandoneón y orquesta*—it was all first rate art, romantic, bohemian, confidential, delicate, *porteño, rioplatense,** and universal, sentimental, superfriend, and supra*tanguero*.

For forty years of the second half of the twentieth century, the genius of Astor Piazzolla reorganizes and moves past old concepts and prejudices to clear away all doubt. It is the venerable formula, Astor Piazzolla and tango, following the wise advice of Madame Boulanger and made true by his venturesome and unfairly tragic destiny. That tango future so seductive and triumphant, sensed so many times, turned out to be in the three thousand compositions he revealed to us.

In essence then, if classic is what remains as a model and universal is what belongs to everyone for all time, Piazzolla's tango is universal and classical music even if he called it "music of cafés," a creation immortal and luminous nonetheless, like a star that has become substance in the sounds of the soul.

* *Rioplatense*: From the Río de la Plata.

The last tour

Anahí Carfi

I knew Astor Piazzolla from the time I lived in Argentina, and I always liked him as a musician. I consider him a classical musician not just because he studied with teachers like Alberto Ginastera or Nadia Boulanger, but also because of the feelings his musical language prompts in me.

In 1987, many years after we had met, guitarist Marco De Santi called me to do a concert with the Italian Society of Chamber Music orchestra in which I was the first violin. The program included, among other works, *Suite Punta del Este* for bandoneon and orchestra and the *Concierto para bandoneón, guitarra, y orquesta*, both by Piazzolla. The composer himself was going to participate.

As can be imagined, I accepted, ecstatic. The concert was held at the Sala Verdi of the Milan Conservatory and was very successful. Afterward we repeated it at Mantova. After that my relationship with Piazzolla, which until then had been just professional, became a friendly exchange of ideas and sensations.

He confessed he wanted to start a new stage in his artistic career. He wanted to take the classical approach to his music making, with small chamber groups. His idea was not to play again with a group and never to play again in stadiums where amplification was needed. Because he needed a classical string quartet and I directed one, the Mantova String Quartet, we decided to play together.

To organize our work we got together at cellist Marco Spano's house in Milan. There we decided to play a program that featured in the first half a string quartet by Ginastera and "Four for Tango" by Piazzolla and then in the second half, with Piazzolla, "Five Tango Sensations" and "Adiós Nonino."

We started a tour that took us through several cities in Italy and Finland. At first we felt a bit intimidated by his presence, but soon he demonstrated that he was a person with a sweet temperament—I

Anahí Carfi was born in Buenos Aires. She began her violin studies with her father, Humberto Carfi, and continued her training with Zino Francescatti and in Italy with Maestro Sergio Lorenzi of the Chigiana de Siena Academy. Since 1973 she has been first violin at the Teatro de la Scala orchestra in Milan.

never saw him angry, just always ready to play. Besides he was excited by the idea of making music in a different way than he had been.

For us, for our quartet, it was a marvelous experience that left a deep imprint in our souls. In time Astor Piazzolla, that great figure in music, seemed just one of us.

After the first concerts he started to feel tired. His wife, Laura Escalada, acknowledged that Astor was not in good health and that the last tests didn't have good results, so much so that the doctors advised him to stop playing and rest, something she also wished for him. And yet the tour took place. When we got to the last concerts, Astor asked us to reinforce our parts so as to make his participation less taxing.

Looking back at that period, in the creative stage he was going through, I think the repertoire we picked did not consider which audience would come. These people expected the Piazzolla of the Quintet, and against their expectations, they would find a more intimate artist who played half a concert of a more classical repertoire.

The situation created some problems. In some cases the police had to intervene because of the protests and the violent audience reaction. To calm the waters, one time Astor decided to satisfy his fans by playing a twenty-minute cadenza in "Adiós Nonino." He reached such heights of inspiration that it was hard for us, when the time came, to re-enter, take our place and continue the piece. We felt as though we were in another world. The success was deafening.

Yet Piazzolla insisted that the audience had to understand that he was changing. I also think now we didn't appear in the best possible places: these were stadiums or theaters not appropriate for chamber music. Astor, as I have said, was not in good health. But he kept saying, "As long as I'm alive, I'll keep playing." We know now that his new musical life was short.

I feel honored to have been artistically and personally close to him in the final part of his intense artistic life. I can say that he shared the last artistic emotions onstage with us, the Mantova String Quartet, and that we helped him live his new creative intentions. At almost seventy, he had started another battle: to make music that would be played in concert halls.

Piazzolla already has a place among the greats in history.

I never gave him away for free.
ATILIO TALÍN

I met him in the early 1960s at the Club Jamaica, a dive where Astor and his Quintet played four sets a night. I went there as a fan. I was even wary of talking to him, fearing the disillusionment one's idols often cause up close. For all us fans, which in truth were just a few, Astor was a figure up there, on an altar.

One of those nights Astor stopped to take a look at my car, parked across the street from the Jamaica. "Don't tell me you like cars, too," I said, and we started talking. He was a very sweet guy, but at the same time he was always on guard. And he had good reasons for it: he was attacked a lot. Perhaps because of this he had few friends throughout his life. One day he asked me, a bit chagrined, "Atilio, I'm going on tour and I need a proxy, a representative to care for the little that I have. Can I count on you?" He asked for my identification card number and wrote a very short power of attorney. Before he signed it I asked him, "Astor, why me? There are other great people who can do the same, such as Natalio Echegaray who is a notary public."

He responded with one of those very direct lines he used to use: "I didn't ask you if you knew somebody. I chose you." I became his representative and I did it *ad honorem* to the last day.

Soon after our first arrangement when he came back from a tour, the business relationship expanded. He said, "Atilio, I am being very unfair with you. You take care of my things, and others make the money. Wouldn't you also like to be my artistic manager?" He didn't ask me if I accepted the offer or not. Astor was like that. He assumed I did with another line: "I only ask you one thing. You know a lot about cars: sell me like a Mercedes; never give me away for free."

I honored his request. Astor went on tour in Japan, for example,

Atilio Talín was Astor Piazzolla's friend and served as his manager and agent for twenty years. With business interests in real estate and automobiles, Talín is also on the board of the Fundación Nuevo Tango.

making more, but much more, than other musicians did. I didn't give him away. It was something that was not hard to do. When I said Piazzolla was the best popular musician, it wasn't a sales pitch. I was saying what I believed in my heart. And that line about him being the best popular musician in the world was not my invention: many people who know about such things believed it then and believe it now.

As a manager, I received ten percent of the Quintet's fee plus another ten percent of Astor's fee and another percentage, between fifteen and twenty percent, for other contracts such as those for film music. Because the arrangement was a bit complicated, one day I told him, "Astor, let's write this down somewhere, just in case something happens to us." His response: "*Che*, you do bother a lot with these things." So he picked up a sheet of music paper, wrote down everything we had agreed on, and signed it—right on the score paper. That was all there was between us. We never had an argument about

Piazzolla with manager Atilio Talín waiting for a press conference to begin in November 1976. Photo by Ángel Rainoldi

a penny, and Astor was no dummy about numbers. My intention
was that he not get into economics. One person worrying about
money was enough. That was my role. Astor had to concentrate only
on his music, which was his great passion. And for that passion, we
should not forget, he even forgot his family.

The second power of attorney he gave me was so broad that other
managers tried to use it as a model with their charges, but their
artists did not allow it. That underscores how much trust Astor had
in me. When he was declared incapacitated by the judge, at the request of his wife, Laura Escalada, those powers were nullified. The
transfer of all my records was done before a notary public, after law-
yers and accountants approved all my work.

Making money, Astor was no Frank Sinatra. He just wanted to
make enough to make his year, have a little extra for insurance, and
treat himself to three months' rest in his house in Punta del Este.
And I know how generous he was with his kids, Diana and Daniel,
of whom I have good memories, when he returned from his exhaust-
ing tours.

My work as Astor's representative was not limited to administer-
ing his money. There was a bit of everything. The job was almost
managing his life: taking care of family problems, handling his crises
with his love relationships, and even attending to his legal messes.

Astor was a giant in music and a kid in many aspects of his life.
Some of his statements to the press, said in a moment of anger or
knowingly, ended up before a judge. On the other hand, no one ever
had a financial claim against him. He was a man of great integrity
who fulfilled his commitments.

Sometimes he complained about contracts he had signed. Such
was the case with his arrangement with Aldo Pagani. I don't believe
it was so damaging to his interests. Pagani, who is a very sharp busi-
nessman, invested a lot of money and time in Astor. He put Piazzolla's music in orbit. Now and forever he is a world figure.

I should be very direct and very honest when I talk about Astor.
He was a very contradictory character, but at the same time a man of
great kindness. He said no to everything—at first. A bit later, after

reflecting, he would call me back and we would start over. At the beginning of our relationship the phone would ring at six in the morning, then I fixed it so it would start ringing at seven and, finally, at eight. Astor didn't do this to be mean. He just was like that. I have never met a person with such a capacity for work, with such love for music, with such respect for his profession. He was never a minute late for an appointment.

Astor suffered a lot in his life. There was in him a certain melancholy; not even his better moods washed away the sadness you could see in his eyes. He struggled a lot to have a name that was known worldwide. It also hurt him that many Argentines couldn't even imagine what he meant artistically outside his country.

He died after painful agony. President Carlos Menem—I say this for the first time in my life—went to visit him at different clinics no fewer than six times. He had become fond of Astor; he used to cradle his head. That ending was so unfair, because to keep being Piazzolla onstage he had stopped smoking and was following a strict diet.

To the last day of his lucid life, before the stroke, he always was Astor Piazzolla. In this regard I should recall two anecdotes.

We were in Los Angeles at the home of Lalo Schifrin, a true friend of many years. Right in front of me, Schifrin confessed to him: "Astor, I have it all," which he said with a wave indicating the house, large and luxurious, "but I have lost the desire for many things." Astor, on the other hand, kept dreaming until his last thought.

He told me one of those dreams by phone, just days before 4 August 1990: "Atilio, last night I dreamed I played again with the Quintet."

A partner, a teacher, a father figure

GARY BURTON

We met in Buenos Aires in 1965. I was twenty-two and on tour with Stan Getz, and we were booked in the same club, alternating sets with Astor and his group. Up to that point I had never heard of him or any tango music for that matter. We had no expectations that on this trip we would find something so sophisticated, so captivating, and were amazed at the musicianship and the beautiful, contemporary nature of the music.

We did three nights at that place [the 676], but I don't remember talking with him. But I loved his music so I bought a bunch of his records and brought them back to the States.

I never really expected to see him again because in those days he never toured in the U.S., but I continued listening to his records, playing them for people, telling them they should check this out, what fantastic music this was, how they should hear this guy. I'm sure some people thought I was obsessed.

I never imagined I would ever see him again. Then, almost twenty years later, in 1984, I was in Paris, playing a concert with Chick Corea, and he walked up to me after the concert and said, "Hi, do you remember me?" and of course I did. It turns out he was living in Paris. He asked me if I wanted to do a project sometime, and I said, "Any time—I'd love to."

He talked to me like he'd known me really closely since we played that time in B.A., and in the meantime *I* thought he would not remember *me*. Apparently I had made an impression on him, and he said, "Yeah, all the local musicians talked a lot about this young vibes player with Getz."

I went home and never heard from him and two more years went

Born in 1943 and raised in Indiana, Gary Burton taught himself to play the vibraphone and, at age seventeen, made his recording debut in Nashville with guitarists Hank Garland and Chet Atkins. After attending Berklee College of Music in Boston, he joined pianist George Shearing and subsequently saxophonist Stan Getz. Burton's own bands have been pioneers in rock-jazz fusion, and he has won four Grammys.

by and I assumed nothing would happen. Musicians often have moments of passing enthusiasm, and I just chalked it up to that. Then one day I was walking through the lobby at Berklee College of Music, and the receptionist stops me to tell me I had a call from Paris. I took it and it was Astor, asking me if I was still interested. I said, "Oh, yes, definitely," and it turns out he was going home to B.A. for holidays and I was going to B.A. to play for a couple of weeks, so we agreed to meet and talk about what the project would be. I asked him not to start writing anything until we had a chance to talk about the

Vibist and composer Gary Burton visiting with Piazzolla and his last group, the Sextet. Left to right, top row: bandoneonist Daniel Binelli, Burton, cellist José Bragato, Piazzolla, pianist Gerardo Gandini. Bottom row: bassist Héctor Console and guitarist Horacio Malvicino.

mechanics of the vibraphone so that we wouldn't have to end up rewriting the vibraphone parts.

So when we met I thought we were just going to talk. He came to the club where I was playing, and it turns out he'd already written all the music.

I was a little nervous. Had this been a jazz thing I would have felt very comfortable that I could play the music, but this was something I'd never done before. But we sort of went ahead on the basis of this enthusiasm we both had.

I told my manager to set some things up. At this time we didn't have a record in mind. We only thought about touring. But it turned out that Nesuhi Ertegun at Atlantic Records was a big fan of Piazzolla, having grown up in Paris and knowing his music for years, so he wanted to do a record. Now suddenly we had a three-week tour in Europe, a record deal, and maybe a tour in Japan—and I still hadn't played a note of the music. It was intimidating.

I remember that at that first meeting in Buenos Aires, Astor was so excited I couldn't get a word in edgewise. He was not listening to my concerns at all, and he struck me as someone who was used to getting his way. My bassist, Steve Swallow, who was sitting next to us in the dressing room and witnessed our conversation, even asked me afterward if I was sure I knew what I was getting into.

Actually I did begin to have concerns and second thoughts. But I was committed, and I was such a fan of his music, I couldn't back out. Still I had heard stories about Astor's legendary temper and his penchant for creating controversy, and I worried that I would be the recipient of some of this behavior. But he was always absolutely wonderful to me, like a father, patient, considerate. He loved my playing and was very complimentary.

He also helped me get comfortable with the musical situation. In his music, instead of soloing at length as we do in jazz, I found myself soloing in small bits and pieces throughout the performances of the written compositions. But he treated me with great respect and deference and was patient and helpful in explaining what he wanted in the music. He later would tell me to use my written part as a guide and make it sound "something like it." He taught me a lot about phrasing and use of dynamics. It was a challenge at first to find the flow of going back and forth between written and improvised phrases, but he kept showing me how to do it.

I learned a tremendous amount of musicianship from him and his music. For me, playing with Astor was not just another gig. This was one of the two or three most important experiences in my career. It changed my playing.

But I also saw him be vicious with promoters during the tour, throw tantrums, and have screaming arguments, always in Spanish or Italian. I remember Astor arguing with a Spanish promoter who hadn't organized the details of the concert well, and everything was chaotic. Astor took the guy backstage and yelled at him in Spanish for half an hour.

He told me he was embarrassed to have me as a guest and see a gig of ours so poorly organized. He said it made him feel embarrassed for himself and his musicians for me to see this. I wasn't bothered at all. These things happen often to jazz musicians, too.

The second time he blew up was when a promoter in Italy didn't have the fee in dollars and wanted to pay him in Italian lira. He made the promoter fly with us to Switzerland the next day, change the money personally at the airport bank, and give it to Astor, after which the promoter caught a plane back to Rome.

I've never seen anything like it before or since. When Astor wanted something, he usually got it. But to me, he couldn't have been nicer or more helpful. I have nothing but great memories of him and our experience together.

Naturally I was shocked and saddened when I got a call from Astor's sister-in-law telling me about his being stricken in Paris and his return to Buenos Aires. There was hope then that he might recover. I thought I might even see him when I was next in Argentina on a tour. But during the days I was in Buenos Aires, he was not doing well, and I didn't have a chance to see him. Some time later I got word that he had passed away. I thought it was especially sad that this man, who had so much energy, drive, and zest for life, was imprisoned in his body for his last year.

When I did *Astor Piazzolla Reunion,** for me it was like closing the circle. After his passing I had assumed our partnership was over, but then I realized there was some unfinished business between us. We had planned a South American tour, we had talked about another project, and then it had ended.

As a jazz musician, I tend to compare Astor to a combination of Duke Ellington and Miles Davis, and I was glad I had the chance to play with him as much as I did. But *Reunion* was a way to complete our work. It was a chance for me to recapture that magic, say good-bye, and make my personal tribute to his music.

---

* *Astor Piazzolla Reunion*, Concord Records, 1998, is an album of tango, mostly Piazzolla's compositions, featuring the members of Piazzolla's Quintet.

My Crazy Bandoneon

LEOPOLDO FEDERICO AND ROBERTO DI FILIPPO

The bandoneon has one sound opening up and another closing down. This is a crucial difference and can be appreciated in the playing: while the instrument is opening, there comes a key point when the lack of air demands that the bandoneon be closed. That's the most important challenge that this instrument offers, this and the imperfect mechanics of the keyboard. The octaves do not follow the order they have in the piano, for example.

It's standard to measure the technique of a bandoneonist by two criteria: first, if he plays solo and the gasping of the instrument is almost imperceptible, and second, if the opening and closing of the bandoneon does not affect the musical phrasing. This is very difficult, but it can be done by studying the part and marking when to open and when to close.

Playing opening up can seem the easy way, a temptation to the less talented. But at the same time it has its dangers: the wrists begin to twist, then harden, and this causes the loss of agility in the fingering.

In the 1946 Orchestra, Piazzolla played the main part, the most potent, leaving for his second bandoneonist the highest pitched line, a difficult line precisely because of its position on the keyboard. The highest notes are the farthest from the wrists and cannot be comfortably played with the tip of the fingers.

This chapter, which Piazzolla didn't get to do, appears here thanks to the help of bandoneon experts Leopoldo Federico and Roberto Di Filippo. "My Crazy Bandoneon" is also a tribute to the memory of Di Filippo, who passed away in Buenos Aires on 15 February 1991.

Piazzolla considered the instrument perfect on the left hand and almost perfect on the right. This was because he didn't like the sound of five or six notes in the fifth octave, from E to B. He always said, "They sound like a little flute."

In Piazzolla technique and feeling came together, but the particular sound he achieved benefited from his great harmonic knowledge. In addition, beyond the bandoneon, Piazzolla's musical knowledge made it possible for the Quintet to sound like a twenty-piece orchestra. The old line that a good bandoneonist can be appreciated when playing solo leads to a piece of advice for young players who might attempt to study this instrument. Listen to Piazzolla's version of

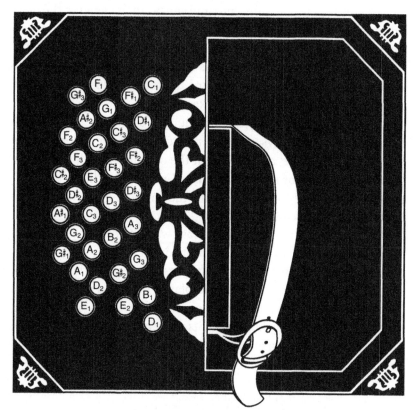

The bandoneon: left hand opening.
Octave register: C_1, C_2, C_3 (middle C), C_4, C_5
Drawings by Roberto Fernández

"En las sombras" by Joaquín Mora. That celestial sound reveals a superior artist. That was Astor: he played well solo, in an orchestra, and opening or closing the bandoneon.

Young players are not advised here to try to imitate him. We have before us an extraordinary case, a self-taught player. Piazzolla grew up in an environment, New York, where he didn't have anyone to listen to, to copy, to imitate. Just the opposite, in Argentina there are great bandoneon players and excellent teachers.

What must be copied from Astor is his drive to reach the greatest heights in his musical studies. The evolution of Piazzolla the bandoneon player paralleled his musical ascent. In the 1946 Orchestra or

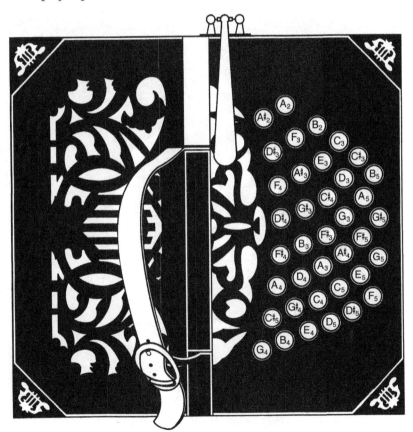

The bandoneon: right hand opening.

the Buenos Aires Octet he had us—Leopoldo Federico, Roberto Di Filippo—to complement his lead bandoneon. Perhaps we are mistaken in mentioning ourselves but this is not about praise. It is about telling the truth.

Astor plays better every day. When he chose to be the only bandoneonist in his groups, he was forced to resolve, by himself, what before he had managed with a second player. The bandoneon played with one hand, the right one, was not enough. The final product was remarkable: Astor plays his part and two or three more, with an infinite variety of chords. Obviously he uses both hands.

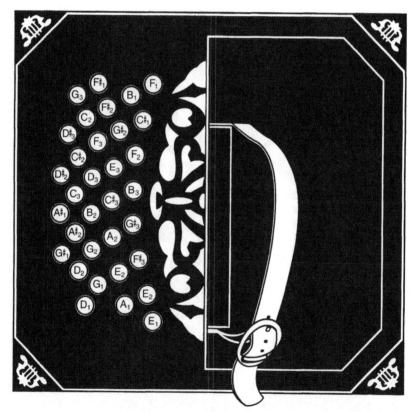

The bandoneon: left hand closing.

He also broke the mold on more than one issue. The bandoneon was considered an instrument that was played sitting down. He broke with tradition. The theory suggests that when the musician played standing up, the two heads, where the keyboards are, would tend naturally to fall to either side, requiring an extra effort to hold the instrument. Piazzolla ignored such difficulties—the bandoneon weighs around ten kilograms [approximately 22 pounds]—and besides he was capable of standing up for two hours, playing with the same proficiency from the first to the last note. Even in that he was different from everyone else.

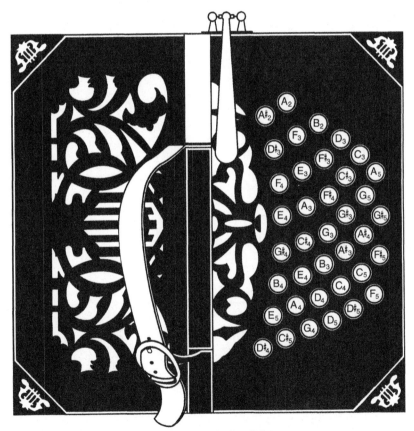

The bandoneon: right hand closing.

Piazzolla's Musicians and Singers

BANDONEON

Binelli, Daniel (b. 1946)
Sextet

Bandoneonist, arranger, and bandleader, a modernist who has worked with jazz and rock musicians, including both Mederos and Piazzolla. Among the best bandoneonists of his generation and perhaps the one who best reflects Piazzolla's concept of the new music of Buenos Aires.

Di Filippo, Roberto (1924–1991)
Fiorentino orchestra, 1946 Orchestra

Piazzolla, perhaps his biggest admirer, said no one surpassed Di Filippo as a bandoneon player. He also played oboe in the orchestra of the Teatro Colón. When Di Filippo died on 15 February 1991, Piazzolla was already deathly ill and never learned of his friend's passing.

Federico, Leopoldo (b. 1927)
1946 Orchestra, Buenos Aires Octet

After Piazzolla perhaps the most important bandoneonist of the 1940s and 1950s generation.

Pane, Julio (b. 1947)
Sextet

Along with Binelli, Walter Ríos, and Néstor Marconi, Pane is a member of the 1970s generation of brilliant bandoneonists whose technique becomes more polished every day.

CELLO

Bragato, José (b. 1915)
Buenos Aires Octet
The greatest cellist in tango history, a personal friend of Piazzolla, and a careful archivist and collector of his works.

CONTRABASS

Console, Héctor (b. 1939)
Quintet
Bass player from the new generation. His work with Piazzolla took him to the top levels of tango.

Díaz, Enrique ("Kicho") (1918–1992)
Quintet, *María de Buenos Aires* orchestra, Nonet
Considered by many the premier tango bassist. Played with Piazzolla off and on from 1961 to 1975, when he joined the Sexteto Mayor. His work with Aníbal Troilo and Astor Piazzolla is considered a model.

Greco, Hamlet (1920–1979)
String Orchestra, Buenos Aires Octet
In 1949 Greco was chosen to fill the first contrabass chair in the Argentine National Symphony Orchestra.

Vasallo, Juan (1927–1995)
String Orchestra, Buenos Aires Octet
Bassist who played a prominent role in other orchestras in tango's vanguard, including Gobbi's and Francini's.

ELECTRIC BASS

Cevasco, Adalberto (b. 1946)
Electronic Octet
Jazz musician who later became involved with popular music.

ELECTRIC GUITAR

López Ruiz, Oscar (b. 1938)
One of the two best-known electric guitarists in Piazzolla's history, the other being Horacio Malvicino. López Ruiz was Piazzolla´s

confidant and strong supporter in the most difficult times of the composer's musical career.

Malvicino, Horacio (b. 1929)
Buenos Aires Octet, Quintet, Electronic Octet, Sextet

Well-known Piazzolla guitarist and considered the most *tanguero* of them all. A solid supporter of Piazzolla.

Tirao, Cacho (b. 1941)
Quintet, *María de Buenos Aires* orchestra

Electric guitarist with Piazzolla. Tirao's technique on the nylon-string guitar made him a soloist; he was among the most important musicians of his generation.

FLUTE, SAXOPHONE

Schneider, Arturo (b. 1929)
María de Buenos Aires orchestra, Electronic Octet

Master flutist and good alto sax player, Schneider collaborated with several tango groups of diverse styles.

PERCUSSION

Corriale, José ("Pepe") (1915–1997)
María de Buenos Aires Orchestra, Nonet

Among the first percussionists dedicated to tango, although he also played other genres.

Piazzolla, Daniel (b. 1944)
Electronic Octet (Percussion and Synthesizer)

Son of Astor. Perhaps, as with Bach's family, he has lived under the shadow of a famous father. He has composed several excellent pieces.

Roizner, Enrique ("Zurdo") (b. 1939)
Electronic Octet

Another jazz musician called on by Piazzolla and one who enjoys great prestige among musicians.

PIANO

Amicarelli, Dante (1917–1996)
Quintet

A pianist and popular musician of great versatility, not just a tango player. Piazzolla greatly admired his ability to sight read just about any piece.

Cirigliano, Juan Carlos (b. 1939)
Electronic Octet

A formally trained musician, Cirigliano teaches and directs a music institute he founded in Buenos Aires.

Figari, Carlos (1917–1994)
Orchestra, 1944–1945

After becoming a member of Aníbal Troilo's orchestra in the 1950s, he formed his own ensemble rooted in Troilo's style.

Gandini, Gerardo (b. 1936)
Sextet

A classically trained musician, composer, and teacher, Gandini, like Piazzolla, was a student of Alberto Ginastera. He played piano in the Sextet.

Gosis, Jaime (1913–1975)
String Orchestra, Quintet, *María de Buenos Aires* orchestra

A student of the great teacher Vicente Scaramuzza, Gosis was fluid in all genres. Piazzolla called him his best pianist.

Manzi, Osvaldo (1924–1976)
Quintet, Nonet

Manzi played with several traditional tango orchestras, but his curiosity took him to the vanguard of Argentine popular music.

Schifrin, Lalo (b. 1932)
String Orchestra, Paris 1955

Resident of the United States, Schifrin is known worldwide for his work for film and television.

Stampone, Atilio (b. 1926)
1946 Orchestra, Buenos Aires Octet

Pianist and composer whose groups and compositions are identified with the tango vanguard.

Tarantino, Osvaldo (1928–1994)

Quintet, Nonet

Many tango musicians consider Tarantino the pianist with the greatest swing in tango history.

Ziegler, Pablo (b. 1944)

Quintet

Another notable Piazzolla musician with jazz schooling. For twelve years he was the pianist of the last Quintet.

VIOLIN

Agri, Antonio (1932–1998)

Quintet, Nonet, *María de Buenos Aires* orchestra, Electronic Octet

The greatest Argentine tango violinist of the last thirty years of the twentieth century, Agri performed in several of Piazzolla's groups.

Bajour, Simón (b. 1928)

Quintet

The classical music world knows him by his true Polish name, Szymsia Bajour. A violinist with the Quintet, he performed on the stages of all continents.

Baralis, Hugo (b. 1914)

1946 Orchestra, Buenos Aires Octet, *María de Buenos Aires* orchestra, Nonet

Longtime Piazzolla violinist who played in most of the composer's groups, with a style similar to Elvino Vardaro's.

Francini, Enrique Mario (1916–1978)

Buenos Aires Octet

A great tango violin virtuoso whose style was similar to Simón Bajour's.

Suárez Paz, Fernando (b. 1941)

Quintet

Piazzolla fans can't decide who was his best violinist: Suárez Paz or Agri. Suárez Paz's style is similar to that of Francini.

Vardaro, Elvino (1905–1971)

String Orchestra, Quintet

Composer, bandleader, and classic tango violinist who played in Piazzolla's groups from 1955 to 1961. Many students of tango say that the Elvino Vardaro Sextet of the 1930s, of which there are no recordings, was the keystone of the modern form.

VOCALISTS

Baltar, Amelita (b. 1940)
Quintet, *María de Buenos Aires*

(María Amelia Baltar) The Piazzolla-Ferrer oeuvre was written for her, a singer known for her low contralto, good phrasing, and great personality onstage. Once a traditional folk singer, Baltar was picked by Piazzolla in 1968 to sing María in his *María de Buenos Aires*. Her biggest hit was Piazzolla-Ferrer, "Balada para un loco" (1969).

Campoamor, Aldo (1910–1968)
1946 Orchestra

The classic tango singer of his time, he played an important role in the 1946 Orchestra.

De Rosas, Héctor (b. 1931)
Quintet, *María de Buenos Aires*

A brilliant baritone. The tango created by the Quintet found in him its ideal voice. He often has said, with good reason, "I was the sixth musician."

Goyeneche, Roberto (1926–1994)
Quintet

Piazzolla used to say of Goyeneche and Edmundo Rivero that they distinguished themselves from other tango singers because they didn't try to imitate Carlos Gardel, an apt observation. Nicknamed "El Polaco" (The Pole), Goyeneche was a premier tango singer. He worked with the top orchestras and musicians, including Piazzolla.

Jairo (b. 1949)
Piazzolla-Ferrer repertoire, 1980s

(Mario Rubén González) Searching for high-quality repertoire, he also recorded Piazzolla–Jorge Luis Borges. Jairo was born in Argentina and has become well known in France.

Lavié, Raúl (b. 1937)
Quintet

A great personality as a singer and actor, and still an important tango voice at the turn of the twentieth century.

Milva (b. 1939)

Quintet

(Maria Ilva Biocatti) Italian singer of great vocal technique and stage presence. Her collaboration with Piazzolla proved rewarding for both: she dove into tango; he became better known around the world.

Rivero, Edmundo (1911–1986)

Astor Piazzolla–Jorge Luis Borges, *El tango*

A unique artist in Argentine popular song in general and tango in particular. He had an original style, and his dark voice was revolutionary in tango.

Sobral, Jorge (b. 1930)

String Orchestra

Television actor and singer, his work in tango and Argentine folk music brought him fame throughout Latin America.

Trelles, José Ángel (b. 1943)

Quintet, Electronic Octet

A 1970s singer dedicated to the new popular music, not only in tango but in all Argentine and Latin American popular music.

Vázquez, Nelly (b. 1940)

Quintet

Originally a lyric singer, with Piazzolla Vázquez adapted her voice to the needs of the just-formed Quintet. Later as a soloist she was identified as the classic tango singer.

Discography of Recordings
by Astor Piazzolla

This discography, based on the original in *Astor Piazzolla: A Manera de Memorias* (Buenos Aires: Editorial Atlántida, 1992) by Natalio Gorin, has been updated by the author as of December 2000. This discography focuses on Piazzolla's conceptual work, meaning commercial releases of recordings of his original compositions or arrangements of music by others for his orchestras. Therefore his work for hire as a conductor and arranger in his New York period of 1958–1959—with Trio Los Bandidos, José Duval, Pete Terrace, The Di Mara Sisters, Machito, and others—is not included. Neither are tracks on a folk recording by pianist Eduardo Lagos, nor reissues in different countries. For this discography, the original is what counts. Also not included are the compilations, with two exceptions because of their importance: *Piazzolla 1943–1982*, selected by Aquiles Giacometti for RCA Victor, and *Tangamente* (Nonet). When a great artist disappears many recordings heretofore unknown come to light. There are commercial abuses, such as the *Suite Punta del Este* version released in 1993 with such awful sound quality that it can be justified only by the fact that it puts on record a piece Piazzolla did not get to record as he would have liked. But there are also valuable contributions, such as *Ensayos* by the Quintet released in 1995. Recordings are listed by date of release.

The author appreciates the collaboration of Víctor Oliveros, Alberto Romeo, José Luis Tavorro (all from the Centro Astor Piazzolla of the City of Buenos Aires), Jorge Bustos (of the Grupo Piazzolla of the City of Rosario, Province of Santa Fe), Ramiro Carámbula (Montevideo, Uruguay), and César Luongo (USA) for their assistance in this discographic work.

1945–1946

Fiorentino y su orquesta. Conducted by Astor Piazzolla. Odeon. 78 rpm.

30201 Si se salva el pibe (F. Pracánico, C. Flores). Corrientes y
Esmeralda (F. Pracánico Aico, C. Flores).

30202 Diez años pasan (J. Razzano, C. Castillo). Nos encontramos
al pasar (R. Kaplún, J. M. Suné).

30203 Cotorrita de la suerte (A. J. de Franco, J. P. de Grandis).
Rosas de otoño (G. Barbieri, J. Rial).

30204 En las noches (F. Fiorentino, E. Cadícamo). La chiflada (A.
Aieta).

30205 Soy una fiera (F. Martino). Seis días (M. Sucher, C. Bahr).

30206 María (A. Troilo, C. Castillo). Fruta amarga (H. Gutiérrez,
H. Manzi).

30207 Dolor de tango (C. Vivan, Yaravi). Oro falso (V. and H.
Espósito).

30208 Amigazo (J. de Dios Filiberto, F. Brancati). Color de rosa
(A. and P. Polito).

30209 El trovero (A. Irusta, R. Tuegols). Viejo ciego (S. Piana, C.
Castillo).

30210 Burbujas (C. Figari, C. Castillo). Quién te ha traído
(F. Fiorentino, A. Piazzolla, V. Velázquez).

30211 De vuelta al bulín (J. Martínez, P. Contursi). Volvió una
noche (C. Gardel, A. Le Pera).

30212 En carne propia (M. Sucher, C. Bahr). Otros tiempos y otros
hombres (C. Ortiz, E. Cadícamo).

1946–1949

Astor Piazzolla. Orquesta típica. Odeon. 78 rpm.

30351 El recodo (A. Junissi). Sólo se quiere una vez (C. V. Flores,
C. Frollo).

30352 Orgullo criollo (P. Laurenz, J. De Caro). Adiós marinero
(A. Gallucci, R. Yiso).

30353 El milagro (A. Pontier, H. Expósito). El desbande (A. Piazzolla).

30354 El pillete (G. de Leone). Ojos tristes (R. Iriarte, A. Navar-
rino).

30355 Inspiración (P. Paulos, L. Rubinstein). Como abrazado a un
rencor (R. Rossi, M. Podestá).

30356 El rápido (R. Firpo). Pigmaleón (A. Piazzolla, H. Expósito).

30357 Haragán (E. Delfino, M. Romero). Tiernamente (A. Bardi, M. Batistella).

30358 La rayuela (J. De Caro). En la huella del adiós (H. Stamponi, H. Expósito).

30359 Se armó (A. Piazzolla). De mi bandoneón (R. Pérez Prechi).

30360 Quejas de bandoneón (J. de Dios Filiberto). Tu pálido final (V. Demarco, A. F. Roldán).

30361 Tapera (H. Manzi, H. Gutiérrez). Taconeando (P. Maffia, J. Staffolani).

30362 Chiclana (J. De Caro). Che Bartolo (R. Sciammarella, E. Cadícamo).

30363 Tierra querida (J. De Caro). Se fue sin decirme adiós (A. Piazzolla, A. F. Roldán).

30364 Ahí va el dulce (J. Canaro, O. Sosa Cordero). Cargamento (A. Gallucci, R. Hormaza).

30365 Cafetín de Buenos Aires (E. S. Discépolo, M. Mores). República Argentina (S. Lipesker, R. Ghiso).

30366 Villeguita (A. Piazzolla). Todo corazón (J. De Caro).

1950–1951

Astor Piazzolla. Orquesta típica. T. K. Discos. 78 rpm.

S-5026 Chiqué (P. L. Brignolo). Triste (F. De Caro, P. Maffia).

S-5036 La cumparsita (G. M. Rodríguez, E. P. Maroni, P. Contursi). Dedé (A. Piazzolla).

1955

Sinfonía de tango. String Orchestra. Allegro LDM 10004 LP.

Picasso (A. Piazzolla). Mi tentación (Chiloe, Moranez). Sens unique (A. Piazzolla). Estamos listos (A. Burli). Chau París (A. Piazzolla). Bando (A. Piazzolla). Luz y sombras (A. Piazzolla). Tzigane tango (A. Piazzolla).

In this period a recording was made on the Barclay and Festival labels that included Nonino, Prepárense, S.V.P. Imperial, Guardia Nueva, Contrastes, Marrón y azul, and Río Sena. (All music by A. Piazzolla.) With the orchestra was Lalo Schifrin, piano.

1956

Astor Piazzolla. String Orchestra. T. K. Discos E-10100. 78 rpm.
Lo que vendra (A. Piazzolla). Sensiblero (J. Plaza).

1957

Tango progresivo. Buenos Aires Octet. Allegro ALL 6001 LP.
Lo que vendrá (A. Piazzolla). La revancha (P. Laurenz). Tema
otoñal (E. M. Francini). Boedo (J. De Caro, D. Linyera). Mi refugio
(J. C. Cobián). Taconeando (P. Maffia, H. Staffolani).

Octeto Buenos Aires. Disk Jockey DIS 15001 LP.
Haydee (H. Grané). Marrón y azul (A. Piazzolla). Los mareados
(J. C. Cobián). Neotango (L. Federico, M. Flores). El marne (E. Aro-
las). Anone (H. Baralis). El entrerriano (R. Mendizábal). Tangol-
ogy (H. Malvicino). Arrabal (J. Pascual). A fuego lento (H. Salgán).
LINEUP: Astor Piazzolla and Leopoldo Federico (bandoneons);
Atilio Stampone (piano); Enrique Mario, E. M. Francini, and Hugo
Baralis (violins); José Bragato (cello); Juan Vasallo (contrabass);
Horacio Malvicino (guitar).

Astor Piazzolla. String Orchestra. Music Hall 65001 LP.
Azabache (E. M. Francini, H. Expósito). Lo que vendrá (A. Piazzolla). Negracha (O. Pugliese). Taconeando (P. Maffia, H. Staffolani).

Tango en Hi Fi. String Orchestra. Music Hall 12033 LP.
Tango del ángel (A. Piazzolla). Melancólico Buenos Aires (A. Piaz-
zolla). Loca bohemia (F. De Caro, D. Linyera). Siempre París (V.
and H. Expósito). Tres minutos con la realidad (A. Piazzolla). La
cumparsita (G. M. Rodríguez, E. P. Maroni, P. Contursi). Fuimos
(J. Dames, H. Manzi). Del bajo fondo (O. Tarantino). Inspiración
(P. Paulos, L. Rubinstein). Prepárense (A. Piazzolla).
LINEUP: Astor Piazzolla (bandoneon), Elvino Vardaro (violin), José
Vasallo (contrabass), José Bragato (cello), with Jorge Sobral (voice)
on Siempre París and Fuimos.

Astor Piazzolla. String Orchestra. Odeon 51997. Single.
Vanguardista (J. Bragato). Marrón y azul (A. Piazzolla).

Lo que vendrá. String Orchestra. Music Hall 90-890-2 LP.
Lo que vendrá (A. Piazzolla). Miedo (E. Vardaro, J. Arola). Yo soy
el negro (A. Piazzolla, C. Gorostiza). Sensiblero (J. Plaza). Tres minutos con la realidad (A. Piazzolla). Noche de amor (F. Franco). La
tarde del adiós (F. López, R. Lambertucci). La cachila (E. Arolas).
With Jorge Sobral (voice) on Yo soy el negro and La tarde del adiós.

*As on Diapason AC 87 which has similar content, two tracks on this
recording, Bando and Contrastes, were written by Astor Piazzolla and
recorded by a certain New Time Quintet. They are not listed here because
this is not Piazzolla's Quintet. The passing years, the badly done CD
releases, the mixing of original recordings, and the ignorance of commen-
tators and recording companies have created great confusion.*

1960

5 º año nacional. Quintet. Music Hall 45-E-97 LP.
5º año nacional. Fin de curso. El goy. El boletín. Aplazado. (All
music by A. Piazzolla.)

1961

Piazzolla bailable y apiazzollado. Quintet. RCA Victor AVL 3340 LP.
Prepárense (A. Piazzolla). Tierrita (A. Bardi). María (A. Troilo,
C. Castillo). Bandoneón arrabalero (J. Deambroggio). Redención
(A. Gobbi). Don Juan (E. Poncio). El arranque (J. De Caro). Chiqué
(R. L. Brignolo). Triunfal (A. Piazzolla). La casita de mis viejos
(J. C. Cobián, E. Cadícamo). Cristal (M. Mores, J. M. Contursi).
Quejas de bandoneón (J. de Dios Filiberto).
LINEUP: Astor Piazzolla (bandoneon), Elvino Vardaro (violin),
Jaime Gosis (piano), Oscar López Ruiz (guitar), Kicho Díaz (con-
trabass), with Nelly Vázquez (voice) on María, Bandoneón arra-
balero, La casita de mis viejos, and Cristal.

Piazzolla interpreta a Piazzolla. Quintet. RCA Victor AVL 3383 LP.
Adiós Nonino. Berretín (P. Laurenz). Contrabajeando (A. Piazzolla, A. Troilo). Tanguísimo. Decarisimo. Lo que vendrá. La calle
92. Calambre. Los poseídos. Nonino. Bando. Guitarzo (H. Malvicino). (All music by A. Piazzolla except where noted.)
LINEUP: Astor Piazzolla (bandoneon), Jaime Gosis (piano), Simón
Bajour (violin), Kicho Díaz (contrabass), Horacio Malvicino
(guitar).

1962

Vanguardia. Quintet. Antar PLP 5049 LP.
> Por la vuelta (J. Tinelli, E. Cadícamo). Triunfal (A. Piazzolla). Nostalgias (J. C. Cobián, E. Cadícamo). Adiós Nonino (A. Piazzolla).

Piazzolla. Quintet with singer Daniel Riolobos. RCA Victor 31 C-1479. Single.
> Garúa (A. Troilo, E. Cadícamo). Uno (M. Mores, E. S. Discépolo).

Piazzolla. Quintet with singer Héctor De Rosas. RCA Victor 3AE 3106.
> Enamorado estoy (O. Zito, J. Márquez). Cuesta abajo (C. Gardel, A. Le Pera). Sur (A. Troilo, H. Manzi). Malena (L. Demare, H. Manzi).

Nuestro tiempo. Quintet. CBS 835 1 LP.
> Introducción al ángel (A. Piazzolla). Muerte del ángel (A. Piazzolla). Milonga triste (S. Piana, H. Manzi). Sin retorno (A. Coronato). Imágenes 676 (A. Piazzolla). Nuestro tiempo (A. Piazzolla). Rosa río (A. Piazzolla, J. C. Lamadrid). Simple (O. Manzi). Todo fue (A. Piazzolla, D. Piazzolla). Los mareados (J. C. Cobián, E. Cadícamo).
> LINEUP: Astor Piazzolla (bandoneon), Osvaldo Manzi (piano), Antonio Agri (violin), Kicho Díaz (contrabass), Oscar López Ruiz (guitar), with Héctor De Rosas (voice) on Milonga triste, Rosa río, and Todo fue.

1963

Tango para una ciudad. Quintet. CBS 8392 LP.
> Tango para una ciudad I. Tango para una ciudad II. Cafetín de Buenos Aires (M. Mores, E. S. Discépolo). Iracundo. Éxtasis. Revirado. El mundo de los dos (A. Piazzolla, A. Gómez). Buenos Aires hora cero. Maquillaje (V. and H. Expósito). Fracanapa. (All music by A. Piazzolla except where noted.)
> LINEUP: Same as for *Nuestro tiempo*, above, with Héctor De Rosas (voice) on Cafetín de Buenos Aires, El mundo de los dos, and Maquillaje.

Tango contemporáneo. New Octet, featuring Ernesto Sábato and Alfredo Alcón. CBS 9039 LP.
> Lo que vendrá (A. Piazzolla). Divagación (A. Piazzolla). Introduc-

ción a héroes y tumbas (A. Piazzolla, E. Sábato). Noposepe (J. Bragato). Ciudad triste (O. Tarantino). Sideral (E. Balcarce). Réquiem para un malandra (A. Piazzolla, D. Piazzolla). Recuerdos de bohemia-milonguita (E. Delfino).

LINEUP: Astor Piazzolla (bandoneon), Jaime Gosis (piano), Antonio Agri (violin), José Bragato (cello), Ocar López Ruiz (guitar), Kicho Díaz (contrabass), Leo Jacobson (percussion), Jorge Barone (flute), Héctor De Rosas (voice), Ernesto Sábato and Alfredo Alcón (recited texts).

Nuevo Octeto. Antar-CBS 2210. Recorded in Uruguay in 1963. Single.
  Bragatisimo (A. Piazzolla). Ciudad triste (O. Tarantino).
  LINEUP: Same as for *Tango contemporáneo*, above.

1964

Piazzolla—Roberto Yanés. Orchestra with singer Roberto Yanés. CBS 33099.
  Cafetín de Buenos Aires (M. Mores, E. S. Discépolo). Fuimos (J. Dames, H. Manzi). Margarita Gauthier (J. Mora, J. J. Nelson). Griseta (E. Delfino, J. González Castillo).

20 años de vanguardia. Orquesta típica, String Orchestra, Octet, and Quintet. Philips 85510 PY LP.
  El recodo (A. Junissi). Orgullo criollo (J. De Caro, P. Laurenz). Prepárense. Imperial. Bandoneón, guitarra y bajo. Lunfardo. Tango ballet. Caliente. Contemporáneo. (All music by A. Piazzolla.)
  1946 ORCHESTRA: Astor Piazzolla, Leopoldo Federico, Abelardo Alfonsín, and Ernesto Baffa (bandoneons); Hugo Baralis, Antonio Agri, Domingo Mancuso, Andrés Rivas, Carmen Cavallaro (violins); Cayetano Giana (viola); José Bragato (cello); Kicho Díaz (contrabass).
  1954 STRING ORCHESTRA: Astor Piazzolla (bandoneon); Osvaldo Manzi (piano); Antonio Agri, Hugo Baralis, Domingo Mancuso, David Díaz, Aquiles Aguilar, José Niesow, Juan Schiaffino, Claudio González (violins); Francisco Sammartino and Cayetano Giana (violas); Oscar López Ruiz (guitar); Kicho Díaz (contrabass).
  OCTET: Astor Piazzolla and Leopoldo Federico (bandoneons); Atilio Stampone (piano); Enrique M. Francini and Hugo Baralis (violins); José Bragato (cello); Kicho Díaz (contrabass); Horacio Malvicino (guitar).

Quintet: Astor Piazzolla (bandoneon); Osvaldo Manzi (piano); Antonio Agri (violin); Oscar López Ruiz (guitar); Kicho Díaz (contrabass).

1965

Concierto en el Philarmonic Hall de New York. Quintet. Polydor 27136 LP. Recorded in Buenos Aires.

Tango diablo. Romance del diablo. Vayamos al diablo. Canto de octubre. Mar del plata '70. Todo Buenos Aires. Milonga del ángel. Resurrección del ángel. La mufa. (All music by A. Piazzolla.)

LINEUP: Astor Piazzolla (bandoneon), Jaime Gosis (piano), Antonio Agri (violin), Kicho Díaz (contrabass), Oscar López Ruiz (electric guitar).

El tango: Jorge Luis Borges—Astor Piazzolla. Orchestra and Quintet with Edmundo Rivero, singer, and Luis Medina Castro, recited texts. Polydor 27128 LP.

El tango. Jacinto Chiclana. Alguien le dice al tango. El títere. A don Nicanor Paredes. Oda íntima a Buenos Aires. El hombre de la esquina rosada. (Poems by J. L. Borges, music by A. Piazzolla.)

LINEUP: Astor Piazzolla (bandoneon), Edmundo Rivero (voice), Luis Medina Castro (recitation), Antonio Agri and Hugo Baralis (violins), Jaime Gosis (piano and celesta), Roberto Di Filippo (oboe), Margarita Zamek (harp), Antonio Yepes (timbales, handbells, xylophone), Leo Jacobson (percussion), Mario Lalli (viola), José Bragato (cello), Kicho Díaz (contrabass), Oscar López Ruiz (guitar).

Melenita de oro. Quintet. Polydor 10069.

Verano porteño. Al compas de los tamangos. C'est l'amour. Tres sargentos. (All music by A. Piazzolla.)

1967

Piazzolla. Quintet. Polydor 10092. Single. 33 rpm.

Revolucionario. Retrato de Alfredo Gobbi. (All music by A. Piazzolla.)

LINEUP: Astor Piazzolla (bandoneon), Osvaldo Manzi (piano), Antonio Agri (violin), Kicho Díaz (contrabass), Oscar López Ruiz (guitar).

La historia del tango: La guardia vieja. Orchestra. Polydor 27142 LP.
El choclo (A. Villoldo). Ojos negros (V. Greco). La cumparsita (G.
M. Rodríguez, E. P. Maroni, P. Contursi). La cachila (E. Arolas).
La maleva (M. Pardo, A. Buglione). A media luz (E. Donato). Mi
noche triste (S. Castriota, P. Contursi). Sentimiento gaucho (F.
Canaro). Nunca tuvo novio (A. Bardi). Entre sueños (A. Aieta).
Quejas de bandoneón (J. de Dios Filiberto). Alma de bohemio
(R. Firpo).
LINEUP: Astor Piazzolla (bandoneon), Osvaldo Manzi (piano),
Antonio Agri (violin), Oscar López Ruiz (guitar), Kicho Díaz (con-
trabass), and an orchestra featuring twelve violins, four violas, four
cellos, vibraphone, handbells, xylophone, and soprano.

La historia del tango: Época romántica. Orchestra. Polydor 27145 LP.
Taconeando (P. Maffia, H. Staffolani). Griseta (E. Delfino). Los
mareados (J. C. Cobián, E. Cadícamo). Loca bohemia (F. De Caro).
Recuerdo (O. Pugliese). Boedo (J. De Caro, D. Linyera). En las
sombras (J. Mora). Pampero (O. Fresedo, E. Bianchi). La revancha
(P. Laurenz). Noche de amor (F. Franco).
LINEUP: Same as for *La historia del tango: La guardia vieja*, above,
with violin solos by Hugo Baralis, Enrique M. Francini, and Antonio Agri on Boedo and cello solo by José Bragato on Recuerdo.

Selección superestereo. Orchestra. Philips 6347 024.
Uno (M. Mores, E. S. Discépolo). Sur (A. Troilo, H. Manzi).
Malena (L. Demare, H. Manzi). Percal (D. Federico, H. Expósito).
This is an unfinished work that was to be called La historia del tango-
epoca moderna.

1968
María de Buenos Aires. Orchestra with singers Amelita Baltar and
Héctor De Rosas. Trova TLS 5020-2 LP.
Alevare. Tema de María. Balada para un organito loco. Milonga car-
rieguera. Fuga y misterio. Poema valseado. Tocata rea. Miserere
canyengue. Contramilonga a la funerala. Tangata del alba. Carta a
los árboles y a las chimeneas. Aria de los analistas. Romanza del
duende. Allegro tangábile. Milonga de la anunciación. Tangus Dei.
(All music by A. Piazzolla; lyrics by H. Ferrer.)

LINEUP: Astor Piazzolla (bandoneon), Horacio Ferrer (recited text), Amelita Baltar and Héctor De Rosas (voice), Jaime Gosis (piano), Antonio Agri and Hugo Baralis (violins), Néstor Panik (viola), Víctor Pontino (cello), Kicho Díaz (contrabass), Cacho Tirao (guitar), Arturo Schneider (flute), José Corriale (percussion), Tito Bisio (vibraphone, xylophone, handbells).

1969

Piazzolla con Roberto Goyeneche. RCA Victor 31A 1605.
Balada para un loco. Chiquilín de Bachín. (All music by A. Piazzolla, H. Ferrer.)

Piazzolla con Egle Martin. Polydor 10132.
Retrato de mí mismo (A. Piazzolla). Graciela oscura (A. Piazzolla, U. Petit de Murat). Las rosas golondrinas (A. Piazzolla, H. Expósito). Verano porteño (A. Piazzolla).

Adiós Nonino. Quintet. Trova TLS 5027 LP.
Adiós Nonino. Otoño porteño. Michelangelo '70. Coral. Tangata. (All music by A. Piazzolla.)
LINEUP: Astor Piazzolla (bandoneon), Dante Amicarelli (piano), Antonio Agri (violin), Kicho Díaz (contrabass), Oscar López Ruiz (guitar).

Astor Piazzolla—Amelita Baltar. Quintet. Trova TS 33-741. Single. 33 rpm.
Chiquilín de Bachín. Milonga en Ay menor. (All music by A. Piazzolla, H. Ferrer).
LINEUP: Astor Piazzolla (bandoneon), Dante Amicarelli (piano), Antonio Agri (violin), Oscar López Ruiz (guitar), Kicho Díaz (contrabass).

Piazzolla en el Regina. Quintet. RCA Victor AVLS 3924 LP.
Invierno porteño. Verano porteño. Otoño porteño. Primavera porteña. Buenos Aires hora cero. Retrato de Alfredo Gobbi. Revolucionario. Kicho. (All music by A. Piazzolla.)
LINEUP: Astor Piazzolla (bandoneon), Osvaldo Manzi (piano), Antonio Agri (violin), Kicho Díaz (contrabass), Cacho Tirao (guitar).

1970

Astor Piazzolla—Horacio Ferrer. Piazzolla (bandoneon), Ferrer (recited text). RCA Victor AVLP 3982 LP.

Fábula para Gardel. Canción de las venusinas. Te quiero che. Chiquilín de Bachín. Balada para él. Balada para mi muerte. Balada para un loco. La última grela. Juanito laguna ayuda a su madre. Preludio para la cruz del sur. (All music by A. Piazzolla and H. Ferrer.)

Pulsación. Orchestra. Trova ST 5038 LP.

Pulsación 1. Pulsación 2. Pulsación 4. Pulsación 5. Fuga y misterio. Contramilonga a la funerala. Allegro tangábile. Tocata rea. Tangata del alba. (All music by A. Piazzolla.)

LINEUP: Astor Piazzolla (bandoneon), Jaime Gosis (piano), Antonio Agri and Hugo Baralis (violins), Víctor Pontino (cello), Néstor Panik (viola), Kicho Díaz (contrabass), Cacho Tirao (guitar), Arturo Schneider (flute and sax), José Corriale (percussion), Tito Bisio (vibraphone, xylophone, handbells). In all versions of Pulsación, Dante Amicarelli (piano) replaces Jaime Gosis, Simón Zlotnik (viola) replaces Néstor Panik, and José Bragato (cello) replaces Víctor Pontino.

Piazzolla—Troilo. Astor Piazzolla and Aníbal Troilo, bandoneon duets. RCA Victor AVS 4659.

Volver (C. Gardel, A. Le Pera). El motivo (J. C. Cobián, E. Cadícamo).

Con alma y vida. Quintet. RCA Victor 3AE 3717.

Casapueblo. Flaco Aroldi. Con alma y vida. Tres en magoya. (All music by A. Piazzolla.)

1971

Concierto para quinteto. RCA Victor AVS 4013 LP.

Concierto para quinteto (A. Piazzolla). Invierno porteño (A. Piazzolla). Primavera porteña (A. Piazzolla). La casita de mis viejos (J. C. Cobián, E. Cadícamo). Mi refugio (J. C. Cobián, N. Córdoba). Loca bohemia (F. De Caro). Flores negras (F. De Caro). En las sombras (J. Mora). Margarita Gauthier (J. Mora, J. J. Nelson). Recuerdos de bohemia (E. Delfino).

LINEUP: Astor Piazzolla (bandoneon), Osvaldo Manzi (piano), Antonio Agri (violin), Kicho Díaz (contrabass), Cacho Tirao (guitar).

The first three pieces are played by the Quintet; the rest are bandoneon solos by A. Piazzolla except the last one, in which he is accompanied by bandoenonists Antonio Ríos, Leopoldo Federico, and Rodolfo Mederos.

1972

Música popular contemporánea de La Ciudad de Buenos Aires. Nonet. RCA Victor AVS 4069 LP.

> Tristezas de un Doble A. Zum. Homenaje a Córdoba. Preludio 9. Divertimento 9. Fuga 9. En 3 x 4. (All music by A. Piazzolla.)
>
> LINEUP: Astor Piazzolla (bandoneon), Osvaldo Manzi (piano), Antonio Agri and Hugo Baralis (violins), Néstor Panik (viola), José Bragato (cello), Oscar López Ruiz (guitar), José Corriale (percussion), Kicho Díaz (contrabass).

Música popular contemporánea de La Ciudad de Buenos Aires, Vol. 2. Nonet. RCA Victor AVS 4125 LP.

> Vardarito. Oda para un hippie. Onda nueve. Verano porteño. Baires 72. Buenos Aires hora cero. (All music by A. Piazzolla.)
>
> LINEUP: Same as for *Música popular contemporánea*, above, except for Osvaldo Tarantino (piano).

El Gordo triste: Piazzolla y Amelita Baltar. Orchestra. RCA Victor 3-AE-3842.

> El Gordo triste (A. Piazzolla, H. Ferrer). Los paraguas de Buenos Aires (A. Piazzolla, H. Ferrer). En 3 x 4 (A. Piazzolla) (Nonet). Las ciudades (A. Piazzolla, H. Ferrer).

Piazzolla y Amelita Baltar. Orchestra. RCA Victor 31-A-2059.

> La primera palabra (A. Piazzolla, H. Ferrer). No quiero otro (A. Piazzolla, H. Ferrer).

1973

Astor Piazzolla. RCA Victor 31-A-2341.

> Vardarito (Nonet). Un día de paz (Orchestra). (Both by A. Piazzolla).

Mina—Piazzolla. Nonet. EMI 1612. Recorded in Italy.
  Balada para mi muerte (A. Piazzolla, H. Ferrer).

  This piece also appears on a recording by Mina. She sings two versions, both with the Nonet, one in Spanish; the other, in Italian.

Piazzolla. Nonet. RCA Victor 31-4-2286.
  El penúltimo. Jeanne y Paul. (All music by A. Piazzolla.)

1974

Libertango. Orchestra. Trova XT 80083 LP. Recorded in Italy. Original label: Carosello.
  Libertango. Meditango. Undertango. Adiós Nonino. Violentango. Novitango. Amelitango. Tristango. (All music by A. Piazzolla.)

Piazzolla—Gerry Mulligan: Reunión cumbre. Orchestra. Trova DA 5000 LP. Recorded in Italy. Original title and label: *Summit*, Carosello.
  Hace veinte años. Cierra tus ojos y escucha. Años de soledad. Deus

Piazzolla with his short-lived but remarkable Nonet, backing singer Mina in Italy in 1972.

tango. Veinte años después. Aire de Buenos Aires (G. Mulligan). Reminiscencia. Reunión cumbre. (All music by A. Piazzolla except where noted.)

Piazzolla—Amelita Baltar. Orchestra. Trova TF 1001.
Pequeña canción para Matilde (A. Piazzolla, P. Neruda). Violetas populares (A. Piazzolla, M. Trejo).

Astor Piazzolla—Edmonda Aldini. Orchestra with singer Edmonda Aldini. Ricordi SMRL 6117 LP. Recorded in Italy.
La primera palabra. Balada para él. Las Venusinas. Balada para un loco. Preludio para el año 3001. La bicicleta blanca. Balada para mi muerte. Preludio para un canillita. (All music by A. Piazzolla and H. Ferrer.)

1975

Ney Matogrosso. Continental (Brazil) 1-01-101-140. Single.
As ilhas (G. Carneiro, A. Piazzolla). 1964 (II) (J. L. Borges, A. Piazzolla).

A strange album. Piazzolla did the arranging, conducted the orchestra, and played bandoneon. The recording was produced by Aldo Pagani. Yet the single, included later in a Ney Matogrosso album, does not feature Piazzolla in the credits.

Suite Troileana—Lumiere. Orchestra with Antonio Agri, solo violin. Trova DA 5005 LP. Recorded in Italy. Original title and label: *Lumiere*, Carosello.
Bandoneón. Zita. Whisky. Escolaso. Soledad. Muerte. El amor. La evasión. (All music by A. Piazzolla.)

Guy Marchand—Astor Piazzolla. Orchestra. Riviera 12.022. Single. 45 rpm. Recorded in France.
Moi je suis un tango (Libertango) (A. Piazzolla, G. Marchand). Mister Tango (Undertango) (A. Piazzolla, G. Marchand).

In this collaboration, Piazzolla conducts the orchestra and plays bandoneon. The two tracks were recorded in Italy (see Libertango*) with new titles related to the lyrics written by Marchand.*

1976

Muralla china: Piazzolla—Antonio Agri. Orchestra with Astor Piazzolla, bandoneon; Antonio Agri, violin. Trova DA 5019 LP. Recorded in Italy. Original title and label: *Il pleût sur Santiago*, Carosello.
    Presagio (A. Piazzolla). Muralla China (A. Piazzolla, G. Carneiro). Olhos de resaca (A. Piazzolla, G. Carneiro). As ilhas (A. Piazzolla, G. Carneiro). Uomo del sud (A. Piazzolla) (violin version). Uomo del sud (bandoneon version). Se potessi ancora (A. Piazzolla, S. Bardotti).

These pieces were later used in the soundtrack of Il pleût sur Santiago *with the following titles: Salvador Allende, Combate en la fábrica, La maison de Monique, Bidonville, Il pleût sur Santiago, and Jorge adiós.*

Balada para un loco: Piazzolla. Orchestra with singer José Ángel Trelles. Trova DA 5006 LP. Instrumentals recorded in Italy.
    Balada para un loco (A. Piazzolla, H. Ferrer). Ojos de resaca (A. Piazzolla, G. Carneiro). La muralla china (A. Piazzolla, G. Carneiro). Los pájaros perdidos (A. Piazzolla, M. Trejo). Balada para mi muerte (A. Piazzolla, H. Ferrer). Se potessi ancora (A. Piazzolla, S. Bardotti). Las islas (A. Piazzolla, G. Carneiro). Chiquilín de Bachín (A. Piazzolla, H. Ferrer).

Astor Piazzolla—Marie Paule Belle. Orchestra with singer Marie Paule Belle. Polydor 2473056 L.P. Recorded in France.
    Je vis ma mort a chaque instant (A. Piazzolla, Françoise Mallet Joris, and Michele Grisolía).

Piazzolla arranged and conducted this piece on an album that contains nine additional songs by other composers.

1977

Piazzolla 77. Orchestra. Trova DA 5011 LP. Recorded in Italy. Original label: Carosello.
    Ciudad tango. Pla-sol-la-sol. Largo tangábile. Persecuta. Windy. Moderato tangábile. Canto y fuga. (All music by A. Piazzolla.)

Viaje de bodas: Piazzolla—Antonio Agri. Astor Piazzolla (bandoneon), Antonio Agri (violin). Trova DA 5010 LP. Recorded in Italy. Original label: Carosello.

> La felure. Bruno y Sarah. Jardines de África. Viaje de bodas. Le kata. El camino re corrido. Noches de Marruecos. La idea fija. La familia. Los pájaros perdidos (A. Piazzolla, M. Trejo). (All music by A. Piazzolla except where noted.)

Armaguedón. Orchestra. Trova DA 5012 LP. Recorded in Italy. Original label: Carosello.

> Luis Carrier. Armaguedón. Correo de genes. Solo, siempre solo. Teatro de París. Calle de Londres. Museo de Madame Tussaud. Les halles. Station taxis. Parque de Saint Cloud. Hotel P. L. M. frente al espejo. Canal de Ostende. Parque de Saint Cloud (2). Canción para un hombre triste. Station taxis (2). Hotel P. L. M. (2). Barrio Marais. Luis Carrier (2). Canal de Ostende (2). Pánico en el teatro. Station taxis (3). Juego teatral. Orquesta del teatro. Final. (All music by A. Piazzolla.)

Piazzolla en el Olimpía de París. Electronic Octet. Interdisc CIC 3378. Cassette. Recorded in France. Original label: Carosello.

> Libertango, Meditango, Zita. Adiós Nonino. Violentango. (All music by A. Piazzolla.)
>
> LINEUP: Astor Piazzolla (bandoneon), Tommy Gubistch (guitar), Gustavo Beytelman (piano), Ricardo Sanz (bass), Luis Cerávolo (percussion), Osvaldo Caló (organ), Daniel Piazzolla (synthesizer), Luis Ferreyra (flute, sax).

1978

Piazzolla 78. Orchestra. Trova DA 5015 LP. Recorded in Italy. Original label: Carosello.

> Mundial 78 (Thriller). Marcación (Panic). Penal (Tango Fever). Gambeta (Chador). Golazo (Goooal). Wing (Baires Promenade). Corner (Milonga Trip). Campeón (Tango Blues). (All music by A. Piazzolla.)
>
> *The title of this album was changed in 1990 to* Chador. *In parentheses are the new titles assigned to these tracks when the name of the recording was changed.*

1979

Biyuya. Quintet. Interdisc SLIM 3055 LP. Original label: Carosello.
Biyuya. Movimiento continuo. Chin chin. Verano del '79. Mare-
jadilla. Escualo. (All music by A. Piazzolla.)
LINEUP: Astor Piazzolla (bandoneon), Pablo Ziegler (piano), Fernando Suárez Paz (violin), Oscar López Ruiz (guitar), Héctor Console (contrabass).

1982

Piazzolla—Goyeneche. Quintet. RCA Victor AVS 4999 LP.
Tristezas de un Doble A (A. Piazzolla). La muerte del ángel (A.
Piazzolla). Chiquilín de Bachín (A. Piazzolla, H. Ferrer). El Gordo
triste (A. Piazzolla, H. Ferrer). Cambalache (E. S. Discépolo). La
última curda (A. Troilo, C. Castillo). Balada para un loco (A. Piazzolla, H. Ferrer).
LINEUP: Same as for Biyuya, above.

*Garua (A. Troilo, E.Cadícamo) was added to the release RCA BMG 74321
18920-2. The track, featuring Goyeneche accompanied by Piazzolla on bandoneon, was not included in the original release because of time limitations.*

Volver. Quintet. Tonodisc DLF 8069 LP.
Siempre se vuelve a Buenos Aires (A. Piazzolla, E. Blázquez). Dos
amigos. Alfredo y Beatriz. Caminata. Tema de amor. Vista aérea.
La piecita. Procesión. Sexómano. Fracaso. Los magos. (All music by
A. Piazzolla except where noted.)

Piazzolla 1943–1982. RCA TLP 2 50032 LP. Double album.
Inspiración (P. Paulos, L. Rubinstein, Aníbal Troilo Orchestra).
Adiós Nonino. Calambre. Prepárense. Redención (A. Gobbi). Tri-
unfal. Balada para un loco (A. Piazzolla, H. Ferrer with singer
Robertero Goyeneche). Chiquilín de Bachín (A. Piazzolla, H. Ferrer
with singer Roberto Goyeneche). Verano porteño. Invierno por-
teno. Concierto para quinteto. La casita de mis viejos (J. C. Cobián,
E. Cadícamo). Milonga triste (S. Piana, H. Manzi). El motivo (J. C.
Cobián, P. Contursi, and bandoneon duet with Aníbal Troilo).
Tristezas de un Doble A. El Gordo triste (A. Piazzolla, H. Ferrer
with singer Amelita Baltar). Un día de paz. Garúa (A. Troilo, E.
Cadícamo with singer Robertero Goyeneche). La muerte del ángel.
(All music by A. Piazzolla except where noted.)

Georges Moustaki—Piazzolla. Astor Piazzolla (solo bandoneon).
Polydor 6052 LP. Recorded in London, England.
  Hacer esta canción (A. Piazzolla, G. Moustaki). La memoria (A.
  Piazzolla, G. Moustaki). La llaman locura (G. Moustaki). Amante
  del sol y de la música (G. Moustaki). Tenemos tiempo (G. Mous-
  taki, D. Milchberg).

  From this same period is Mon corps (A Piazzolla, G. Moustaki), a piece
  which Moustaki included in a CD produced in France in 1987 (Blue Sil-
  ver 8238.)

Oblivion. Orchestra. EMI 64 2402211 LP. Recorded in Italy. Music
written for the film *Enrico IV* by Marco Bellochio.
  Oblivion (1). Remembrance. Cavalcata. Oblivion (2). Oblivion
  (3). Enrico IV. Tanti anni prima. Oblivion (4). (All music by A.
  Piazzolla.)
  LINEUP: Astor Piazzolla (solo bandoneon), Juan Pablo Torres (solo
  trombone), Angelo Arienti (solo guitar). Oboe soloist not indicated.

Piazzolla—Jairo. RCA Victor AVI 4939 LP. Recorded in France.
  Hay una niña en el alba (A. Piazzolla, H. Ferrer).

  Piazzolla accompanied Jairo on the bandoneon only on this track. The LP
  was released under the title Jairo: My Best Songs. *They also recorded*
  Gotango (A. Piazzolla, J. M. Cherino), but it wasn't included on this
  recording.

Live in Wien. Quintet. Messidor 45916 LP. Recorded live in Vienna,
Austria.
  Fracanapa. Verano porteño. Caliente. Decarísimo. Libertango.
  Revirado. Invierno porteño. Adiós Nonino. (All music by A. Piaz-
  zolla.)
  LINEUP: Astor Piazzolla (bandoneon), Pablo Ziegler (piano), Fer-
  nando Suárez Paz (violin), Oscar López Ruiz (guitar), Héctor Con-
  sole (contrabass).

1983
Woe. Astor Piazzolla and the String Quartet of the Graunke Orchestra
of Munich. Recorded in Italy. Eleven Music. LP.
  Sleeping. Midnight. Woe. Look Out. Desire. Awake. Woe Pass
  Away. (All music by A. Piazzolla.)

Live in Lugano. Quintet. Ermitage 124 ADD. Recorded live at the Palazzo dei Congressi, Lugano, Switzerland, 13 October 1983.

Adiós Nonino. Escualo. Invierno porteño. Libertango. Biyuya. Fracanapa. Lunfardo. Revirado. Caliente. Decarísimo. Milonga del ángel. Muerte del ángel. Resurrección del ángel. (All music by A. Piazzolla.)

LINEUP: Same as for *Live in Wien*, above.

1984

Piazzolla—Alberto Cortez: Gardel como yo lo siento. Quintet with singer Alberto Cortez. MH 14.697-1 LP.

Mi Buenos Aires querido (C. Gardel, A. Lepera).

This is the only track that brings Piazzolla and Cortez together.

1985

Milva—Piazzolla. Quintet. Polydor 825 125-1-B LP. Recorded live at the Bouffes du Nord Theater in Paris.

Balada para mi muerte (A. Piazzolla, H. Ferrer). Los pájaros perdidos (A. Piazzolla, M. Trejo). Decarísimo (A. Piazzolla). Años de soledad (A. Piazzolla, M. Le Forestier). Balada para un loco (A. Piazzolla, H. Ferrer). Vamos nina (A. Piazzolla, H. Ferrer). Yo olvido (A. Piazzolla, D. McNeil). Che tango che (A. Piazzolla, J. C. Carriere). Preludio para el año 3001 (A. Piazzolla, H. Ferrer). Finale entre Brecht et Brel (A. Piazzolla, C. Lemesle).

LINEUP: Same as for *Live in Wien*, above.

Piazzolla tango. Music Hall 14797-8 LP. Liège Philarmonic conducted by Leo Browner. Cacho Tirao (solo guitar). Recorded live in Liège, Belgium.

Adiós Nonino. Concierto para bandoneón y guitarra. (All music by A. Piazzolla.)

The first symphonic version of Adiós Nonino was heard in 1980 with Piazzolla as soloist with the National Symphony Orchestra directed by Simón Blech. This version appeared in 1995 on a recording of works by various composers titled Panorama de la música Argentina *(Cosentino Irco 306 CD).*

Piazzolla—André Heller. Quintet with singer André Heller. Polydor LP. Recorded in Vienna, Austria.

Maria Magdalena. Der alte Pierre. Lindenberg. (All music by
A. Piazzolla, A. Heller.)
LINEUP: Same as for *Live in Wien*, above.

The Quintet accompanied Heller.

1986

El exilio de Gardel. Quintet. RCA Victor TLP 60200 LP.
   Dúo de amor. Ausencias. Tanguedia III. Mumuki. Tanguedia. El
   día que me quieras (C. Gardel, A. Le Pera). (All music by A. Piazzolla except where noted.)
   LINEUP: Same as for *Live in Wien*, above.

El nuevo tango: Piazzolla and Gary Burton. Quintet. WEA 80720 9 LP.
Recorded live at the Montreux Jazz Festival, Montreux, Switzerland.
   La milonga se acerca. Vibrafonisimo. Pequeña Italia. Nuevo tango.
   Sueño de Laura. Operación tango. (All music by A. Piazzolla.)
   LINEUP: Astor Piazzolla (bandoneon), Gary Burton (vibraphone),
   Pablo Ziegler (piano), Fernando Suárez Paz (violin), Horacio
   Malvicino (guitar), Héctor Console (contrabass).

   La muerte del angel, left out of the original LP because of time limitations,
   was included on the CD WEA 2292-55069-2.

Hora cero. Quintet. American Clave AMCL 1013 CD. Recorded in the
U.S.
   Tanguedia III. Milonga del ángel. Concierto para quinteto. Milonga
   loca. Michelangelo '70. Contrabajísimo. Mumuki. (All music by A.
   Piazzolla.)
   LINEUP: Astor Piazzolla (bandoneon), Pablo Ziegler (piano), Fer-
   nando Suárez Paz (violin), Horacio Malvicino (guitar), Héctor
   Console (contrabass).

1987

Tristezas de un Doble A. Quintet. Messidor 15970 CD. Recorded live at
the Konzert Haus, Vienna, Austria, 1986.
   Tristezas de un Doble A. Tanguedia. Biyuya. Lunfardo. Tangata.
   (All music by A. Piazzolla.)
   LINEUP: Astor Piazzolla (bandoneon), Pablo Ziegler (piano), Fer-
   nando Suárez Paz (violin), Héctor Console (contrabass), Horacio
   Malvicino (guitar).

1988

Concierto para bandoneón y orquesta. St. Luke's Orchestra conducted by Lalo Schifrin with A. Piazzolla, bandoneon. WEA 80767 Cassette. Recorded in the U.S.

> Concierto para bandoneón y orquesta. Tres tangos para bandoneón y orquesta. (All music by A. Piazzolla.)

Sur. Quintet. RCA Victor TLP 90127 LP.

> Vuelvo al sur (A. Piazzolla, F. Solanas). Regreso al amor. Tristeza separación. Regreso al amor (2). Los sueños. Tristeza separación (2). Los sueños (2). (All music by A. Piazzolla except where noted.)
> LINEUP: Same as for *Tristezas de un Doble A*, above.

Tango apasionado. American Clave 1019. Recorded in the U.S.

> Prologue tango apasionado. Milonga for Three. Street Tango. Milonga picaresque. Knife Fight. Leonora's Song. Prelude to the Cyclical Night. Butcher's Death. Leijia's Game. Milonga Reprise. Bailongo. Leonora's Love. Finale tango apasionado. Prelude to the Cyclical Night (Part II). (All music by A. Piazzolla.)
> LINEUP: Astor Piazzolla (bandoneon), Pablo Zinger (piano), Fernando Suárez Paz (violin), Paquito D' Rivera (sax), Andy González (electric bass), Rodolfo Alchourrón (guitar).

> *Not to be confused with Pablo Ziegler, the Uruguayan-born Pablo Zinger, based in New York, often works with saxophonist Paquito D'Rivera.*

1989

La camorra. Quintet. American Clave 1021. Recorded in the U.S.

> Soledad. La camorra I. La camorra II. La camorra III. Fugata. Sur. Los sueños. Regreso al amor. (All music by A. Piazzolla.)
> LINEUP: Astor Piazzolla (bandoneon), Pablo Ziegler (piano), Fernando Suárez Paz (violin), Horacio Malvicino (guitar), Héctor Console (contrabass).

> *This is a historic recording, the last recording of the Quintet.*

1990

Concierto para quinteto. Quintet. Alfa (no number). Double CD. From a recording of a live performance at the Gran Rex Theater in Buenos Aires in 1981.

Invierno porteño. Otoño porteño. Concierto para quinteto. Biyuya.
Muerte del ángel. Adiós Nonino. Palabras de Piazzolla. Tristezas de
un Doble A. Tangata. Verano porteño. Libertango. (All music by A.
Piazzolla.)

LINEUP: Astor Piazzolla (bandoneon), Pablo Ziegler (piano), Fernando Suárez Paz (violin), Oscar López Ruiz (guitar), Héctor Console (contrabass).

1991

Five Tango Sensations. Astor Piazzolla and the Kronos Quartet. None-
such-Warner 559-79254-2. Recorded in the U.S. in 1990.

Asleep. Loving. Anxiety. Despertar. Fear. (All music by A. Piazzolla.)

LINEUP: Astor Piazzolla (bandoneon). Kronos Quartet: David Har-
rington (violin), John Serbo (violin), Hank Dutt (viola), Joan
Jeanrenaud (cello).

This is a historic recording, Piazzolla's last recorded in a studio.

1992

Finally Together. Sextet. Lucho 7704-2 CD. Recorded live in Amsterdam in 1989.

Buenos Aires hora cero. Tanguedia III. Milonga del ángel. Camorra
III. Preludio y fuga. Sex-tex. Luna. La yumba (Osvaldo Pugliese).
Adiós Nonino (Piazzolla's Sextet and the Osvaldo Pugliese Orches-
tra). (All music by A. Piazzolla except where noted.)

LINEUP: Astor Piazzolla and Daniel Binelli (bandoneons), Gerardo
Gandini (piano), José Bragato (cello), Héctor Console (contrabass),
Horacio Malvicino (guitar).

Música de la película "El infierno tan temido." Soundtrack with the
Quintet. Ans Records 12011-2 CD. Original label: Carosello.

El infierno tan temido. Isa Risso. Tema de gracia. Desesperado.
Tanguería. Gracia amor. Effeti. Fotografía. Final. (All music by
A. Piazzolla.)

Musica de la película "La intrusa." Soundtrack with the Quintet. Ans
Records 12013-2 CD. Original label: Carosello.

A intrusa (Part I). Milonga. Celos (Part I). Malambo. Amanecer.

La intrusa (Part II). Eduardo y Juliano (Part I). Eduardo y Juliano (Part II). Pensamiento. Espejo. Eduardo y Juliano (Part III). Luna, luna. Duelo facón. La intrusa (Part III). Celos (Part II). (All music by A. Piazzolla.)

1993

The Lausanne Concert. Sextet. Milan Sur, BMG, CDA 631 CD. Recorded live in 1989.

Tanguedia III. Milonga del ángel. Buenos Aires hora cero. Adiós Nonino. Mumuki. Contrabajísimo. Reality. Operación tango. Nuevo tango. Camorra II. (All music by A. Piazzolla.)

LINEUP: Astor Piazzolla and Daniel Binelli (bandoneons), Gerardo Gandini (piano), Carlos Nozzi (cello), Ángel Ridolfi (contrabass), Horacio Malvicino (guitar).

Titles have been changed: Reality actually is Sex-tet, Operación tango is This is Luna, and Camorra II is Tres minutos con la realidad. The title changes could be honest mistakes by the label or a misguided attempt to differentiate this recording from others by the Sextet.

Introducción al ángel. Quintet. Melopea. CAMSE 5041 CD. From a live recording at Radio Municipal, Buenos Aires, in 1963.

Introducción al ángel. La muerte del ángel. Buenos Aires hora cero. La calle 92. Adiós Nonino. Fracanapa. Chiqué (Brignolo). Prepárense. Los poseídos. Revirado. Lo que vendrá. (All music by A. Piazzolla.)

LINEUP: Astor Piazzolla (bandoneon), Antonio Agri (violin), Jaime Gosis (piano), Oscar López Ruiz (guitar), Kicho Díaz (contrabass).

Tangamente. Nonet. Just a Memory. JAM 9107. Original label: Eleven Music. A three-CD set presenting the music of Piazzolla from 1968 to 1973 from the RCA Victor and Trova catalogs, including pieces by the Nonet recorded live in Rome in 1972 at the Instituto Italolatinoamericano.

CD 1. 1968–1969. Musica instrumental de la operita *María de Buenos Aires*: Fuga y misterio. Tocata rea. Contramilonga a la funerala. Tangata del alba. Allegro tangábile. Amelita Baltar interpreta a Piazzolla-Ferrer: Ballada para un loco. Preludio para el año 3001. Balada para mi muerte. Adiós Nonino. Otoño porteño. Michelangelo 70. Coral. Tangata (Silfo y Ondina).

CD 2. 1969, 1972. Pulsación 1969. Homenaje a Cordoba. Fuga 9.
En 3 x 4. Oda para un hippie. Baires 72. Zum. Buenos Aires hora
cero. Vardarito. Onda 9. Muerte del ángel. Tristezas de un Doble A.
CD 3. 1972–1973. Verano porteño. Divertimento 9. Preludio 9.
Adiós Nonino. Mufa 72. Amelita Baltar con Astor Piazzolla
1972: Los paraguas de Buenos Aires. Las ciudades. La primera
palabra. No quiero otro. Vamos Nina. Astor Piazzolla y su
Conjunto 9 1973: El penúltimo. Jeanne and Paul. (All music
by A. Piazzolla.)

Little information is available about these versions of Buenos Aires hora
cero and Muerte del ángel as having been played by the Nonet and much
less about their having been recorded. The boxed set was released by Aldo
Pagani.

Libertango. Quintet, Grand Orchestra. Saludos amigos 62037 CD.
Adiós nonino. Mumuki. Verano porteño. Chin chin. Libertango.
Suite Punta del Este. (All music by A. Piazzolla.)
LINEUP: Astor Piazzolla (bandoneon), Fernando Suárez Paz (vio-
lin), Pablo Ziegler (piano), Oscar López Ruiz (guitar), Héctor Con-
sole (contrabass).

The Quintet recordings are from a performance at the Teatro Nazionale in
Milan, 15 October 1984. The Grand Orchestra recordings are from a per-
formance at the Teatro Municipal de Caracas, Venezuela, on 2 April 1981.
These recordings are of low sound quality, but both have historical
significance. Piazzolla planned to record Suite Punta del Este *in 1990, but*
on 4 August of that year he suffered the stroke from which he did not
recover. The Milan performance is the last by Piazzolla in that city.

1994
The Central Park Concert. Quintet. Chesky Records JD 107 CD.
Recorded live in 1987.
Verano porteño. Lunfardo. Milonga del ángel. Muerte del ángel.
Astor's Speech. Camorra. Mumuki. Adiós Nonino. Contrabajísimo.
Michelangelo. Concierto para quinteto. (All music by A. Piazzolla.)
LINEUP: Astor Piazzolla (bandoneon), Pablo Ziegler (piano), Fer-
nando Suárez Paz (violin), Héctor Console (contrabass), Horacio
Malvicino (guitar).

The piece listed as Camorra *is actually* Tanguedia III.

Aconcagua: Tres tangos. Symphony orchestra with Astor Piazzolla, solo bandoneon. AAA Pagani Caneo 3532 CD. Recorded at Kaiser-lauten Studio, Germany, in 1983.

> Aconcagua. Allegro marcato. Moderato. Presto. Tres tangos. Allegro tranquillo. Moderato místico. Allegretto molto marcato. (All music by A. Piazzolla.)
>
> *Aconcagua is not a new piece but actually* Concierto para bandoneón y orquesta *retitled by publisher Aldo Pagani after Piazzolla's death.*

Astor Piazzolla y su nuevo conjunto. Music of the World 12520 CD. A live recording of Piazzolla's Electronic Octet at La Ciudad in Buenos Aires, Argentina, in 1976.

> Libertango. Amilitango. L'evasion. Buenos Aires hora cero. Años de soledad. Los pájaros perdidos (A. Piazzolla, M. Trejo, S. Bardotti). Bandoneon. Zita. Adiós Nonino. Balada para mi muerte (A. Piazzolla, H. Ferrer). Balada para un loco (A. Piazzolla, H. Ferrer). (All music by A. Piazzolla except where noted.)
>
> LINEUP: Astor Piazzolla (bandoneon), Juan Carlos Cirigliano (piano), Adalberto Cevasco (bass), Horacio Malvicino (guitar), Daniel Piazzolla (synthesizer and percussion), Arturo Schneider (flute and sax), José Ángel Trelles (voice).
>
> *Technically poor but an important document. The cover of the CD, released in Europe in 1994, reads, "From Argentina, Astor Piazzolla and his new group." The recording is dated 1976. Piazzolla died in 1992.*

Una tarde en Buenos Aires. Orchestra. CD 2885 P-Vine/Blues Interactions. Japan. Original label: Tico LP-1065 (USA) 1959.

> Celos (Gade). Adiós muchachos (Sanders-Vedani). Orquídeas bajo la luz de la luna (Youmans). El choclo (A. Villoldo). A media luz (E. Donato, C. C. Lenzi). Nieblas del riachuelo (J. C. Cobián, E. Cadícamo). Nostalgías (J. C. Cobián, E. Cadícamo). Porque (O. and E. Fresedo). El día que me quieras (C. Gardel, A. Lepera). Derecho viejo (E. Arolas). Sus ojos se cerraron (C. Gardel, A. Lepera). Cuando camino bajo la lluvia (A. Piazzolla?).

Llevame bailando. Quintet. CD 2877 P-Vine/Blues Interactions. Japan. Original label: Tico LP 1066 (USA) 1959.

> Laura (Mercer, Raskin). Triunfal. Oscar Peterson. Abril en París (D. Harburg). Boricua. Para lucirse. Canción de cuna en la tierra de los pájaros (G. Shearing). Plus ultra. La dama sofisticada (D. Elling-

ton, Mills, Parish). Contratiempo. Algo raro. La coquette (F. Gon-
zaga). (All music by A. Piazzolla except where noted.)
LINEUP: Astor Piazzolla (bandoneon), Al Caiola (guitar), Eddie
Costa (piano), Chet Amsterdam and George Duvivier (bass), Carlos
Rauch, Johnny Pacheco, and Tito Puente (percussion).

*This CD, like the one above, appeared in Buenos Aires without the original
label, with all the markings of a pirate release.*

1995

Piazzolla ensayos. Quintet. Jazz Fusión Records. JF 9503 CD.
Contrabajeando. Lo que vendrá. Intimidad de ensayo. Tango para
una ciudad. Bando. Tres minutos con la realidad. Melancólico
Buenos Aires. Triunfal. Adiós Nonino. Cristal (J. M. Contursi, M.
Mores). Uno (E. S. Discépolo, M. Mores). (All music by A. Piaz-
zolla except where noted.)
LINEUP: Astor Piazzolla (bandoneon), Jaime Gosis (piano), Elvino
Vardaro (violin), Horacio Malvicino (guitar), Kicho Díaz (contra-
bass).

Amateur recordings of rehearsals in late 1960, early 1961.

Bandoneón sinfónico. Athenas Colours Orchestra conducted by Manos
Hadjidakis. Milan Latino 34268-2 CD. Recorded live in Athens, Greece,
on 3 July 1990.
Tres tangos para bandoneón y orquesta. Adiós Nonino. Concierto
para bandoneón y orquesta. (All music by A. Piazzolla.)

*According to Laura Escalada de Piazzolla in the CD booklet, this concert
was Astor Piazzolla's last performance.*

1996

57 minutos con la realidad. Sextet. Intuition Record. INT-3079/2.
1. Tres minutos con la realidad. 2. Mumuki. 3. Sexteto. 4. Adiós
Nonino. 5. Imágenes. 6. Milonga para tres. 7. Buenos Aires hora
cero. 8. Pasajes oscuros dos estrellas. 9. Preludio a la cyclical night.
(All music by A. Piazzolla.)
LINEUP: Astor Piazzolla and Daniel Binelli (bandoneons), Horacio
Malvicino (guitar), Gerardo Gandini (piano), Héctor Console (con-
trabass), José Bragato (cello).

*Tracks 1 through 4 were recorded in July 1989 at the television studios of
the BBC. Tracks 5 through 8 were recorded in November 1989 at Connyús*

Studio, Neunkirchen, Germany. Track 9 was recorded in August 1982 at Radio City Studio, NY. Additional recording in September 1993 at RPM Studio, NY. Edited and mastered in December 1995 and January 1996 at Sound Byte Studio, NY. On tracks 1 and 2, Andy González replaced H. Console. On track 7, Carlos Nozzi and Ángel Ridolfi replaced H. Console and J. Bragato, respectively.

Tango Piazzolla: Astor Piazzolla Key Works 1984–1989. Music Collection International. MC CD 165. Recorded at Studio Delphine, Paris, December 1984; Studio ICP, Brussels, November 1984; Studio Panda, Buenos Aires, April 1985; and Studio Ion, Buenos Aires, December 1987.

1. Vuelvo al sur. 2. Ausencias. 3. Oblivion. 4. Tanti anni prima. 5. Tango-tango. 6. Tristeza, separación. 7. Los sueños. 8. Dúo de amor. 9. Tanguedia I. 10. Milonga del ángel. 11. Adiós Nonino. 12. Nuevo tango. 13. Camorra II. 14. Regreso al amor. (All music by A. Piazzolla.)

LINEUP: Astor Piazzolla (bandoneon), Susana Lago (voice, piano, and synthesizer), Pablo Ziegler and Gerardo Gandini (piano), Roberto Goyeneche (voice), Miguel Ángel Solá (recitation), Kurzwell Omar Espinosa (acoustic guitar and acoustic Gibson guitar), Horacio Malvicino and Oscar López Ruiz (guitars), Alain Huteau (alto sax and drums), Jean-Louis Carlotti, Héctor Console, and Ángel Ridolfi (contrabass), Daniel Cabrera and Daniel Binelli (bandoneons), Fernando Suárez Paz (violin), Carlos Nozzi (cello).

Tracks 1, 6, 7, and 14 were taken from the original soundtrack of Sur, *a film by Fernando Solanas. Tracks 2, 5, and 8 are from the film* El exilio de Gardel *by Solanas. Tracks 3 and 4 are from the film* Enrico IV *by Marco Bellochio. Tracks 9–13 were recorded live by the Sextet at Moulin and Danses, Lausanne, Switzerland, on 4 November 1989. They feature Ridolfi (contrabass) and Nozzi (cello), which makes this CD a bit of a novelty.*

1997

Libertango. Quintet. Milan Sur 51138-2 CD. Recorded at the Teatro Roxy, Mar del Plata, Argentina, in February 1984.

Verano porteño. Lunfardo. Decarísimo. Milonga del ángel. Muerte del ángel. Resurreción del ángel. Tristezas de un Doble A. Escualo. Mumuki. Contrabajísimo. Libertango. Chin chin. (All music by A. Piazzolla.)

LINEUP: Astor Piazzolla (bandoneon), Fernando Suárez Paz (violin), Pablo Ziegler (piano), Oscar López Ruiz (guitar), Héctor Console (contrabass).

Do not confuse this Libertango with the earlier release of the same title. Apparently there is not much originality in record companies.

La muerte del ángel. Quintet. Milan Sur 51140-2 CD. Recorded live at the Teatro Odeón, 1974.

Verano porteño. Los poseidos. Milonga del ángel. Muerte del ángel. Adiós Nonino. Otoño porteño. Retrato de Milton. (All music by A. Piazzolla.)

LINEUP: Astor Piazzolla (bandoneon), Osvaldo Tarantino (piano), Antonio Agri (violin).

The record label offers no other information, but at the time the Quintet featured Kicho Díaz (contrabass) and Horacio Malvicino (guitar). There is an excellent improvisation by Osvaldo Tarantino in Otoño porteño in what is his only recording with the Quintet. Retrato de Milton, dedicated to Brazilian pop singer Milton Nascimento, was called Retrato de mí mismo before and Luna later, in the Sextet period of 1989. The date of the concert is not known, but the year could have been 1973. After dissolving the Nonet and before leaving for Europe, Piazzolla did some shows with the Quintet.

Tres minutos con la realidad. Sextet. Milan Sur 51339-2 CD. Recorded live at Club Italiano of Buenos Aires in April 1989.

Luna. Sexteto. Tres minutos con la realidad. Camorra II. Camorra III. Tango ballet. (All music by A. Piazzolla.)

LINEUP: Astor Piazzolla and Julio Pane (bandoneons), José Bragato (cello), Gerardo Gandini (piano), Horacio Malvicino (electric guitar), Héctor Console (contrabass).

Although identified as a "concert" at the Italiano, this was actually a rehearsal before invited guests.

Piazzolla en el Colón. Nonet and the Teatro Colón Philharmonic Orchestra conducted by Pedro Ignacio Calderón. CD Sello La Batuta. Recorded live at Teatro Colón in Buenos Aires on 11 June 1983.

Adiós Nonino (symphonic arrangement). Vardarito (Nonet). Fuga y misterio (Nonet). Verano porteño (Nonet). Concierto de nacar (Nonet with orchestra). Concierto para bandoneón y orquesta. (All music by A. Piazzolla.)

LINEUP (Nonet): Astor Piazzolla (bandoneon), Fernando Suárez Paz and Hugo Baralis (violins), Pablo Ziegler (piano), Enrique Roizner (percussion), José Bragato (cello), Héctor Console (contrabass), Delmar Quarleri (viola), Oscar López Ruiz (guitar).

Because of legal agreements, this CD was released under this name only in Argentina. In the rest of the world it was released as Concierto de nacar *(Milan Sur 51139-2) with a bonus track by the Nonet:* Buenos Aires hora cero. *This Milan Sur CD contains a grave error. Track 7 is not* Adiós Nonino *and track 8 is not* Adiós Nonino (bis). *In fact, those are the second and third movements of the* Concierto para bandoneón y orquesta. *We insist that the version on the La Batuta label is impeccable.*

Live at the BBC 1989. Sextet. CD INT 3226-2. Recorded at the Bristol Studios of the BBC in June 1989.

Tanguedia III. Milonga del ángel. Sextet. Michelangelo. Mumuki. Tango Zero Hour. Adiós Nonino. Tres minutos con la realidad. (All music by A. Piazzolla.)

LINEUP: Astor Piazzolla and Daniel Binelli (bandoneons), Horacio Malvicino (guitar), Gerardo Gandini (piano), José Bragato (cello), Héctor Console (contrabass).

1998

This information is included because of the artistic importance of these works.

Yo-Yo Ma: Soul of the Tango—The Music of Astor Piazzolla. Sony SK 63122. This CD features a virtual duet with Yo-Yo Ma and Piazzolla from a track originally recorded in 1987. For this new piece entitled "Tango Remembrances," Los Angeles–based Argentine composer and arranger Jorge Calandrelli incorporated bits of outtakes of Piazzolla's bandoneon playing from the album *The Rough Dancer and the Cyclical Night (Tango apasionado)*.

Gary Burton: Astor Piazzolla Reunion—A Tango Excursion. Concord CCD 4793-2. This release features vibraphonist Gary Burton with the members of Piazzolla's last Quintet. It includes the tango "Mi refugio," a virtual duet with Burton dubbed over Piazzolla's recording from 1970.

Chronology

1921   Astor Pantaleón Piazzolla is born on 11 March 1921 in the city of Mar del Plata, province of Buenos Aires, Argentina.

1925   Family settles in New York, where they live until 1936 except for a brief interval in Mar del Plata in 1930.

1929   Father gives him his first bandoneon.

1933   Takes music lessons with pianist Béla Wilda, a disciple of Rachmaninoff.

1934   Meets Carlos Gardel and plays a cameo in the movie *El día que me quieras*.

1936   Family returns to Argentina for good.

1939   Joins Aníbal Troilo's orchestra.

1941   Studies with Alberto Ginastera.

1943   Takes piano lessons with Raúl Spivak.

1944   Leaves Troilo to lead the orchestra of singer Francisco Fiorentino.

1946   Debuts leading his own orchestra (the 1946 Orchestra).

1949   Writes his first film score, for *Con los mismos colores* by Argentine director Leopoldo Torre Ríos.

1950   Disbands his 1946 Orchestra.

1953 Wins the Fabien Sevitzky Prize, a cash award and scholarship to study in France, and premieres his *Buenos Aires* Symphony (*Tres movimientos sinfónicos*) in Buenos Aires.

1954 Studies in Paris with the renowned Nadia Boulanger.

1955 Upon his return, founds the Buenos Aires Octet, for many the fault line between traditional and contemporary tango.

1959 In New York writes his most popular piece, "Adiós Nonino."

1960 Back in Buenos Aires forms his most famous group, the Quintet.

1965 For the first time releases an album comprising only his original compositions, *Piazzolla en el Philarmonic Hall de New York*.

1965 Releases *El tango*, an album for which he collaborates with the poet Jorge Luis Borges.

1968 Premieres the operetta *María de Buenos Aires* with a libretto by Horacio Ferrer.

1969 Writes "Balada para un loco," lyrics by Horacio Ferrer.

1971 Founds Conjunto 9 (Nonet); puts aside his Quintet for several years.

1974 Records in Italy with saxophonist Gerry Mulligan.

1976 Organizes the Electronic Octet.

1978 Forms the second Quintet, with which he will tour the world for eleven years.

1983 Performs at the Teatro Colón in Buenos Aires.

1985 Is named Illustrious Citizen of Buenos Aires.

1986 Wins the French critics' César Award for best film music for *El exilio de Gardel*.

1986 Records with Gary Burton.

1987 Records *Concierto para bandoneón y orquesta* with Lalo Schifrin.

1988 Records *La camorra*, his last album with the Quintet.

1989 Organizes the Sextet, his last group, formally New Tango Sextet.

1990 In New Orleans, Russian cellist Mstislav Rostropovich premieres Piazzolla's *Le grand tango* for cello and piano.

1990 Records his last album, *Five Tango Sensations*, with the Kronos Quartet.

1990 A cerebral hemorrhage and stroke fell him in Paris on 4 August.

1992 He never recovers. Piazzolla dies in Buenos Aires on 4 July.

Bibliography

Sources

Ferrer, Horacio. *El libro del tango: Arte popular de Buenos Aires.* Buenos Aires: Ossorio-Vargas, 1970; Barcelona: Antonio Tersol, 1980.

Kuri, Carlos. *Piazzolla: La música límite,* 2d ed. Buenos Aires: Ediciones Corregidor, 1992.

López Ruiz, Oscar. *Piazzolla, loco, loco, loco: 25 años de laburo y jodas conviviendo con un genio.* 2d ed. Buenos Aires: Ediciones de la Urraca, 1994.

Piazzolla, Diana. *Astor.* Buenos Aires: Emecé, 1987.

Speratti, Alberto. *Con Piazzolla.* Buenos Aires: Galerna, 1969.

Additional information

Azzi, María Susana, and Simon Collier. *Le Grand Tango: The Life and Music of Astor Piazzolla.* Oxford and New York: Oxford University Press, 2000.

Chase, Gilbert. *Guide to the Music of Latin America.* 2d ed. Washington: Pan American Union, 1962; reprinted New York: AMS Press, 1972.

Collier, Simon. *The Life, Music & Times of Carlos Gardel.* Pitt Latin American Series. Pittsburgh: University of Pittsburgh Press, 1986.

Collier, Simon, Artemis Cooper, María S. Azzi, and Richard Martin. *Tango!: The Dance, the Song, the Story.* London: Thames & Hudson, 1997.

Ferrer, Horacio. *El siglo de oro del tango.* Buenos Aires: Horacio Ferrer —Manrique Zgo Ediciones, 1996.

García Mendez, Javier Peñon, and Arturo Peñon. *The Bandonion: A Tango History.* Trans. Tim Barnard. London, Ontario: Nightwood Editions, 1988.

Pampin, Manuel, ed. *La historia del tango*. Buenos Aires: Ediciones Corregidor, 1976.

Pellettieri, Osvaldo, ed. *Radiografía de Carlos Gardel*. Buenos Aires: Editorial Abril, 1987.

Salas, Horacio. *El tango*. Buenos Aires: Editorial Planeta Argentina, 1986.

Sierra, Luis Adolfo. *Historia de la orquesta típica: Evolución instrumental del tango*. Buenos Aires: Ediciones Corregidor, 1966.

A comprehensive Web site can be found at *http://www.piazzolla.org*.

Index

Italicized page numbers refer to illustrations.

Accardi, Salvatore, 114, 182
Agri, Antonio, 79–80, 82, 110, 114, *137*,
   160, 180, 182
   with Quintet, *52*, *53*, *54*, 58, 185
Ahumada, Julio, 41
Amicarelli, Dante, 180–181
Antonioni, Michelangelo, 171
Aristarain, Adolfo, 171
Arnold, Alfred, 35, 144
Arolas, Eduardo, 43
Assad, Odair, 17
Assad, Sergio, 17
Astiz, Alfredo, 88–89
Ayestarán, Lauro, 191
Aznavour, Charles, 192

Bach, Johann Sebastian, 19, 93, 97, 125,
   126, 129, 142
Badi, Libero, 90
Bajour, Simón (Szymsia), 173
Baltar, Amelita, 106, 118–120, *119*,
   123–124, 182, 183, 185, *190*
   as singer, 49, 86–87, *114*, *137*, 179
Band, Heinrich, 34
Baralis, Hugo ("Huguito"), 59, 62–63, *74*,
   75, 100, 117, *137*
Bardi, Agustín, 43
Barenboim, Daniel, 169
Bariloche, Camerata, 188

Barletta, Alejandro, 100–101
Bartók, Béla, 16, 107, 129, 149
Basabru, Fernando, 22
Basso, José, 46,
Baudo, Vicenzo, 29
Bergman, Ingmar, 170
Bernstein, Leonard, 71
Binelli, Daniel, 35, 44–45, 92, 161, *162*,
   163, 188, *203*
Bioy Casares, Adolfo, 90
Biral, Thelma, 90
Blázquez, Eladia, 89–90
Blech, Simón, 129–130
Bocca, Julio, 152
Bolognini, Astor, 93
Bores, Tato, 136
Borges, Jorge Luis, 9, 103–105, *104*, 152,
   165–167, 177–178
Borocotó. See Lorenzo, Ricardo
Boulanger, Nadia, 16, 19–20, 25, 47,
   69–73, *70*, 83, 94, 131–132, *131*,
   168–169, 193, 195, 196
Boulez, Pierre, 83
Boyé, Mario, 47
Bozán, Sofia ("La Negra"), 40
Bragato, José, *74*, 75, 91–92, 100, *162*, *203*
Brignolo, Ricardo Luis, 173
Burton, Gary, 20, 22, 40, 82, 85–86, 114,
   133, 153, 176, 202–206, *203*

Cadícamo, Enrique Domingo, 63, 66, 166
Calderón, Pedro Ignacio, 129–130, 183
Calloway, Cab, 13, 37, 47
Caló, Miguel, 16, 41, 43, 128
Camilo, Michel, 188
Campanella, Joseph, 32
Canaro, Francisco, 48
Caniggia, Claudio Paul, 187
Carfi, Anahí, 154, 161, 188, 196–197
Carlevaro, Agustín, 193–194
Casadesus, Robert, 71
Castellanos, Alberto, 96
Castillo, Cátulo, 63, 191
Castro, Juan José, 72, 112
Centofanti, Rosa. See Piazzolla, Rosa
    Centofanti de
Cevasco, Adalberto, 83
Cirigliano, Juan Carlos, 58, 83
Clarke, Stanley, 163
Clausi, Gabriel, 42
Cobián, Juan Carlos, 44, 47
Colombier, Michel, 152
Console, Héctor, 82, 91–92, *154, 162, 203*
Contursi, José María ("Catunga"), 66
Copes, Juan Carlos, *76*, 77–78, 165
Copland, Aaron, 69, 71, 114, 130, 192
Corea, Chick, 83, 85, 147, 163, 165, 202
Correale, José, *137*
Cortázar, Julio, 91, 171
Cura, Julio, 89

Dan, Leo, 172
Dantas, Arturo, 193
D'Aquila, Andrés, 98, 125, 141
D'Arienzo, Juan, 18, 61
Dávalos, Julia Elena, 90
Davis, Miles, 85–86, 112–113, 163, 188,
    206
De Angelis, Alfredo, 43
Debussy, Claude, 16
De Caro, Francisco, 44, 128
De Caro, Julio, 32–33, 43–44, 93, 192
Delfino, Enrique, 126, 194
Delon, Alain, 107
De los Ríos, Waldo, 106–107, 148

Demare, Lucas, 171
De Moraes, Vinicius, *114*, 115, 169–170,
    182, 191
De Narke, Victor, 90
De Rosas, Héctor, 88, *137*
De Santi, Marco, 196
Díaz, David, 59, 62
Díaz, Enrique ("Kicho"), 80–81, *137*, 173,
    179–180
    with Quintet, *52, 54*, 58
    with Troilo's orchestra, 62, 101
Di Cico, Enrique ("Minotto"), 100, 142
Di Filippo, Roberto, *46*, 100–101, 129, 142,
    143, 155, 176, 207–211
Di Meola, Al, 150, 163
Discépolo, Armando, 171
Discépolo, Enrique Santos, 25, 66, 171
Dorsey, Tommy, 136
Duarte, María Eva (Evita Perón), 155

Echegaray, Natalio, 198
Ellington, Duke, 77, 206
Emerson, Keith, 149
Ertegun, Nesuhi, 204
Escalada, Laura, 18, 50, 66, *104*, 124, 135,
    184, 197, 200
    and love, 118–120, *121*, 186
Esteban, El Negro, 32
Evans, Gil, 48, 112–113, 149–150
Expósito, Homero, 62, 166
Expósito, Virgilio, 62

Fabiani (bandoneon repairman), 143
Falla, Manuel de, 144, 193
Federico, Leopoldo, *74*, 75, 86, 92, 142,
    143, 176, 207–211
Fellini, Federico, 128, 170
Ferrer, Horacio, 49, 88, 166, 178–179, *190*,
    191–195
    and "La bicicleta blanca," 78
    and "El Gordo triste," 68, 159
    and *María de Buenos Aires*, 137, *137*
Ferri, Olga, 89–90
Fiorentino, Francisco, 45, 129
Françaix, Jean, 71

Francini, Enrique Mario, 43, *74*, 75, 100
Fresedo, Osvaldo, 46
Frondizi, Arturo, 170
Fuchs, Teodoro, 72

Galván, Argentino, 41, 62–63, 65
Gandini, Gerardo, 58, 80, 203
García, Charly, 85, 149
García Lorca, Federico, 193
García Márquez, Gabriel, 170
Gardel, Carlos, 26, 79, 83–85, 93, 98, 142,
    174–175, 176
  as tango star, 14, 15, 16, 21, 25, 63, 88
  and teenage Piazzolla, 37, 40, 61, 95–97,
    95, 126
Gassman, Vittorio, 170
Gershwin, George, 17, 60, 94–95
Getz, Stan, 114, 136, 202
Gide, André, 72
Gilberto, Joao, 115
Gillespie, John Birks ("Dizzy"), 106,
    112–113, 114, 188
Ginastera, Alberto, 25, 32, *73*, 106, 112,
    154, 168, 191, 196
  as teacher, 61–62, 65, 69, 72–73, 115,
    129, 155
Girri, Alberto, 90
Gobbi, Alfredo, 16, 43, 49, 98–100, *99*,
    101, 168, 172, 173, 176
Gómez, Albino, 115
Goñi, Orlando, 16, 43, 59–60, 62, 101–102
González, Felipe, 91
Gonzalez, Fernando, 13–22, 35
González Azcona, Quito, 164, 178, 185
González Castillo, José, 126
Gorin, Natalio, *10*, 9–11, 17–21, 105, 110,
    120, 124, 153, 163, *188*
Gosis, Jaime, 80, 82, 128, *137*, 173, 186
  with Quintet, *52*, *53*, 58
Goulda, Frederich, 136
Goyeneche, Roberto ("El Polaco"), 49, 86,
    88, 179
Grane, Héctor, 69
Greco, Vicente, 43
Greely, George, 75–78

Grela, Roberto, 192
Grondona, Mariano, 172
Guarany, Horacio, 91
Guerra, Maximiliano, 152
Guerrero Marthineitz, Hugo, 50
Guido, José María, 170
Guidoni, Jean, 149

Hanrahan, Kip, 22

Ibars, Antonio, 35
Illía, Arturo, 170, 172
Itelman, Ana, 77

Jagger, Mick, 149
Juárez, Manolo, 148
Juárez, Ruben, 88

Kenton, Stan, 47, 113
Khachaturian, Aram, 193
Kohon, David, 181
Kremer, Gidon, 169
Kuhn, Rodolfo, 171
Kuri, Carlos, 169

La Motta, Jake, 32
Laurenz, Pedro, 20, 41, 44, 48, *55–57*, 128,
    142, 143, 145, 182
Lauro, Francisco ("El Tano"), 17, 40,
    42–43, 59
Lavié, Raúl, 88
Legrand, Michel, 111
Legrand, Mirtha, 167
Leguizamón, Gustavo ("Cuchi"), 148
Leopoldo, Federico, 207–211
LePera, Alfredo, 96–97
Lerner, Alejandro, 149
Lhote, André, 67, 70, 131
López Ruiz, Oscar, 81, 82, 173, 179–180,
    182, 184
  with Quintet, *52*, *54*, 58
Lorenzo, Ricardo ("Borocotó"), 46–47
Lynch, Marta, 171

Maffia, Pedro, 40, 41, 43–44, *55–57*, 80, 128
  style, 142, 143, 145, 182
Malraux, André, 72
Malvicino, Horacio, 22, 82–83, *162*, 168, 172, 173, 176, *203*
  in Buenos Aires Octet, *74*, 75
  with Quintet, 81, *154*
Mancera, Nicolas ("Pipo"), 133, 136
Manetti, Asunta. See Piazzolla, Asunta Manetti de
Manzi, Homero, 66, 166
Manzi, Osvaldo, *53*, 58, 82
Maradona, Diego, 46–47, 187
Marconi, Néstor, 142
Markevitch, Igor, 71, 130
Martin, Egle, *119*
Matarazzo, Maysa, 115
Mederos, Rodolfo, 44–45, 163
Mejía, Ricardo, 172
Menem, Carlos Saúl, 155–156, 201
Menotti, César Luis, 135
Messiaen, Olivier, 16, 83
Metheny, Pat, 150
Milva (Maria Ilva Biocatti), 87, *87*
Mina (Ana Maria Mazzini), *232*
Mitterrand, François, 91
Monicelli, Mario, 171
Montero, Carlos, 130
Monti, Marikena, 124, 183
Mora, Joaquín, 44, 209
Morada, Franja, 89
Moreau, Jeanne, 94, *104*, 105–106, 110–111, 149
Moreno, Zully, 167
Mores, Mariano, 45, 48, 155, 192
Moretto, Gustavo, 163
Mozart, Wolfgang Amadeus, 17, 129
Muller, Mr. (German bandoneon player), 144–145
Mulligan, Gerry, 16, 20, 51, 82, 85–86, *108*, *109*, 132
  and *Summit*, 108–110, 134, 153, *158*, *184*

Nascimento, Milton, 115
Natola, Aurora, 73
Nicolini, Aldo, *74*
Nievas, Roberto, 174
Nieves, María, *76*, 77
Nisinman, Marcelo, 35, 40

Ocampo, Victoria, 115
Oliveros, Víctor, 168, 185, *188*
Oréfiche, Armando, 193
Oréfiche, Chiquito, 193
Ortega, Palito, 172

Paez Vilaró, Carlos, 181
Pagani, Aldo, 105, *134*, 159–160, 165–166, 174, 175, 188
  contract with, 134, 184–185, 200
  and *Summit*, 153, *158*
Panik, Néstor, *137*
Pascual, José, 41
Pauloni, Homero, 33, 42, 125, 128
Pauloni, Líbero, 42, 128
Pelé, 170
Perón, Evita. See Duarte, María Eva
Perón, General Juan Domingo, 155, 167
Peterson, Oscar, 47
Philippe, Gerard, 105
Philippe, Pierre, 149
Piazzolla, Asunta Manetti de (Nonina) (mother), 13, *28*, 30–31, 33, 38, 93–94, 125, 131–132, 156
Piazzolla, Daniel (son), *108*, 173, 184, 185, *188*, 200
  as child, 67, *116*, 117, 118, 121, 131
  and Electronic Octet, 83, *85*
Piazzolla, Daniel Astor (grandson), 144
Piazzolla, Diana (daughter), 67, *116*, 117, 118, 121, 131, 184, *188*, 200
Piazzolla, Pantaleón (grandfather), 29, 93
Piazzolla, Rosa Centofanti de (grandmother), 93
Piazzolla, Vicente (Nonino) (father), 13, 75, 93–94, 102, 144, 156, 175
  and Astor as adult, 41, 60, 131–132

and Astor as child, *28*, 29–33, 38, 125, 141
  death, 78, 164
  as woodcarver, 96, 98
Picasso, Pablo, 189
Pinochet, General Augusto, 90
Pinter, Harold, 170
Pocholo (pianist), 128
Pomponio, John, 32
Ponti, Carlo, 111
Pontino, Victor, *137*
Ponty, Jean-Luc, 105
Puccini, Giacomo, 16
Puente, Ernest Anthony ("Tito"), 188
Pugliese, Lidia, 184
Pugliese, Osvaldo, 16, 18, 43, 48–49, *102*,
  102–103, 168, 184, 192
  playing Piazzolla's music, 86
  and politics, 91
  and style, 79, 98
  and Troilo, 62

Racciatti, Donato, 48
Ramírez, Ariel, 44
Ravel, Maurice, 16, 71, 94–95, 112, 130, 194
Rinaldi, Susana, 124, 183
Rissi, Dino, 170
Rivero, Edmundo, 86, 88
Rodríguez, Juan Miguel ("Toto"), 59
Roizner, Enrique ("El Zurdo"), 83
Rolando (bass player), 128
Romualdo (bandoneon repairman), 144
Rovira, Eduardo, 44–45
Rubinstein, Arthur, 72, 111–112, 129, 143,
  173, 193

Sábato, Ernesto, 49
Salgán, Horacio, 40, 43, 58, 103, 192
Saluzzi, Dino, 44–45, 142
Salvo, Kiko, 185
Samson, Victor, 66
Sandrelli, Stephania, 111
Sandrini, Luis, 171
Santa Ana, Walter, 90
Santoro, Claudio, 191

Sapochnick, Pedro, 59
Sasiaín, Mario, 128
Scabutiello, Nicola, 30, 33
Scaramuzza, Vicente, 101
Scherchen, Hermann, 129
Schifrin, Lalo, 82, 106, 132, *139*, 140, 201
Schneider, Arturo, *137*
Selinger, Miguel ("Miguelito"), 180, 185
Serrat, Joan Manuel, 90
Sevitzky, Fabien, 130–131, *131*
Shapiro, Michal, 34
Shorter, Wayne, 188
Sierra, Luis Adolfo, 132
Solanas, Fernando ("Pino"), 89
Sommers, Stanley (originally
  Sommerkovsky), 36–37
Sosa, Mercedes, 44, 153
Spano, Marco, 196
Speratti, Alberto, 86, 118
Spinetta, Luis Alberto, 163
Spivak, Raúl, 129
Stampone, Atilio, *46*, *74*, 75
Stamponi, Héctor ("Chupita"), 41, 100, 192
Stern, Isaac, 136
Sting, 48, 113, 138, 149–150
Stravinsky, Igor, 17, 72, 79, 83, 113–115,
  129, 130, 149, 154
Suárez Paz, Fernando, 79–80, 82, *154*, 186
Subiela, Eliseo, 171
Swallow, Steve, 204

Talín, Atilio, 174, 198–201, *199*
Tarantino, Osvaldo, *54*, 58, 80, 181–182,
  192
Tatum, Art, 47
Tauriello, Juan Carlos, 89–90
Tinayre, Daniel, 89–90
Tirao, Oscar Emilio ("Cacho"), *53*, 58, 81,
  137
Torre Nilsson, Leopoldo, 46, 171
Torre Ríos, Leopoldo, 46
Toscanini, Arturo, 193
Trelles, José Ángel, 88
Trintignant, Jean Louis, 110–111

Trintignant, Nadine, 110–111
Tristano, Lennie, 16
Troilo, Aníbal, 14, 16, 21, 31, 41, 43, 71,
    83–85, 101–102, 156, 168, 192, 194
    and *Amurado*, 49
    and bandoneon, 142–145
    as celebrity, 172
    and Piazzolla arrangements, 46, 132
    with Piazzolla in orchestra, 32, 40,
        59–68, *61*, *64*, 73, 103, 111, 128–129,
        167
    playing Piazzolla's music, 86
    style, 79, 80, 95, 171, 176, 182
    and *Suite Troileana*, 160–161
Troilo, Zita, 31, *64*, 68, 143, 160

Valentino, Rudolph, 15
Valéry, Paul, 72, 105
Valladares, Leda, 148
Vardaro, Elvino ("Vardarito"), 41, 49, 61,
    62, 80, 128, 142, 173

Varela, Héctor, 156
Vasallo, Juan, 75
Vega, Carlos, 191
Videla, Lieutenant General Jorge Rafael,
    89–91
Villegas, Enrique ("El Mono"), 136
Vitale, Lito, 149
Vivaldi, Antonio Lucio, 79

Wilda, Béla, 97, 125–126, 128, 129, 142
Wolff, Dedé, 111, 121
    marriage to, *116*, 75, 78, 117–118,
        128–129, 133
    in Paris, 69, 131
    and Troilo, 67

Yo-Yo Ma, 17, 22, 169
Yupanqui, Atahualpa, 148

Ziegler, Pablo, 22, 58, 82, *154*, 181, 186
Zimmerman, C., 34

CPSIA information can be obtained at www.ICGtesting.com
Printed in the USA
LVOW04s1936111214

418361LV00031B/1731/P